TRUMPETS OF THE LORD

Bramwell Booth Speaks

Daily Readings
selected by

CATHERINE BRAMWELL-BOOTH

HODDER AND STOUGHTON
LONDON · SYDNEY · AUCKLAND · TORONTO

Foreword

By General Erik Wickberg

In 1947 Commissioner Catherine Bramwell-Booth published a book of daily readings selected from her father's writings. The title was *Bramwell Booth Speaks*.

It is a source of satisfaction to me personally that a reprint should have been decided upon and the new title, *Trumpets of the Lord*, is not without significance.

General Bramwell Booth was promoted to Glory in 1929 and the number of Salvationists and others, who knew him personally and remember his meetings and his administration is rapidly diminishing. My own memories are few and intermittent, but his personal interest in a young Cadet and Officer, his warmth and his spiritual authority left traces which all the years have never been able to sweep away.

But it was much later that I began to realise the extent of his written ministry. In the first place I can only marvel at the number of books and articles that he found time and inspiration to write. All his life he carried an enormous burden of administrative work, and as possibly few others, I have had occasion to assess the wisdom and foresight with which this 'masterbuilder' laid the foundations of the organisation that has become known as the international Salvation Army.

But I have also come to admire more and more the quality of his writings. His mind and heart were steeped in the message of the Bible, which he knew so well. Here in this book is no attempt to analyze in depth the biblical passages from an exegetical point of view. Here are truly devotional readings, perhaps deceptively simple in language, but heart-warming and compelling in their aim to make our love for Christ lead us on to love the sinner.

His daughter, in her preface to the first edition, said that these readings 'are primarily intended for Salvationists'. How important that we, Soldiers of the Cross today, should be reminded of the simplicity of our faith, the dynamics of the love of God and the greatness and urgency of our mission. Bramwell Booth speaks of all these things in a low pitch, yet with a heart aglow with that love. Here are no quotable anecdotes, no rhetorical phrases, no startling dialectics. Here is the depth and simplicity of absolute faith in the presence and power of Jesus, our Lord.

Bramwell Booth suffered increasingly from deafness, but his spiritual hearing was tuned to the voice of a loving Father, and because he implicitly believed in the reality of the Kingdom of God, he wanted all the trumpets to sound to call the wanderers home. He must have known the quotation from Saint Augustine that 'you do not love your neighbour as yourself, unless you try to draw him to that good which you are yourself pursuing, namely that he may love God with a perfect affection'.

February, 1973

Preface

THESE daily readings chosen from my father's writings are primarily intended for Salvationists and are taken in the main from writings originally addressed to them. Whilst dwelling upon his words I have realized afresh how his thoughts flowed ever toward God. He saw mankind, as it were, from God's side ; saw man's capacity, by the Holy Ghost's power, for godlikeness ; saw man precious to God.

It has been said : 'To serve God is to love Him above everything and everything for His sake.' After this fashion Bramwell Booth served his God and his fellows ; and for his own people, his Salvationist family, he yearned with passionate desire that they should claim their inheritance in Christ and thus be ' in the world ' as Jesus, our lovely Forerunner, was, and as He designed His followers should be.

To press home the word to the individual heart and conscience is, then, Bramwell Booth's aim. He wants what he says to be so clearly plain that the meaning will be open to the least tutored mind ; he *wants* the word to be ' applied to every heart and mine ! ' Does any one come short ? He *wants* to help that one to cry, ' Lord, is it I ? ' Are some weak, fearful ? He *wants* them to be certain that God can make *them* strong and bold.

From his own heart's vision he tells of Jesus Christ with a simple directness designed to kindle our faith to full assurance that we, too, may perceive our Saviour, possess Him, manifest Him, by the Holy Spirit, to the little world of our familiars, in the home, the factory, the Corps* ; Yes, and more ! go into the highways and byways of the great world outside to *tell of Him*, our Lord and our God.

For my father the sum of joy was to love the Redeemer and to know His love ; life's chief grief that so many still lived without that experience. A dying Christian said, ' I weep because Love is not loved ! '† So from his earliest manhood felt Bramwell Booth. Hence his insistence on the awfulness, the horribleness of sin, the monstrosity that hides God from men and destroys them in the process. He believed that the ' saved ' must grow in grace, but also in realizing the vileness of sin. He wanted Salvationists to grasp something of its fearful effect in cutting men off from God. I have chosen a number of passages dealing with sin, because an important proportion of the General's words to his people are about sin and the Saviour's power to save and to keep the soul from sinning.

Bramwell Booth saw The Salvation Army, or rather the individual Salvationist, as called and chosen to fight at Christ's side, who, as John puts it, ' was manifested that He might destroy the works of the devil.' These messages aim at arousing us to desiring and resolving to do our duty toward sinners better, and to be better devil-haters.

One could find the doctrines of The Salvation Army in these passages and see how the exposition of the doctrine always leads the writer to Christ, the Author. But if doctrine has a part in this collection of readings it is that some souls may be helped to live in closer harmony with their belief, to accord more nearly in action and feeling with the truth.

* Fighting unit of Salvation Army forces.

† Giacapone da Todi.

That this might be so has been my hope and prayer while compiling this book.

All the verses linked to readings are from the Salvation Army Song Book, save one or two marked out by inverted commas which were quoted by General Bramwell Booth himself.

CATHERINE BRAMWELL-BOOTH.

London, 1947.

Thanks are due to Mrs. Bramwell Booth for kind permission to use extracts from copyright works.

William Bramwell Booth,

eldest son of William and Catherine Booth, Founders of The Salvation Army, was born in 1856. Converted as a boy, he early assisted his father in the organization of the Mission which became, in 1878, The Salvation Army. As The Army's Chief of the Staff from 1880 to 1912, he was responsible for the administration of its rapidly growing activities at home and abroad. His teaching and preaching of Holiness as a practical experience did much to strengthen the spiritual life of Salvationists and Christian people, some of whom came from the European Continent and from America to attend his Holiness Meetings.

Bramwell Booth succeeded his father as General of The Salvation Army in 1912, and under his leadership The Army's missionary, social and youth work made phenomenal advances. The full-time Officer-force of The Army had increased from 16,000 in 1912 to 25,000 when on June 16, 1929, he died.

In an Address to Salvation Army Officers on his eightieth birthday, General William Booth wrote of his son, Bramwell : ' He possesses capacities for government in all its branches, whether those of leadership or administration, in a remarkable degree. . . . He is dear to you all on the ground of his practical godliness, his familiarity with the principles of The Army, and his devotion to them. His unswerving impartiality in dealing with the characters and movements of Officers the world over endears him to all who know him ; while his unflagging energy, his untiring industry and his readiness and capacity for dealing with details, as well as with fundamentals, make him a worthy example to every Officer in The Army. The service he has rendered me, and you, and I think I may say the world as well, through these long years, in the construction and building up of this great Movement, is beyond my power to describe . . . but I can acknowledge that service, and commend him and his devoted wife to the fullest confidence and affection of you all.'

Oh that men would praise the Lord for His goodness, and for His wonderful works to the children of men! For He satisfieth the longing soul, and filleth the hungry soul with goodness.— Psalm 107 : 8, 9.

We are beginning a New Year; shall we not make it a year of desperate, determined seeking for God? And whether we write, or cook, or serve, or suffer, or work underground, or fly, or sail on the seas; whether we eat or drink, or whatsoever we do, *in that very thing, seek after Him.* Be resolved that *we* will taste and see, in our own everyday experience, that He *is* to be found by those who seek Him, that He *is* faithful that promised!

> Father, let me dedicate
>   This new year to Thee,
> In whatever worldly state
>   Thou wilt have me be;
> Not from sorrow, pain, or care
> Would I ask that Thou should spare;
> This alone shall be my prayer:
>   Glorify Thy name.

Jesus our Lord . . . whereby are given unto us exceeding great and precious promises : that by these ye might be partakers of the divine nature.—
2 Peter 1: 2, 4.

God is my record, how greatly I long after you. . . . And this I pray, that your love may abound yet more and more . . . till the day of Christ.—
Philippians 1. 8–10.

I am so glad to think that the New Year will bring the old wish with new feeling and hope to many hearts—a happy New Year !

But what about a New Year's gift ? Well, the gift I most covet for The Army is a fresh and over-flowing baptism of love for souls. I am sure this is the greatest need of some Corps, and some Officers, and some Soldiers. I am not at this moment thinking of winning souls. This is infinitely important, of course. We shall not be able to go forward as a Salvation Army if we cannot go on winning souls. But just now I am full of thought and desire about loving souls. I want God's love for them to be shed abroad afresh in our hearts. I want our love for them to be sanctified and inflamed and fanned by His love. I want the love of Christ—the Bethlehem love—the Lazarus love—the Gethsemane love—the Calvary love to be in us.

> Jesus, Thou Lover of souls !
>   Oh, let me drink of Thy Spirit,
> Make me a lover of souls.

. . . **The Lord, bless His name ; shew forth His salvation from day to day. Declare His glory . . . among all people.**—Psalm 96 : 2, 3.

I rejoice—as I have rejoiced a thousand times before—that all over the world men recognize in the uniform of the Salvationist a reminder of the claims of God. Look at it how you may, that is a gain to the world ; it is a gain to the Church of Christ ; it is a gain to the Kingdom of Righteousness ; it is something to be thankful for. It is something to increase our faith in God. It is the witness of the world generally to the great central fact of our history—namely, that we stand for religion ; *that we acknowledge God.*

Here is a witness from the world itself that the first great outstanding feature of The Salvation Army, that which has impressed itself first and foremost upon the mind of the multitude, is not that we are humanitarian, or social, or philanthropic—although we are all these put together—but *that we are religious.*

> We are witnesses for Jesus
>   In the haunts of sin and shame,
> In the underworld of sorrow
>   Where men seldom hear His name ;
> For to bind the broken-hearted
>   And their liberty proclaim,
> We are witnesses for Jesus
>   In the haunts of sin and shame.

3

The Pharisees . . . said unto His disciples, Why
eateth your Master with publicans and sinners ?
But when Jesus heard that, He said unto them,
They that be whole need not a physician, but they
that are sick. . . . I am not come to call the
righteous, but sinners to repentance.—Matthew
9: 11–13.

This means that we shall mix with the people we
want to save, just as our Saviour did. We shall
study them and know them. Then there will be
discoveries! The things which seemed frozen and
dead in the winter of condemnation will awaken
to life! Flowers will come out of the cold clay!
Gold and precious stones will be found amongst the
mud and ' muck '! Fire will be seen in the flints!
Beauty, as the beauty of the rainbow, will appear in
the blackest pitch! Men are very bad, but they are
not altogether bad—there is good in the worst!

> Sinners Jesus will receive !
>   Sound this word of grace to all
> Who the heavenly pathway leave,
>   All who linger, all who fall !
>
> Sing it o'er and o'er again :
>   Christ receiveth sinful men !
> Make the message clear and plain :
>   Christ receiveth sinful men.

You, being dead in your sins . . . hath He
quickened . . , having forgiven you all trespasses.
—Colossians 2 : 13.

' Dead in sins ! ' Jesus never made light of sin.
He used no disguise when He talked of it, no equivocal
terms, no softening words. There is no single suggestion in all His discourses or conversations that He
thought it merely a disease, or a derangement, or a
misfortune, or anything of that kind, or that He
deemed it anything but a ruinous and deadly rebellion against God—the great disaster of the world,
and far-reaching precursor of suffering in the whole
existence of the universe. He said it was bad, bad
all through—in form, in expression, in purpose ;
above all, in spirit and design. That there was no
remedy for it but His remedy. No rains in all the
heavens to wash it, no waters in all the seas to cleanse
it away, no fires in hell itself to purge its defilement.
The only hope was in the blood of His sacrifice. And
so He came to shed it, to save the people from their
sins.

> What can wash away my sin ?
>   Nothing but the Blood of Jesus.
> What can keep me always clean ?
>   Nothing but the Blood of Jesus.
>
> Here will I seek the flow
> That washes white as snow ;
> No other fount I know,
>   Nothing but the Blood of Jesus.

Jesus answered and said unto them, . . . God is not the God of the dead, but of the living. —Matthew 22 : 29, 32.

Jesus . . . said, . . . Labour not for the meat which perisheth, but for that meat which endureth unto everlasting life.—John 6 : 26, 27.

The moment men really see that life is not merely a broken thread, or a socket without an eye, and that death is not just a trap-door to nothingness, they begin—yes ! in that very moment they begin—to look ahead, to look up, to think, to believe, to see that they may rise even to the heights of Heaven or sink to the abyss of Hell. Nay, they begin to see that they must rise to the one or they *will* sink to the other.

Paul seized upon the whole lesson of life beyond the grave in its effect on life here when he said, in his defence before Felix, ' This I confess unto thee, . . . that there shall be a resurrection of the dead, both of the just and unjust. And herein do I exercise myself, to have always a conscience void of offence toward God, and toward men.'

Here is the whole wisdom, the true philosophy of life. Live now in this wise because you must live again ! Keep a good conscience here, because on that will depend your destiny there ! What a fine and enduring purpose is thus revealed in human affairs ! If death ends all, the little that we could do or leave undone will matter nothing. But if, after all, there will be a morning to the night of death, then *everything* which has to do with thought, or conduct, matters.

6

God is our refuge and strength, a very present help in trouble. Therefore will not we fear. —Psalm 46 : 1, 2.

God is present in temptation. When the soul is buffeted by the assaults of the Devil, and we put up resistance to the Tempter, saying, ' Get thee behind me, Satan ! ' *that* is God. It shows the Divine Spirit watching the Devil, and watching us, and coming near to help us. We may win or we may lose, but nothing can alter the fact that God was there close at hand, present with us in our time of trial. It is the same also in sorrow and disappointment. When the thought arises : ' How strange this is ! Why should I be called on to endure such things ? ' and immediately something says within us : ' Well, God does know, and He does care,' and we feel a restraint upon us not to go too far in our grief—that again is God present and working in us. Just as really is it so as if we could see Him with the outward eye or hear Him with the outward ear.

> Peace, doubting heart, my God's I am :
>   Who formed me man forbids my fear ;
> The Lord hath called me by my name ;
>   The Lord protects, for ever near ;
> His Blood for me did once atone,
> And still He loves and guards His own.

7

Let no corrupt communication proceed out of your mouth, but that which is good. . . . And grieve not the Holy Spirit of God, whereby ye are sealed unto the day of redemption. Let all . . . evil speaking, be put away from you.—Ephesians 4 : 29–31.

Depend upon it, God still visits those who speak against His people ; and the most fearful of His judgments upon them is the injury that follows to their own souls. Nothing more quickly infects the whole man with the poison of doubt and hatred—the very spirit of Hell itself—than this practice of evil-speaking. It tarnishes everything it touches and blackens what it cannot consume. It fosters selfishness, destroys sympathy and kills love outright. Talk against one man long enough, and you will come to hate all men ; and then all men will shun you like a leper. Allow the spirit of slander to take possession of your heart, and the joy and sweetness will all go out of your life.

Envy and jealousy alone could make one soul wretched enough to infect Heaven itself with woe. Do not imagine that it is a happy thing to go about the world speaking evil. Better by far to be the slandered than to be the slanderer.

Justice and judgment are the habitation of Thy throne : mercy and truth shall go before Thy face. Blessed is the people that know the joyful sound : they shall walk, O Lord, in the light of Thy countenance.—Psalm 89 : 14, 15.

Jesus saith unto him, I am the way, the truth, and the life : no man cometh unto the Father, but by Me.—John 14 : 6.

It is one of God's witnesses to truth, *that truth will out*. Sooner or later, selfishness and sin will *appear* in their naked deformity, to horrify those who behold them ; and in the end, justice and truth and love are certain to be made manifest in their natural beauty, to convince and to charm and to attract their beholders.

It is not only one of the uses of trial to bring this about, but it is one of the means by which God converts to His own high purposes the miseries and sorrows the Devil has brought in. The one casts us into fiery dispensations of suffering and loss ; the other takes these moments of human anguish and desolation, and makes of them open windows through which a doubting or scoffing world may see what love can do. Thus He makes us to triumph in the midst of our foes, while working in us a likeness to Himself, the all-patient and all-perfect God. Hallelujah !

Be thou strong and very courageous.—Joshua 1 : 7.
There is no fear in love ; but perfect love casteth out fear. . . . He that feareth is not made perfect in love. . . . This commandment have we from Him, That he who loveth God love his brother also.—1 John 4 : 18, 21.

Do we need more *daring* in going after souls ? The whole world has lately been stirred by deeds of daring which have been performed in this dreadful war—in many instances by the youngest officers and by the most obscure privates in the rank. Have we not, all of us, thought of such things with great admiration ? A large part of the world positively worships such daring, such devotion, such self-forgetfulness. But none will admire or extol or worship it more than those who were rescued by it from death.

Now I believe there is something of the same kind, of capacity for gratitude, in the miserable and condemned souls around us. When they see us plunge in for them in the face of difficulty, when they see us run risks for their Salvation, when they see us suffer on their account, when they see us dare to sacrifice ourselves—our time and ease, our wealth of mind and heart and body—in order to save them, that very courage commands their esteem and makes them more ready to receive and act upon the truths we proclaim.

Thus saith the Lord, thy Redeemer, . . . I am the Lord thy God which teacheth thee . . , which leadeth thee by the way that thou shouldest go. O that thou hadst hearkened to My commandments ! then had thy peace been as a river. —Isaiah 48 : 17, 18.

Those who want peace must give up the fight. It goes without saying that you cannot have peace and have war at the same time. Men cannot be right with God and wrong with Him at the same moment. If they want peace, they must stop the fight—lay down their weapon—cease pushing God out of their lives—make an end of refusing His calls,—give up going against His commandments and quenching His Spirit in their hearts.

Here is one of the chief reasons for which I hate the drink, and dread the pleasure houses, and detest the worldly companionships and influences under which so many choose to live ; for all these things help men to fight against God. Well, all this must come to an end if you want peace ; and there is no time to lose !

> Though I wandered far from Jesus
>   In the paths of sin,
> Yet I heard Him gently calling,
>   ' Wanderer, come in ! '
>
> Now I live for Christ, my Saviour,
>   Live to do His will ;
> Though the path be dark and thorny
>   Yet I'll conquer still.
>
> Yes, He gives me peace and pardon,
>   Joy without alloy.

11

God . . . which doeth great things past finding out ; yea, and wonders without number.—Job 9 : 2, 10.

Where sin abounded, grace did much more abound.—Romans 5 : 20.

The history of our world is a record of wonders—wonders unsuspected, or at least unseen—wonders discovered—wonders achieved, all linked in an advancing unity, and in their purpose and relation to each other showing the highest wonder of all—the presence and power of God. Our earliest knowledge is of the wonders of the earth's creation ; and all its marvels are to culminate at last in the great wonders of. Resurrection and Judgment. There will have been wonders all along the intervening time. Talk of miracles ! Think of the wonders of life ! of the wonders wrought by human thought and labour and endurance. And there have been wonders also in the moral sphere, no less remarkable. Wonders of courage—think of all that pluck has accomplished ! Wonders of virtue—are they not the most enduring of all ? Wonders of love—is it possible, for example, to measure what has been done in the world by the force of mothers' love alone ? And there have been spiritual wonders more wonderful than all the rest—the wonders of Grace, and the wonders wrought by Faith.

Jesus said, . . . A new commandment I give unto you, That ye love one another ; as I have loved you, that ye also love one another. By this shall all men know that ye are My disciples, if ye have love one to another.—John 13 : 31, 34, 35.

We see men everywhere striving after liberty—suffering, toiling, fighting and dying to win it. And yet we know that, great as it is, greatly as we admire and value it ourselves, it is destined to prove little more than a myth unless when men find it they find love also.

This is our message. This is our secret. This is the inner meaning of the great Commandment of God which sums up all the law and the prophets, ' Thou shalt love the Lord thy God with all thy heart, and with all thy soul, and with all thy strength, and with all thy mind ; and thy neighbour as thyself.' This is the leaven which must be hid in the life of man till the whole be leavened—a holy love. This is the salt without which everything else in human life will lose its savour. Love ! Love ! Love ! Nothing without love.

> Nothing on earth do I desire,
> But Thy pure love within my breast :
> This, only this, do I require,
> And freely give up all the rest.

Beloved, . . . beware lest ye . . . fall from your own stedfastness. But grow in grace, and in the knowledge of our Lord and Saviour Jesus Christ. —2 Peter 3 : 17, 18.

Wisdom is a thing of the heart more than of the brain, and the wisdom of God is really a revelation of the love of God. To be ' wise unto Salvation ' is to learn the lesson of love. To be 'wise to win souls ' is first to love souls. To feel that ' it is more blessed to give than to receive,' is the fruit of love. How different this from the calculating wisdom of this world !

Dear comrade, and friend, are you taking care that the Divine Life in you shall grow after this Christ-like fashion ? When I hear Christian people say : ' Oh, I have so little love, so little faith, so little joy,' I generally find that it is so because they stifle and quench the blessed yearnings of the Divine Spirit to seek the souls of others ; because they leave unanswered the urgings and promptings of duty which God in their conscience is demanding ; because they neglect prayer, and self-denial, and heart-searching, and the word of God. What wonder if love and faith are feeble, and joy is like to die !

**Verily He took not on Him the nature of angels ;
but . . . in all things it behoved Him to be made
like unto His brethren, . . . for in that He Himself hath suffered being tempted, He is able to
succour them that are tempted.**—Hebrews 2 : 16–18.

Our Lord was alone in the wilderness. Satan is a
cowardly enemy. He chooses for his onslaughts our
hours of loneliness and of separation from the happy
associations of all that is likely to support and aid us
in the conflict. It was so with our dear Master, and
as the servant is not above his Lord, it is often so
with us.

It was a time of physical weakness. Jesus had
fasted for forty days and forty nights, and He was
an hungered. And has it not been often our strange
experience also that in the time of physical depression,
of weariness, of sickness, our enemy has assaulted us
with suggestions which would have been powerless
had we been well and strong ? This also, then, our
Master understands. Even in this He is touched with
the feeling of our infirmity, for He was tempted in
like manner and amid the like circumstances.

> Still nigh me, O my Saviour, stand,
>   And guard in fierce temptation's hour ;
> Hide in the hollow of Thy hand,
>   Show forth in me Thy saving power ;
> Still be Thy arms my sure defence,
> Nor earth nor Hell shall pluck me thence.

**Verily, verily, I say unto you, The servant is not
greater than his lord ; neither he that is sent
greater than he that sent him.**—John 13 : 16.

**Then saith He unto them, My soul is exceeding
sorrowful, even unto death : tarry ye here, and
watch with Me. And He went a little farther, and
fell on His face, and prayed. . . . And He cometh
unto the disciples, and findeth them asleep, and
saith unto Peter, What, could ye not watch with
Me one hour ?**—Matthew 26 : 38–40.

There are few more instructive or more touching
things in the life of our Lord Jesus Christ than His
evident appreciation of human sympathy. What we
call ' companionship ' had real charm for Him. And
as He valued the consolations arising from human
friendship and love, so also He had to suffer the loss
of them. But the bitterest sorrow which can come
to a leader was added to His cup, when He witnessed
the failure of His trusted disciples in the hour of trial.

Now, when we are called upon to suffer in the same
way, may we not be brought into very intimate
fellowship with Jesus ? Shall we complain because
the servant is not above his Lord ? Shall we doubt
His love and care and power, because He does not
always shield us from that same blast of loneliness
which swept over His own soul in the Garden, when
for the second, aye, and for the third time, He found
His three disciples asleep ?

Jesus saith, . . . from your hearts forgive . . . every one his brother.—Matthew 18 : 22, 35.

Offences will come—they must come. There is not one of us but will, at some time, be wounded in the house of our friend ; or sold and betrayed by one we trusted ; or maligned by one we loved. It must be so —the Master said it would be so. We shall be mistaken and misjudged. Hasty words will be spoken in anger about us and ours, and birds of ill omen will carry them to us. Our good will be called evil ; our very sorrows will become reasons for visiting us with reproaches and reproofs. When we look for comfort we shall receive stripes, and our tears will, for a season, become our meat by day and night. It has always been so. It always will be so.

Well, amidst it all, we must forgive. Oh, when I hear Salvationists say, ' I cannot forgive,' my heart stands still. It is such a contradiction. It is like saying that the sun cannot give light, or that the earth cannot go round, or that the winds cannot blow. Forgiveness is as natural to love as fragrance is to flowers.

The angel of His presence saved them.—Isaiah
63 : 9.
**I can do all things through Christ which
strengtheneth me.**—Philippians 4 : 13.

What courage the consciousness of Christ's presence
will give to the weakest of His children. By the
grace which He imparts even the least of them can
say, ' In His presence what dare I in sin ? And in
His presence what dare I not in service.' They can
say with David, ' I have set the Lord always before
me : because He is at my right hand, I shall not be
moved.'

It is by the presence of God that we may most
clearly realize His guidance in our daily life. And in
this also the weakest and most ignorant may be
trained.

What transformation, what elevation of character
would result from the cultivation of this sense of
God's presence ! And it *is* the privilege of each one
to walk in ' fellowship . . . with the Father, and with
His Son, Jesus Christ.'

> Friendship with Jesus,
>   Fellowship Divine !
> Oh, what blessèd, sweet communion !
>   Jesus is a Friend of mine.

**He that overcometh, the same shall be clothed
in white raiment ; and I will . . . confess his
name before My Father and before His angels. He
that hath an ear, let him hear what the Spirit saith.**
—Revelation 3 : 5, 6.

If you go on with your work for God, and finish it,
paying no heed to those who, having put their hand
to the plough, look back ; and if, in spite of your
sorrow, you will struggle steadily forward in the face
of the coldness and carelessness of those between
whom and you there was once the tenderest love,
God will not only carry you through your appointed
labour for the world, but He will restore many of those
others to their allegiance to Him and His.

Let us, then, press forward, without one backward
glance, until we finish our work. Let us thank God
for those who are faithful ; let us hope and pray for
those who fail, expecting to see them restored, healed
and purified.

Not all the powers of Hell can fright
A soul that walks with Christ in light,
    He walks and cannot fall ;
Clearly he sees, and wins his way,
Shining unto the perfect day,
    And more than conquers all.

Ten thousand snares my path beset :
Yet will I, Lord, the work complete
    Which Thou to me hast given ;
Regardless of the pains I feel,
Close by the gates of Death and Hell,
    I press along to Heaven.

**Put off . . . the old man, which is corrupt
according to the deceitful lusts ; . . . and . . .
put on the new man, which after God is created in
righteousness and true holiness.**—Ephesians 4 :
22, 24.

The change of nature or character, which we undoubtedly see in some of God's people, is a true
miracle. Here is one of the permanent wonders of God's
dealings with men. They are not only made correct
in outward acts, but changed in tastes, in desire, in
preference—that is, in their very nature.

Now, this is all in direct opposition to the ordinary
laws of the moral world. All character tends to
become permanent ; bad natures become fixed in bad
tendencies, in bad preferences, in bad choices ; and
bad men grow more and more powerless to change
themselves.

When, therefore, we see those who have from their
youth up been accustomed to do and be evil, changed
to do and love what is good : we are compelled to
exclaim—this is none other than the work of the
Divine Spirit. Lo ! God is here.

> Lo, a new creation dawning !
> Lo, I rise to life Divine ;
> In my soul an Easter morning ;
> I am Christ's and Christ is mine.

The love of Christ constraineth us ; . . . He died for all, that they which live should not henceforth live unto themselves.—2 Corinthians 5 : 14, 15.

What a great heart of passionate love was Christ's ! Blessed be His Name for ever ! Whether the poverty and suffering and hatred were or were not favourable to it, there it was—the Great Heart of all the world. Can you ever be again content to remain little and narrow, with interests and affections that are little and narrow also ? Will you not rise, as He rose, above the small ambitions of the spiritual pigmies who meet you at every turn, determined to look beyond your own tiny circle and the low aims of those around you ? Depend upon it, you ought to do so. Depend upon it, the holy Saviour can enable you to do so. Depend upon it, the world's great need is ' Great Hearts.' Will you be one ?

> Wanted, hearts to love the masses,
>   Hearts to help Him seek the lost ;
> Hearts to help Him save all classes,
>   Hearts to help Him save the worst ;
> Hearts to share with Him the weeping,
>   Hearts to bear with Him the cross ;
> Hearts to help Him with the reaping,
>   Hearts to trust through gain or loss.

And [Jesus] **said unto them, Take heed what ye hear.**—Mark 4 : 24.

I will hear what God the Lord will speak : for He will speak.—Psalm 85 : 8.

Being situated as they are in families and associated with worldly-minded and ungodly people in their business, many are compelled to hear daily what must prove injurious to the new life of purity, unless, when they hear, they refuse to ' listen,' unless they can learn to close the inner ear, and refuse to let it entertain or dwell upon what may be unworthy and undesirable.

This includes not merely what is positively evil, like filthy talk, but useless, frivolous conversation. Unless the ear is trained to turn away from that which does not serve the highest interest of the soul, the soul must be damaged. The ear then becomes not only an avenue through which temptation assails the soul, but the soul's own inner power of hearing the higher voices is dulled. Let us, then, so train the ear that it becomes a sort of blind alley for whatever does not serve the interest of the life of God, and an open road for all that will deepen the sacred strength of God's revelation. I do believe that the reason the prophets and apostles heard so much from God was that they listened so well.

> Master, speak ! and make me ready,
>   When Thy voice is truly heard,
> With obedience glad and steady
>   Still to follow every word.
> I am listening, Lord, for Thee ;
> Master, speak ! Oh ! speak to me !

Every man that striveth for the mastery is temperate in all things. . . . I therefore so run, not as uncertainly . . . But I keep under my body, and bring it into subjection : lest that by any means, when I have preached to others, I myself should be a castaway.—1 Corinthians 9 : 25–27.

When men assert that any form of impure indulgence, either of the mind, through the eye or the ear, or of the body, by appetite or habit, is natural to them, what do they mean ? Do they mean to say that our nature is only animal ? Is it on a level with the brutes ? Is it a beastly nature ? Is it not something higher than that ? Is it not the nature of one made in the image of God ? Is not the spiritual intended to triumph over the animal ?

The truth is that it is impurity that is unnatural, for it is contrary to, and the very opposite of, man's nature as a whole, founded as that nature is on the principles of reason, of conscience and of self-preservation, of every one of which impurity is the deadly foe. My brother, my sister, that is your true nature which acts out the noble thought of Paul when he said, ' I keep under my body . . . lest . . . I myself '—even Paul the great Apostle—' should be a castaway.' Never, therefore, say of an uncleanness in word or thought or deed that it is excusable because it is inevitable or necessary to your nature. That would be a lie.

Our sins testify against us : . . . and as for our iniquities, we know them ; in . . . lying against the Lord, and departing away from our God, . . . conceiving and uttering from the heart words of falsehood.—Isaiah 59 : 12, 13.

If any man sin, we have an advocate with the Father, Jesus Christ the righteous : and He is the propitiation for our sins : and not for ours only, but also for the sins of the whole world.—1 John 2 : 1, 2.

Sin ! The world's sin. The sin of this one generation. The sin of one city. The sin of one family. The sin of one man—*my* sin ! What shall be done with our sin ? Thanks be to God ! there is an atonement. The Man of whom I write has made a propitiation for our sins, and not for ours only, but for the sins of the whole world. He stands forth the *only Saviour*. None has ever dared even to offer to the sin-stricken hearts of men relief from the guilt of sin. But He does. He can cleanse, He can pardon, He can purify, He can save, *because He has redeemed*.

When Jesus was born in the manger,
   The shepherds came thither to see,
For the angels proclaimed that a Saviour was born
   To save a poor sinner like me.

Paul dwelt two whole years in his own hired house, and received all that came in unto him, preaching the kingdom of God, and teaching those things which concern the Lord Jesus Christ.
—Acts 28 : 30, 31.

Tell men what God has done, what Jesus Christ has suffered for them. Tell them of His condescension. Tell them of His patience. Tell them of His gift. Tell them of a Saviour's shame and anguish and humiliation on their behalf. Make it plain to them in common everyday language, that He was, as the Scriptures say, a Man of Sorrows ; a Man who trod the winepress alone ; a Man who suffered for them with none to help Him ; and that it was their sins and their sorrows, their backslidings and infirmities, which He bore in life and in death. To many, this will have far more effect in bringing about conviction of sin than talking about sin itself.

I entreat you not to leave any man or woman whom you can reach in ignorance of what God has done. And what God has borne on account of sin is concentrated and focused, brought into a single fact which all can comprehend, in the life and suffering and death of the Son of Man.

> In every land where man is found
> Let us make known the story
> Of love Divine ; its praises sound,
> And give to Jesus glory !

When I am weak, then am I strong.—2 Corinthians
12 : 10.

**Jesus stood and cried, saying, If any man thirst,
let him come unto Me, and drink. He that
believeth on Me, as the scripture hath said, out of
his belly shall flow rivers of living water. (But
this spake He of the Spirit, which they that believe
on Him should receive . . .)**—John 7 : 37-39.

Some are much hindered in that pouring forth of
which I am speaking by ill-health. I know well how
the weariness and depression, if not the actual suffering, which are associated with poor health, do make
against the flowing out of these streams of living
water. Small anxieties become great at such times.
The snub or neglect by others which ought scarcely to
be noticed, brings a sting, sorrow which ought to be
sanctified becomes insupportable, and heart and flesh
fail in the presence of difficulties which at other times
would scarcely be counted difficulties at all.

But then, on the other hand, I have seen, oh, so
often! that these things are not a sufficient reason
for the loss of that great force. Some of the most
mighty examples of the power of enthusiasm and of
zeal amounting almost to a fury for God's honour and
the Salvation of souls, have been amongst these very
saints of whom I am thinking.

How many are mine iniquities and sins ? make me to know my transgression and my sin.—Job 13 : 23.

Ye that love the Lord, hate evil.—Psalm 97 : 10.

Consider the moral and physical decay of manhood involved in the sinful sensualism of the day. See how the drinking places, the degenerate stage, the immoral literature, the nasty talk of the street, combine to inflame the baser nature and make the animal in man the master of his destiny ! So that this wonderful creature, the noblest of God's works, sinks lower than the swine, and finds at last the only joys of life in the gratification of a depraved appetite and in the corruption of a filthy lust. Labour is a necessary nuisance ! The service of his generation, a sign of servitude ! The life of restraint, of temperance, of noble aspiration—why, it is all fudge as compared with the joys of quenching a depraved thirst, or of lascivious mirth, or of licentious indulgence !

My God, how I detest the great enemy of Thy throne and righteousness, which has wrought all this havoc ! How vast the fields of human experience which are strewed with the trophies of his desolate victories !

> To the front ! the fight is raging ;
>   Christ's own banner leads the way.
> Every power and thought engaging,
>   Might Divine shall be our stay.
> We have heard the cry for help
>   From the dying millions round us,
> We've received the royal command
>   From our dying Lord who found us.

He addeth rebellion unto his sin, . . . and multiplieth his words against God.—Job 34 : 37.
Let us therefore follow after the things which make for peace.—Romans 14 : 19.

Ohe of the remarkable facts about wrong of every kind is that it so quickly joins forces with other wrong. Sin is the grand support of sin. Self-will is the great stand-by for pride and selfishness. Evil desire and appetite support passion and indulgence. The love of the world encourages unbelief and hate. One lie sustains another lie. One cheat covers up another cheat.

As with sin, so with sinners. They go into partnership against God and His will, and bolster one another up in the awful neglect of His law, and the struggle to resist His claims.

Come, Holy Ghost, Thy mighty aid bestowing !
    Destroy the works of sin, the self, the pride !
Burn, burn in me, my idols overthrowing :
    Prepare my heart for Him—for my Lord crucified !

The name of the Lord Jesus was magnified. And many that believed came, and confessed, and shewed their deeds.—Acts 19 : 17, 18.

Few things surprise me more, either in my public work or in my personal dealing with souls, than the evidences I meet with of unconfessed sin. It would be no exaggeration to say that fully half the misery, uncertainty and weakness I come across arises from this cause. The fact is, that the nature of man was not constructed to harbour evil. Sin is an intruder. Conscience, the fear of God, the capacity of memory, the instinct of self-preservation, all want to acknowledge what is wrong, to expel it and to get rid of its sting. But men knowingly violate all this. They hide their sin. Thus they make untold misery for those about them, and bring final ruin upon themselves.

The teaching of the Bible is perfectly clear on this matter. Confession is a good thing. It gives humility and vigour to the soul. And it is good, also, because it is the condition on which God grants forgiveness. The Old and the New Testaments, Patriarchs, Prophets and Apostles all unite in this—that the confession of sin is the way to forgiveness.

I am Alpha and Omega, the beginning and the ending, saith the Lord, which is, and which was, and which is to come, the Almighty.—Revelation 1 : 8.

Do not turn away with the paralysing fear that it cannot be ; that the life of Jesus can never be lived out again in flesh and blood. He is ' the same yesterday, and to-day, and for ever.' All He was in Bethlehem, to Mary and Joseph ; all He was to His workmates at Nazareth ; all He was in the wilderness, fighting with fiends, in the deserts feeding the hungry, or among the multitude—healing the sick, blessing the little children, casting out devils and preaching the Kingdom ; all He was in Bethany, weeping over Lazarus, and crying, ' Lazarus, come forth ' ; in the garden of His agony, in the darkness of His cross, in the hour of His resurrection, all this—all—all—all— He is to-day. He belongs to the everlasting Now. All He was to the martyrs who died for His Name, all He has been to our fathers, He is to us, and will be to our children, for with Him is no variableness nor shadow of turning. Yes ! This unchanging Christ ' is in us, except we be reprobate,' the Life and Image of God, and the Hope of Glory.

> Oft our trust has known betrayal,
>   Oft our hopes were vain ;
> But there's One in every trial
>   Proves Himself the same.
>
> Yesterday, to-day, for ever,
>   Jesus is the same ;
> We may change, but Jesus never,
>   Glory to His name !

**Shewing to the generation to come the praises of
the Lord, and His strength, and His wonderful
works that He hath done.   For He . . . commanded our fathers, that they should make them
known to their children : . . . that they might set
their hope in God, and not forget the works of God,
but keep His commandments.**—Psalm 78 : 4, 5, 7.

God expects of all parents that they work with
Him in the making of their children into men and
women after the pattern of their Lord.   The little
child is the clay in the mother's hands—she is the
potter ; it is the father's workshop—he is the worker.
In union with God the parents may, indeed, transform
the tiny being into His likeness.   Nothing can prevent
it.   The word of God is sure.   If they will do faithful
work, He will work ; and when He works, who shall
hinder ?   ' Come thou, and all thy house, into the
ark,' is still His command. Oh, let there be stronger
faith, and more earnest effort, for the sanctifying of our
children.   They are in the covenant.

All who are ours must also be—nay, shall be—His,
made over again in His image, to be like Him for
ever.   ' And I will establish My covenant between Me
and thee and thy seed after thee in their generation
for an everlasting covenant, to be a God unto thee,
and to thy seed after thee.'

> Blessèd Jesus, make our children
>   Thine for life and Thine for aye !
> When death's waters overtake them,
>   Be their Rock, their Light, their Stay !
> Tender Shepherd, let us find them
>   On Thy breast in realms of day !

31

God that made the world and all things therein
. . . hath made of one blood all nations of men
. . . in Him we live, and move, and have our being.
—Acts 17 : 24, 26, 28.

All souls are in some respects manifestations of the
life of God. He is not only their Creator and Father
—the great Source, that is, from which they proceed—
but He is the Power which sustains them—the Power
by which they exist at all. In Him, whether we are
good or bad, we live and move and have our being.
It is this intimate relationship with the Divine,
although they may not perceive it, which makes all
men's souls so interesting—so wonderful in their
restlessness—so remarkably incapable of being satisfied with human things, whether those things are low
things, like money and sensuous pleasure and sensuous
indulgence ; or whether they be the higher things,
like knowledge or friendship or love. As the fish is
made to live and move and have its being in the water,
and cannot be at rest, no matter what it may have
besides, unless it have the water, so the soul of man
is made for God, and only God can really satisfy it.

O Love, who formedst me to wear
  The image of Thy Godhead here,
Who soughtest me with tender care
  Through all my wanderings wild and drear :
O Love, I give myself to Thee,
Thine ever, only Thine to be.

We know that the Son of God is come, and hath given us an understanding, that we may know Him that is true, and we are in Him that is true, even in . . . Jesus Christ. This is the true God, and eternal life.—1 John 5 : 20.

A circumstance always impresses me when I consider the force of criticism of The Army's doctrine of Atonement. It is this : the critics can never agree ! Their various theories differ so widely that they become mutually destructive. They are so vastly divergent that, when considered together with the Bible history, they leave on the mind the impression that there is a grave blunder somewhere, and that, after all, the original story is the true story. . . . . While the changing theories of the critics come and go like fitful mists round the lighthouse when fog is on the sea, the Truth stands out with unchanging lustre.

It is also important to remember that there is very little that is new in the criticism that is put forward by so-called modern learning.

Nearly all that we hear nowadays has been heard often before. The language changes, but the thoughts are similar. No one need fear these old weapons. They are nothing more than the old doubts and hatreds dressed up in modern garb ; the old tunes played again and again in perhaps a different key, or in a little shriller tone. Christ and His redeeming work have long survived them and all they could do, and are still marching on.

I will very gladly spend and be spent for you ; though the more abundantly I love you, the less I be loved.—2 Corinthians 12 : 15.

Some are set as solitary witnesses for Jesus in families where they only too often hear that they are ' not wanted.' Some are with companies of workmates, men or women, or both, where they are looked upon in just the same way. Some are in circles of friends or acquaintances where the moment they open their mouths for God and eternal things they are voted a nuisance, and made instantly to feel that they are in the way of the happiness and peace of all around.

What will you do ? Will you give it up because you are not wanted ? Will you run away because the Devil's dupes reckon to make it hard for you ? O Brothers of the Cross and Sisters of the Grace of God, what will you do ?

> I have given up all for Jesus,
>   This vain world is naught to me ;
> All its pleasures are forgotten.
>   In remembering Calvary.
> Though my friends despise, forsake me,
>   And on me the world looks cold,
> I've a Friend that will stand by me
>   When the Pearly Gates unfold.

34

**Having made peace through the blood of His
cross, . . . to reconcile all things unto Himself ;
. . . and you, that were sometime alienated and
enemies in your mind by wicked works, yet now
hath He reconciled in the body of His flesh through
death, to present you holy and unblameable and
unreproveable in His sight.**—Colossians I : 20–22.

Will you not have His cross ? Is there no appeal
to you to-day from that hill side without the city wall?
Does it not speak to you of the power, the sweetness
and nobleness of a life of service, of sacrifice for others,
of toil for His world ? Has it no message for you
of victory over sin and death, of life from the dead—
life, abundant life, in the Blood of the Son of Man !
Believe me, unless you accept His cross, He will
prepare for you a coffin. ' The wages of sin is death.'
It matters not how noble your aspirations, how lofty
your ideals of life and conduct, how faithful your
labour to raise the standard of your own life—*unless
you accept the cross*, all must go into the grave. Your
highest aims, together with your lowest, your most
cherished conceptions, your most deeply loved
ambitions, all must be entombed.

> In the Cross, in the Cross
>   Be my glory ever ;
> Till my raptured soul shall find
>   Rest beyond the River.

I will judge you, . . . every one according to his ways, saith the Lord God. Repent, and turn yourselves from all your transgressions ; . . . make you a new heart and a new spirit : for why will ye die . . . ? For I have no pleasure in the death of him that dieth, saith the Lord God : wherefore turn yourselves, and live ye.—Ezekiel 18 : 30–32.

God our Saviour ; who will have all men to be saved, and to come unto the knowledge of the truth.—1 Timothy 2 : 3, 4.

The fact is, Salvation is a twofold work. It is of God—it is of man. Did not God will man's Salvation he could not be saved. Unless man will his own Salvation he cannot be saved. God is free. Man also is free. He may set up a plan for saving himself ; but no matter how perfect, it will fail unless it have God for its centre. And God, though He has devised the most infinitely complete and beautiful and costly scheme of redemption for man, will none the less fail unless the individual man wills to co-operate with Him. Man is not a piece of clay which God can fashion as He likes. He is not even a harp out of which He can get what strains He will without regard to its strings. There is in man something—a force, an energy—which must act in union with God, and with which God must act in wonderful partnership, if His will is to be accomplished.

> I need Thee every hour ;
> Teach me Thy will,
> And Thy rich promises
> In me fulfil.

36

And the Lord heard it.—Numbers 12 : 2.

The Lord always hears. There is not an evil word
but He catches it. There is not a slander spoken
against His servants that He misses. The words that
were uttered in whispers—·the sedition that came of a
breath spoken in the inner chamber—the Lord heard
them. The calumny that was passed on under a
solemn promise never to tell any one—the Lord heard
it. The disagreeable jest that made such good fun,
at some one else's expense, for some evil-minded
acquaintance—the Lord heard it. The stray word
that was thrown into the conversation just to carry
the little false impression—so clever, so simple,
so natural it was, that it was only just understood—·
the Lord heard it. The suggestion—not exactly about
that person directly, but about his work, or his wife,
or son, or daughter, but so discreetly put that without appearing spiteful it was really injurious to him
—the Lord heard it. Let slanderers beware ; He
always hears. Let them take heed.

> I want the first approach to feel
>   Of pride or fond desire ;
> To catch the wandering of my will,
>   And quench the kindling fire.
>
> Quick as the apple of an eye,
>   O God, my conscience make !
> Awake my soul when sin is nigh,
>   And keep it still awake.

37

Jesus said :
I say unto you, there is joy in the presence of the angels of God over one sinner that repenteth. —Luke 15 : 10.

Seeking souls is The Army's first work, every true Salvationist's vocation, no matter what may be his earthly calling. Come along, then, and let us join together, not only to suffer with our Saviour on account of the people's sin, but to fight by His side for their redemption. Open your eyes to look on the multitude who are without a shepherd ! Open your ears to the cry of the lost as they pass out into the night ! Stretch out your hand to take the clasp of pain ! Open your heart to the sorrows and despair which are breaking the hearts of those who have no hope ! Weep with those who weep, and watch with those who watch.

Jesus talked about opening the doors of the prison, and healing the diseases of the sick and bringing the wanderers home, and making joy where there had never been joy before. Oh, it will all prove so real and practical, if you will only take it and act upon it, and make it personal and immediate for the people you know and meet and amidst whom you actually work and live.

> Yes, the happiness He gives me
> Far outweighs the toil and loss ;
> Sweetest joy I find in leading
> Weary sinners to the Cross.
> Sore temptations may beset me,
> Sorrow on my heart may fall,
> But there's pleasure in His service,
> More than all.

We know that we have passed from death unto life.—1 John 3 : 14.
I know whom I have believed.—2 Timothy 1 : 12.

In the realms of science, in philosophy, in literature, the tendency is in the main to discredit the whole idea of Atonement, and to throw doubts upon the person and work and sacrifice of Jesus. But what of it ? The opinions or reasonings, on any question, of men who are admittedly ignorant of some of the fundamental facts affecting that question, can never be of any serious moment, and the whole army of doubters and critics of Christ are only too ready to acknowledge that they do not know Christ, that they are actually without any revelation of Christ or acquaintance with Him as a personal Saviour.

Who would go to a blind man to be taught about light and colour ? Who would take any notice of a deaf man criticizing the harmonies of musical genius or the melodies of human song ? Who then, can pay much attention to these blind leaders of the blind who, because in their own confusion they do not see the Christ of God, deny His love for others ? These deaf souls who, because they do not hear His voice themselves, deny His gracious words to us ?

> My Jesus to know,
> And to feel His Blood flow,
>   'Tis life everlasting,
> 'Tis Heaven below.

Likewise, ye younger, submit yourselves unto the elder. Yea, all of you be subject one to another, and be clothed with humility : for God resisteth the proud, and giveth grace to the humble. Humble yourselves therefore under the mighty hand of God, that He may exalt you in due time.—1 Peter 5 : 5, 6.

Our young people must learn to bear reproof not only when they deserve to be reproved, but when they do not deserve it, and to be silent and humble when wrongfully accused. We must—oh, we must teach them how God hates the proud spirit and loves those who are meek and lowly in heart ; who, instead of being uppish and quick to take offence, are poor in spirit and little in their own eyes. We must make them to see that . . .

'. . . Meekness is the chosen bent
Of all the truly great, and all the innocent.'

It is important also that we teach them respect for their elders and those set in authority over them. Their parents and Officers have a special claim for this. They are put into the place they occupy by God, and for that reason the young should give them respect and consideration. They should be taught to give attention when spoken to, to greet respectfully, and never to speak rudely or ' answer back.' Especially should they be taught to show gentleness and kindness in dealing with the aged, with the weak or helpless, whether young or old, whether friend or stranger.

The imagination of man's heart is evil from his youth.—Genesis 8 : 21.
The weapons of our warfare are not carnal, but mighty through God. . . . Casting down imaginations, and every . . . thing that exalteth itself against the knowledge of God, and bringing into captivity every thought to the obedience of Christ.—2 Corinthians 10 : 4, 5.

What a horrible effect sin has on the *Imagination*, on all that belongs to the mind of man ! How it gets in there, and occupies men's thoughts so that they are not even listening when God speaks to them by conscience or by His servants, and finally stops their thinking about God altogether. It turns men's minds to dwell on injuries till their hearts burn with hate. It lights the fires of passion and filthy lust by unclean thoughts, and by and by the sinful mind becomes a dreadful infection to the whole man.

> Come, Holy Ghost, all sacred Fire !
>   Come, fill Thy earthly temples now,
> Emptied of every base desire ;
>   Reign Thou within, and only Thou.
> Fill every chamber of the soul ;
>   Fill all our thoughts, our passions fill,
> Till under Thy supreme control
>   Submissive rests our cheerful will.

**The servant of the Lord must . . . be gentle
unto all men.**—2 Timothy 2 : 24.

Kindness will lead to personal thought for those
around us. It did so with Jesus. ' Come ye apart,'
He said on one occasion to the weary disciples, ' and
rest awhile.' And again, after a weary night of toil
on the sea, Peter and some others found Jesus mind-
ful of their bodily needs, with a fire ready on the
shore in the early morning, and He said, ' Bring of
the fish, . . . come and dine.'

My comrades, how many opportunities for practis-
ing this, the true kindness, does every Salvationist's
life afford ! In visiting, how often would a way be
found to some hard heart if there was an offer made
to light a fire in the early morning, or tend it in the
lone night hours, or to do some other little thing of
that sort. In the Meetings, too, how often one kind
word of inquiry about health, or work, or home,
which could be spoken in one moment, would bring
a ray of comfort to hearts that are sick and sore.
Oh, think, and you will find out how to make your
gentleness and kindness a positive foretaste of Heaven
to many whom you now scarcely notice at all.

> ' In the village, in the town,
>   On the railway, in the square,
>   Came a beam of kindness down,
>   Doubling daylight everywhere.'

Fear none of those things which thou shalt suffer ; . . . be thou faithful unto death, and I will give thee a crown of life.—Revelation 2 : 10.

There is no doubt that many people go astray in prayer because they are constantly asking God to deliver them out of trial and sorrow and temptation instead of praying for patience and grace to bear their trials and carry their sorrows and overcome their temptations. This is a common blunder. It must be grievous to God to be dunned by people who are always crying out that they may be spared from this and that, or helped out of something else, instead of crying to Him for life and power and love to show His wonderful grace and goodness amidst the darkness of their grief or want, or in the fierceness of their conflicts. Quite evidently, it is not always His plan to save us from sorrow or trial, but to save us *in* it. God did not choose to save the three Hebrew lads from entering the fiery furnace ; but He shared it— and His strength— with them, and verified the promise, ' When thou passest through the fire, thou shalt not be burned.' His love and grace were manifested, not in escape from the fiery billows, but escape from harm while in them.

Jesus cried with a loud voice, saying, . . . My God, my God, why hast Thou forsaken Me ?
—Matthew 27 : 46.

Before the final struggle in many great conflicts, inward consolations on which so much seems to depend are often mysteriously withdrawn. Why it should be so we do not know ; it is a mystery ; it was so with our Master. Do not let the servant expect to be above his Lord. This terrible moment of seeming separation from the Father, did not, however, make the final victory any the less. And if you are one with Him, and have really set your heart on glorifying Him, and if you can only *endure*, such moments will not take from your victory one shred of its joy. Oh, then, *hold on to your cross*. Even if it seems, as it sometimes may, that God has forsaken you, and that you are left to suffer alone, without either the sympathy of those around you or the conscious support of the indwelling God, *hold on to your cross*. This is the way of Calvary—this is becoming conformable to the death of the Lord Jesus.

> When darkness seems to veil His face,
> I rest on His unchanging grace ;
> In every high and stormy gale
> My anchor holds within the veil.

Be ye kind one to another, . . . forgiving one another, even as God for Christ's sake hath forgiven you.—Ephesians 4 : 32.

This is the old and ever new way of dealing with injuries, especially ' personal injuries.' Is it yours ? Are you seeking thus after reasons for making the wrong done to you appear pardonable ? Is your first response to an affront or insult or slander, or to some still greater wrong, to pray the Father for those whom you believe to be injuring you, that His gracious gift of forgiveness may come upon them ? That is the principle of Calvary. That is the spirit, the mind of Christ.

> Would Jesus have the sinner die,
>   Why hangs He then on yonder tree ?
> What means that strange expiring cry ?
>   Sinners, He prays for you and me :
> ' Forgive them, Father, oh, forgive !
> They know not that by Me they live ! '
>
> Oh, let Thy love my heart constrain,
>   Thy love for every sinner free ;
> That every fallen soul of man
>   May taste the grace that found out me ;
> That all mankind with me may prove
> Thy sovereign, everlasting love !

When they had performed all things according to the law of the Lord, they returned into Galilee, to their own city Nazareth. And the child grew, and waxed strong in spirit, filled with wisdom : and the grace of God was upon Him.—Luke 2 : 39, 40.

The birth and childhood of Jesus were the beginning of His great sacrifice, as well as the preparation for it. The spirit of Bethlehem and the spirit of Calvary are one. He was born for others that He might die for others. The mystery of God in the Babe was the beginning of the mystery of God on the Cross. The one was a part of the other. If they had not ' laid Him in a manger ' for us, they could never have laid Him in the tomb, that He might ' taste death for every man.'

And is it not in this same fashion and for this same purpose that Christ is to be formed in us ? ' He grew.' Progress is the law of happiness, the law of holiness, the law of life. To stand still is to die. It was not enough for the fulfilment of His great mission that He should be born, that He should live—He must grow.

But how, and in what, are we to grow ? In spiritual strength and stature ; that is, from the timid babe to the bold and valiant soldier ; in the power to do the things we ought to do, in the ability to obey the inward voice. It is by the daily acts of loving help that the soul learns to soar on eagles' wings, and shout the truth that God is gracious, and to brave difficulty and danger in His service. They go from strength to strength. Are you so journeying ?

46

Lord, Thou hast been our dwelling place in all generations.—Psalm 90 : 1.

Jesus said : **Abide in Me, and I in you. As the branch cannot bear fruit of itself, except it abide in the vine ; no more can ye, except ye abide in Me.** —John 15 : 4.

God is our true Home. This is one of the very central realities of religion, as our dear old Paul proved. Persecuted, imprisoned, ship-wrecked, living without ordinary human ties of home or love, and thrown when an old man to the lions, he proved that God was the home of his soul right to the very end. In Him he lived, and moved, and had his being, as he declared on Mars Hill. Our comrades in every part of the world have proved the same truth. God has proved to be Home to thousands of them who for His sake have given up home for ever.

> No home on earth have I,
>   No nation owns my soul ;
> My dwelling-place is the Most High,
>   I'm under His control.
> O'er all the earth alike,
>   My Father's grand domain,
> Each land and sea with Him alike,
>   O'er all He yet shall reign.

Thine ears shall hear a word behind thee, saying, This is the way, walk ye in it.—Isaiah 30 : 21.

Up and down the land are those to whom God has spoken, of whom we may say, ' The Lord has commanded ' them to take up their cross. But some one may ask, ' How may I know that the Lord has commanded ? ' That is a difficult question to answer, except in one way : *you will know*. How the conviction will come to you, I cannot tell. You may, in fact, never fully know yourself ; but if the Lord has commanded, you will have an inward assurance that this is so—*you will know* ! It is a terrible thing to neglect that assurance. To do so is not only to go against the light for yourself, but it is probably to withhold the light from those you might have saved from their impending doom.

Yes, the Living God has spoken to some who will read these lines. They are chosen to be His watchmen. They know what they ought to do. *They know !*

By Thine unerring Spirit led,
  We shall not in the desert stray ;
We shall not full directions need,
  Nor miss our providential way ;
As far from danger as from fear,
While Love, Almighty Love, is near.

Jesus answered them, saying, The hour is come, that the Son of man should be glorified. Verily, verily, I say unto you, Except a corn of wheat fall into the ground and die, it abideth alone : but if it die, it bringeth forth much fruit.—John 12 : 23, 24.

Then said Jesus . . . He that sent Me is with Me : the Father hath not left Me alone.—John 8 : 28, 29.

Seed must abide unfruitful unless it is put into the earth alone to weaken and die that it may bring forth fruit. Some of the suns and stars which shine the brightest are those which abide alone in the solitary spaces of the firmament.

So I say to the lonely ones : It may be the same with you. Do not repine. Above all things, do not be selfish. Do not waste your pity on yourself. Do not look for rest within. If you dam the waters of the little spring which God has placed in your breast it will fail—assuredly it will fail, and you will be left without any water at all. But if you will let your little spring flow forth, your brook will become a river ; if you can say, ' Never mind me ; here, I give my sorrow, my loneliness, my disappointment—I give them all to my God to be consecrated by Him and made—little morsels though they be—into bread and water for the famishing around me,' then you will be blessed, and other people will be blessed as well.

The Lord said unto me, . . . thou shalt go to all that I shall send thee, and whatsoever I command thee thou shalt speak. Be not afraid.—Jeremiah 1 : 7, 8.

His word was in mine heart as a burning fire shut up in my bones, and I was weary with forbearing, and I could not stay.—Jeremiah 20 : 9.

But Jeremiah soon relented. It was a sign that he was a true prophet that he was tempted to give up. And it was much more a sign that he was a true prophet that he was obliged to cry out : ' His word was in mine heart—I could not stay.' Yes, that is it. It was not merely that he had taken possession of the word of God, but that the word of God had taken possession of him. It was in him ; it was like an inextinguishable fire in his bones ; it was a part of his very life.

Blessed be God, who has called us in The Army, we know what that means also ! Oh, then, let us hold on to our duty ! Ever on ! It is not difficulties which spoil men. It is not devils that silence them. It is not even temptations to selfishness which destroy them. What does overthrow some of them is going back on God—going back on their own vows ; doing violence to the Holy Ghost, and silencing the inward voice—the living word which He has given them to declare to the souls of men. O my God, do Thou save us from this great peril—from this great sin !

When the road we tread is rough, let us bear in mind,
In our Saviour strength enough we may always find ;
Though the fighting may be tough, let our motto be,
    Go on, go on to victory !

Christ glorified not Himself, . . . Though He were a Son, yet learned He obedience by the things which He suffered ; and being made perfect, He became the author of eternal salvation unto all them that obey Him.—Hebrews 5 : 5, 8, 9.

Jesus Christ's life was a discipline, in the very highest sense of the word. Much of His love for those around Him was disappointed, and His trust betrayed. He was despised where He should have been honoured : rejected where He should have been received. ' He came unto His own, and His own received Him not.' ' Not this man,' they cried, ' but Barabbas.' But out of it all He came forth perfect and entire, lacking nothing—the chiefest among ten thousand, the altogether lovely. It may be a mystery, but it is a fact all the same, that the more the precious and wondrous and eternal jewel was cut and cut again, the more the light and glory of the Dayspring from on High was made manifest to men.

> Worship, honour, power and blessing
>   Thou art worthy to receive ;
> Loudest praises without ceasing
>   Meet it is for us to give.
> Help, ye bright angelic spirits,
>   Bring your sweetest, noblest lays :
> Help to sing the Saviour's merits,
>   Help to chant Immanuel's praise.

The Lord is good, a strong hold in the day of trouble ; and He knoweth them that trust in Him. —Nahum 1 : 7.

Blessed be the name of God for ever and ever : for wisdom and might are His : . . . He changeth the times and the seasons.—Daniel 2 : 20, 21.

Instead of the hard compulsion of some inexorable and unchanging law fixing summer where it must, and planting winter in our midst whether it be well or ill, here is the sweet assurance that the seasons change at His command, and that the winds and the waves obey Him. It is not some abstract and unknowable force, taking no account of us and ours, with whom we have to do ; but a living and ruling Father ; He who maketh small the drops of water that pour down rain ; He who shuts up the sea with doors, and says : ' Here shall thy proud waves be stayed ' ; He who maketh the south winds to blow, and by whose breath the frost is given ; He who teaches the swallow to know the time of her coming, and has made both summer and winter, and the day and the night His servants—*He is our Father*. How precious to feel that our times are in His hands ; and to know that, whether the year be young or old, He will fill it with mercy and crown it with loving-kindness !

> Yes, He sees and knows me daily,
>   Watches over me in love,
> Sends me help when foes assail me,
>   Bids me ever look above.
> Soon my journey will be ended,
>   Life is drawing to a close ;
> I shall then be well attended—
>   This my Heavenly Father knows.

Hannah answered and said . . . my lord, I am a woman of a sorrowful spirit : I have drunk neither wine nor strong drink, but have poured out my soul before the Lord . . . out of the abundance of my complaint and grief have I spoken. . . . Then Eli answered and said, Go in peace : and the God of Israel grant thee thy petition that thou hast asked of Him.—1 Samuel : 1 15–17.

I do not think there is much value in praying, either in private or in public, for anything we do not really desire at the time we pray. We may fill up the time, but it will be to little purpose unless our soul's hunger prompts our words. I would go so far as to say that it would be far better to pray for something we really desire even though it may have no relation whatever to the occasion, than to pray for things for which we have no true desire, simply because we are called upon to pray. Prayer without desire is like a bird without wings, it cannot rise.

It is this desire, this asking God for what springs out of a flame of longing in our own spirits, that lifts true prayer above the mere words employed. We all know that the most beautiful language and choicest thoughts often leave us cold and unmoved, while the bursting, almost incoherent cry moves us deeply, lifts our spirits above the secularities and buzzing trifles around us and makes us plume the wings of our souls.

The way of peace they know not ; and there is no judgment in their goings : they have made them crooked paths : whosoever goeth therein shall not know peace.—Isaiah 59 : 8.

Through the tender mercy of our God . . . the dayspring from on high hath visited us, . . . to guide our feet into the way of peace.—Luke 1 : 78, 79.

Peace is impossible without God's help. Unless the vanquished is willing to let the Victor bring in the Balm, there will be no calm for the storm-driven soul, no rest to the burdened mind and memory, no peace for the guilty conscience. Alas ! I know that men everywhere still cry out for help from other physicians. They go about asking :

' Canst thou not minister to a mind diseas'd,
Pluck from the memory a rooted sorrow, . . .
And with some sweet oblivious antidote
Cleanse the stuff'd bosom of that perilous stuff
Which weighs upon the heart ? '

And the answer is always : ' No, we cannot '—with sometimes the mocking advice to the overburdened spirit, ' Try to do it for yourself ! ' The fact is that love is the only help for the sin and sorrow in man, and even the sweet healing virtues which distil in the heart of God can only heal us when they have conquered all our powers.

Love can bow down the stubborn neck,
    The stone to flesh convert,
Soften and melt and pierce and break
    The very hardest heart.

Help, Lord ; . . . for the faithful fail from among the children of men. They speak . . . with flattering lips and with a double heart.—Psalm 12 : 1, 2.

Not unto us, O Lord, not unto us, but unto Thy name give glory, for Thy mercy, and for Thy truth's sake.—Psalm 115 : 1.

Oh, let us beware ! This temptation to take God's glory and give it to another is still a very real trial to some of us. It is so natural to seek our own. It is so easy to go about after the praise of our gifts and the honour of our own selves. Let us beware ! The people around us even with the best intentions are often so ready to become the tools of Satan with their flatteries, and our own hearts are such poor weak things ! ' Let him that thinketh he standeth take heed lest he fall.'

What am I, O Thou glorious God,
   And what my father's house to Thee
That Thou such mercies hast bestowed
   On me, the chief of sinners, me ?
I take the blessing from above,
And wonder at Thy boundless love.

Honour and might and thanks and praise
   I render to my pardoning God,
Extol the riches of Thy grace
   And spread Thy saving name abroad,
That only name to sinners given
Which lifts poor dying souls to Heaven.

Then spake Jesus to the multitude, and to His disciples, saying, The scribes and the Pharisees sit in Moses' seat : . . . but do not ye after their works : for they say, and do not. . . . Woe unto you, . . . hypocrites ! for ye shut up the kingdom of heaven against men.—Matthew 23 : 1–3, 13.

The kingdom of God is not in word, but in power.—1 Corinthians 4 : 20.

The form of godliness without the power is not only the greatest of all shams, but it is the most easily detected. Hence it is that a large part of mankind is either disgusted to hostility, or utterly estranged from real religion, by theories and ceremonials which, though they may continue to exist in shadow, have lost their life and soul.

Sound doctrine will of itself never save a soul. A man may believe every word of the faith of a Churchman or a Salvationist, and yet be as ignorant of any real experience of religion as an infidel or an idolater. And it is this merely intellectual or sentimental holding of the truth about God and Christ, about Holiness and Heaven, which makes the ungodly mass look upon Christianity as nothing more than an opinion or a trade ; a something with which they have no concern.

Men require something beyond creeds, be they ever so correct ; and traditions, be they ever so venerable ; and sacraments, be they ever so sacred. They ask for power to grapple with what they feel to be base in human nature and to master what they know is selfish and sinful in their own hearts.

56

Then said Jesus . . , If any man will come after Me, let him deny himself, and take up his cross, and follow Me.—Matthew 16 : 24.

Human nature is a collection of likes and dislikes. The great masses of men are governed by their preferences. What they like, they strive after ; what they do not like, they neglect, or refuse, or resist. Many of these preferences, though not harmful in themselves, lead continually to that subjection of the will to self-interest, and help that self-satisfaction and self-love which are the deadly enemies of the soul. Now, true self-denial is the denial, for Christ's sake and the sake of souls, of these preferences. To say to God : ' I sacrifice my way for Thy way—my wish for Thy wish—my will for Thy will—my plan for Thy plan—my life for Thy life '—this is self-denial.

> Behold, the servant of the Lord,
>   I wait Thy guiding hand to feel,
> To hear and keep Thy every word,
>   To prove and do Thy perfect will ;
> Joyful from my own works to cease,
> Glad to fulfil all righteousness.
>
> Me if Thy grace vouchsafe to use,
>   Meanest of all Thy creatures, me,
> The deed, the time, the manner choose ;
>   Let all my fruit be found of Thee !
> Let all my works in Thee be wrought,
> By Thee to full perfection brought.

The fruit of the Spirit is love, joy, peace, long-suffering, gentleness, goodness, faith.—Galatians 5 : 22.

There is a wonderful unity between the Holy Spirit and the work which He, the Holy Spirit, does. Take a familiar illustration of this. When I carry a lighted candle into a dark room I, a person, enter the room as a light-bearer, and at the same time the light is poured out on the darkness of the room. I bring the light, and the light I bring is spread abroad. That is just what the Holy Spirit does. When He, our Personal Deliverer, enters, the light He brings— that is, the light of His own nature—is poured out upon the darkness within.

It is the same with love and zeal. When the Holy Spirit comes in and makes His abode in His sons and daughters, no matter how great or small, how wise or simple they may be, He brings the love and zeal which are His, and begins at once to pour them out upon all our powers, and to spread them abroad in our hearts and in our lives.

> Holy Spirit, Love Divine,
> Glow within this heart of mine ;
> Kindle every high desire,
> Perish self in Thy pure fire !

All scripture is given by inspiration of God, and is profitable for doctrine, for reproof, for correction, for instruction in righteousness : that the man of God may be perfect.—2 Timothy 3 : 16, 17.

Just as many things in nature standing ready and complete for our use are yet useless until we grasp them and, working at them, make them our own ; so, much of the teaching of the Scriptures and many facts of God's dealings with men are of little real service to us until we have taken hold of them for ourselves, examined and prayed about them and applied them to the wants and wounds of our own hearts.

The corn, for instance, hangs ripe and pure upon the stalk, a perfect fruit of the earth, and yet to make full use of it we need to seize it, to thresh and crush it, to convert it into flour and dough and subject it to a violent heat ; and even then we must masticate and digest it for ourselves.

It is the same with much of the most precious of the grain from the harvest fields of truth. Beautiful and valuable as it always is, it is only when we have studied it for ourselves, taken the trouble to thresh it from the incident or history in which God has placed it and, above all, have fearlessly applied it as a test to our own conduct and character, that we get out of it the strength and life and light that it is intended to give.

Come unto Me, all ye that labour and are heavy laden, and I will give you rest. Take my yoke upon you, and learn of Me ; . . . and ye shall find rest unto your souls.—Matthew 11 : 28, 29.

Bear ye one another's burdens, and so fulfil the law of Christ.—Galatians 6 : 2.

The ruler, contending with unruly men ; the workman, fighting for consideration from a greedy employer ; the dark-skinned, sad-eyed mother, sending forth her only babe to perish in the waters of the sacred river of India, thus ' giving the fruit of her body for the sin of her soul ' ; the great multitude of the sorrowful, which no man can number, who refuse to be comforted ; the dying, whose death will be an unwilling leap in the dark—all these, yea, and all others, may find in the law of Christ that which will harmonize every conflicting interest, which will solve the problems of human life, which will build up a holy character, which will gather up and sanctify everything that is good in every faith and in every man, and will unite all who will obey it in the one great brotherhood of the one fold and the one Shepherd.

> Jesus, my Truth, my Way,
>   My sure, unerring Light,
> On Thee my feeble steps I stay,
>   Which Thou wilt guide aright.
>
> My Wisdom and my Guide,
>   My Counsellor Thou art ;
> Oh, never let me leave Thy side,
>   Or from Thy paths depart !

**As the Lord commanded . . . so did Joshua ;
he left nothing undone of all that the Lord commanded Moses.**—Joshua 11 : 15.
**I will delight myself in Thy statutes : I will not
forget Thy word.**—Psalm 119 : 16.
**Servants of Christ, doing the will of God from
the heart.**—Ephesians 6 : 6.

' He left nothing undone of all that the Lord
commanded.' So runs the inspired record of one of
God's great servants. It is a remarkable witness to a
remarkable life. His life was full of valuable service,
and was fruitful in many ways for his nation and his
Lord. But this is a testimony not so much to his
great activity as to the fact that he was saved from
failing to act. He left nothing undone of the things
that the Lord commanded.

Many sincere people make the mistake of supposing
that they may disobey in some things if only they
obey in others. They make, or try to make, a kind of
bargain with God. I cannot find any excuse for it.
The fact is, we are not our own. We have nothing
that is really our own. We are at best the poor
relations of our Lord, dependent upon Him for all
and bound in duty, in gratitude and in honour, as well
as in our own true interests, to observe His wishes
and to do His will in all things.

> Not my own ! My time, my talents,
> Freely all to Christ I bring,
> To be used in joyful service
> For the glory of my King.

I am crucified with Christ : nevertheless I live : . . . and the life which I now live in the flesh I live by the faith of the Son of God, who loved me, and gave Himself for me.—Galatians 2 : 20.

Knowing this, that our old man is crucified with Him, . . . that henceforth we should not serve sin.—Romans 6 : 6.

It is a common mistake to view religion as merely a state of safety. It is not even that unless it is also much beside. It is the creation of a new life, the moulding of a new man, the blending of new powers, the living out of a new revelation, the building up of a new character. And how can that be done except by storm, by sorrow, by trial, by buffeting, by disappointment, by crucifying the old man, by mortifying the flesh, by smashing up self and pride, by the agony of disappointed hopes and the loss of anticipated joys, and by obedience to the law of suffering and love ?

If all were easy, if all were bright,
Where would the cross be ?   and where the fight ?
But in the hardness God gives to you
Chances of proving that you are true.

Let us press on then, never despair,
Live above feeling, victory's there ;
Jesus can keep us so near to Him
That nevermore our faith shall grow dim.

Now is come salvation, and strength, and the kingdom of our God, and the power of His Christ : . . . And they overcame . . . by the blood of the Lamb, and by the word of their testimony ; . . . Therefore rejoice.—Revelation 12 : 10–12.

In the end the Lamb will appear with thousands of thousands of His saints to put an end to wickedness. Jesus will reign—and the kingdoms of the world shall become the kingdoms of our Lord and of His Christ.

Now is the time for faith in the Lamb. Now in these days of death and of the destruction of so much that the world values and needs, and amidst so much that savours of hatred and passion and falsehood : now is the time to prove our own selves, as the Apostle said, whether we be in the faith or not. Now is the time to stand up for Jesus and His Cross. Now is the time to pour out our love on the world—to make men see and feel that we really love God and them ; that religion is love.

> Lo ! He comes with clouds descending,
>   Once for favoured sinners slain ;
> Thousand thousand saints attending,
>   Swell the triumph of His train :
>   Hallelujah !
>   God appears on earth to reign.
>
> Those dear tokens of His passion
>   Still His dazzling body bears ;
> Cause of endless exultation
>   To His ransomed worshippers ;
>   With what rapture
>   Gaze we on those glorious scars !

Helping together by prayer.—2 Corinthians 1 : 11.
The eyes of the Lord are over the righteous, and His ears are open unto their prayers.—1 Peter 3 : 12.

Prayer strengthens and enlarges love. I have had some of the richest blessings from the hand of God, especially in recent years, in pleading with Him for particular people in whom I have been interested in my own Meetings, especially backsliders. My heart is always tender to backsliders. They suffer so much. They have such troubles. They feel (especially if they have been in The Army any length of time and enjoyed its comradeship) so isolated—left like refuse on the shore. In my own spirit I have been so blessed and touched in pleading with God for some particular man or woman who has drawn out my sympathy. I shall soon be seventy years of age, if God allows me to live long enough, and here I am, after nearly sixty years of soul-saving work and trying to bless the people and work for God, and my own heart is touched and made tender, my love for souls is increased, and I am made to realize my own need, *while I am praying for particular souls.*

> O Lord, increase our faith and love,
> So shall we all Thy goodness prove
> And gain from Thine own boundless store
> The fruits of prayer for evermore.

The Lord heard the voice of your words.
—Deuteronomy 1 : 34.
**Out of the abundance of the heart the mouth
speaketh . . . by thy words thou shalt be justified,
and by thy words thou shalt be condemned.**
—Matthew 12 : 34, 37.

True gentleness and kindness in speech are, of
course, foreign to many natures. Words spoken in
haste may not always be wrong ; they may in themselves be practically colourless, and yet because of
the manner in which they are uttered may cause
unnecessary pain. You know that in the Alps an
avalanche is sometimes so delicately poised that even
the vibration of the air caused by a shout will bring
it crashing down with disastrous results for the
people below. If men would advance in the life of
God they must be free not only from idle and wrong
talk, but from hasty, uncharitable and ill-considered
speech.

The tongue is like a mint ; it may turn out base
counters of little or no value, stamped with the sign
of earth and earthy things, or coins of pure gold,
bearing the image of the Divine. The tongue of the
sanctified man or woman may send into circulation
words of priceless value. ' The lips of the righteous
feed many.'

Yea, mine own familiar friend, in whom I trusted, . . . hath lifted up his heel against me. But Thou, O Lord, be merciful unto me.—Psalm 41 : 9, 10.

Man himself is the most-changeable thing in all man's world. It is not merely that our companions and friends and loved ones die, and the dear places that knew them know them no more ; it is not merely that their circumstances change, youth to age and decay, but it is that *they* change. The ardour of near friendship grows cold and fades away ; the trust which once knew no limitations is narrowed down and, by and by, walled in with doubts and fears ; the comradeship which was so sweet and strong, and quickened us to great deeds is changed for other companionships ; the love which seemed so deep and true, and was ready to ' look on tempests ' for us, becomes but a memory, even if it does not change into a well of bitter waters in our lives.

This fact of human mutability, this inherent changeableness in man, is the key to many of the darkest chapters of the world's history. But, blessed be the name of our God, above the strife of tongues and over the stormy seas of sorrow, when, as Job said, even our kinsfolk have failed and our familiar friends have forgotten us. there is borne to us the voice of One who sticketh closer than a brother, saying, ' I am the Lord ; I change not. I will never leave thee, nor forsake thee.' The more men change, the surer God will be ; the more they forget, the more He will remember ; the further they withdraw, the nearer He will come.

66

**When Jesus knew that His hour was come . . ,
having loved His own which were in the world, He
loved them unto the end.**—John 13 : 1.

Jesus knew the failures begotten of human weakness, as well as the horror of human sin. And so He
made allowances, and was as patient with those who
left Him as He was tender to those who were steadfast. He loved them both.

Go thou, and do likewise. In your home ; in your
family circle ; in your Corps ; in your office ; in your
work, be it what it may ; when men fail and forsake
your Lord, even if all disappoint and desert you,
you must love them still. Be faithful with them, but,
above all, be steadfast in your purpose, and devote
all your zeal and strength to finish the work that God
has given you to do. In short, go forward without
them ; but let your words and thoughts and prayers
for them be like your Master's.

I want, dear Lord, a love that cares for all,
A deep, strong love that answers every call ;
A love like Thine, a love divine,
A love to come or go ;
On me, dear Lord, a love like this bestow.

**Jesus . . . said . . , If a man love Me, he will
keep My words : and My Father will love Him,
and We will come unto him, and make Our abode
with him.**—John 14 : 23.

I love Thee every hour, Thou loving One,
Because Thou first loved me, Thou suffering Son.

> I love Thee, oh, I love Thee,
> Live to love and serve Thee ;
> All I have, my Saviour,
> I give to Thee.

I love Thee every hour, and Thee alone—
My Love, my Life, my Lord, my All-in-one.

I love Thee every hour, and never fear ;
Temptations lose their power, for Thou art here.

I love Thee every hour ; to hear Thy voice,
And do Thy blessed will, is all my choice.

I love Thee every hour, and I am Thine ;
And I have All-in-all, for Thou art mine.

W. BRAMWELL BOOTH.

**Continue in the faith grounded and settled, . . .
be not moved away from the hope of the gospel.**
– Colossians 1 : 23.

Jesus said : **So have I loved you : continue ye in
My love.**—John 15 : 9.

How shall we do it ? By endless suffering and
loving-kindness toward sinners. By humble service
for them, that vaunteth not itself ! By ministering
—not self-seeking—love ! By never-ending patience !
By refusal to yield to any provocation ! By sorrowing
to the depths over iniquity and sin ! By believing and
still believing for the good, be it ever so little, that is
in every soul ! By hoping when all others give up
hoping ! Nay, by hoping all things for those despairing souls who have long ceased to hope for anything ! Oh, dear, precious, beautiful hope—it is one
of the Salvationist's choicest treasures. And by
enduring all things. Yes, the hard and cruel things—
the icy and neglecting things. Love will endure for
others, as Love Himself endured for us.

Oh, grant that nothing in my soul
    May dwell but Thy pure love alone ;
Oh, may Thy love possess me whole,
    My Joy, my Treasure and my Crown.
Strange loves far from my heart remove ;
My every act, word, thought, be love.

**If thine eye offend thee, pluck it out : it is better
for thee to enter into the kingdom of God with one
eye, than having two eyes to be cast into hell fire.**
—Mark 9 : 47.

**Peter said, . . . Why hath Satan filled thine
heart to lie to the Holy Ghost, and to keep back
part . . . ? . . . why hast thou conceived this
thing in thine heart ? thou hast not lied unto men,
but unto God.**—Acts 5 : 3, 4.

How many sincere souls, when they look into their
own hearts, find, to their horror, evil in them where
they least expected it ; find them part stone, when
they should be all flesh ; find them bound to earth
and the love of earthly things, when they should be
free from the world and the love of the world ; find
them occupied, alas ! so often with idols and heart-
lusts, when God alone ought to rule and reign. Here
is a sphere for self-denial.

And if you would thus deny yourself, then examine
yourself. Study the evils of your own nature.
Recognize sin. Call it by its right name when you
speak of it in the solitude of your own heart. If there
are the remains of the deadly poison in you, say so to
God. ' Confess your sins.' Attack them as the
farmer attacks the poison-plant amongst his crops.
That is the ' perfect self-denial '—to cut off the right
hand, and to pluck out and cast away what is as
dear as the right eye, if it offend against the law of
purity and truth and love. But you yourself are to
do it.

Jesus said . . . While ye have light, believe in the light, that ye may be the children of light. —John 12 : 35, 36.

We have no light in ourselves. The most we can say for ourselves at our very best is that we are a kind of lantern. It is God who is the Light! It is He who plants His light in us! It is He, and He alone, who can dispel the darkness of unbelief and fear. *He will do it,* bless His holy Name! For He can make light in the darkest night! He can make gladness amid the deepest gloom of anxiety and care! He is our Sun, and His Light is the Light that works by love.

The great evil of spiritual eclipses is that they obstruct the Light. Men are so prone to turn from the high to the low, to build upon the material and the natural instead of upon the spiritual. What a shadow-maker is this! What a manufactory of darkness is trusting in the human, leaning on the arm of flesh, looking at the clouds!

Our Sun is ever the same! If there are any obstructions which now eclipse His Glory and Beauty, clear them out of the way! Make a free course for the light! No obstructions allowed! Shadows prohibited! Eclipses forbidden! A blue-sky religion! Can you sing the old song?

> ' Not a cloud doth arise
> To darken the skies,
>   Or hide for one moment
> My Lord from my eyes! '

Stand fast in the faith, quit you like men, be strong.—1 Corinthians 16 : 13.

Weakness in many things is not inconsistent with goodness and purity and love. The manger has in this also a message for us. Out of that mystery of helplessness came forth the Lion-Heart of Love, which led Him, for us, to the wine-press alone, and which, while we were yet rebels, loved us with an everlasting love, going, for us, to a lonely and shameful death. Take heart, then, remembering that it is out of weakness we are to be made strong. Be of good courage—to-day may be the day of the enemy's strength, when you are constrained to cry out : ' This is your hour and the power of darkness ! ' but to-morrow will be yours. The weakness and humiliation of the stable must go before the Mount of Transfiguration, the Mount of Calvary, the Resurrection Glory and the exaltation of the Father's Throne. Take heart !

> The cross is not greater than His grace,
> The storm cannot hide His blessèd face !
> I am satisfied to know that with Jesus here below
> I can conquer every foe.

On My servants and on My handmaidens I will pour out in those days of My Spirit.—Acts 2 : 18.

This promise of God, that He will pour out His Spirit, is one of the most wonderful in the whole history of man. It is, in fact, a promise to the world as a whole, to the entire family of Christ in the world, and also to each of the individuals who compose that family. It is especially of that promise of a personal gift that I am thinking here.

Now, the Holy Spirit is a Person. He comes to the heart of a man as a Person. He makes demands, and makes promises, which could only be made by a Person. When Jesus Christ said, as He was about to leave His disciples, ' I will send you another Comforter, and He shall abide with you,' it is quite clear that He meant to convey the idea that Some One would come to them who should be a substitute for Himself.

> Come, Thou Witness of His dying ;
> Come, Remembrancer Divine !
> Let us feel Thy power, applying
> Christ to every soul—and mine !

Our light affliction, which is but for a moment, worketh for us a far more exceeding and eternal weight of glory ; while we look not at the things which are seen, but at the things which are not seen.—2 Corinthians 4 : 17, 18.

Consider what an entirely new light might be thrown upon God's dealings with us, in affliction and pain, if it should appear in the world to come that, in much which is now most mysterious and torturing to us, we had been bearing one another's burdens ! Every one knows how often love makes us long to bear grief and pain for those dear to us ; every one has seen a mother suffer, in grateful silence, both bodily pain and heart-anguish, in her child's stead, preferring that the child should never know. Suppose it should turn out, hereafter, that many of the afflictions which now seem so perplexing and so grievous have really been given us to bear in order to spare and shield our loved ones, and make it easier for them— tossing on the stormy waters—to reach Home at last ? Would not this add a whole world of joy to the glory which shall be revealed ? And would it not transform many of the darkest stretches of our earthly journey into bright memorials of the infinite wisdom and goodness of our God ?

> Thy everlasting truth,
>   Father, Thy ceaseless love
> Sees all Thy children's wants, and knows
>   What best for each will prove.

Peter . . . lifted up his voice, and said . . .
hearken to my words : for these are not drunken,
as ye suppose. . . . But this is that which was
spoken by the prophet Joel ; And it shall come to
pass in the last days, saith God, I will pour out of
My Spirit . . . : and your sons and your daughters
shall prophesy.—Acts 2 : 14–17.

Paul said, **Remember, that by the space of three
years I ceased not to warn every one night and day
with tears.**—Acts 20 : 31.

Be desperately in earnest! This is a great security
against the evil of formalism, even if it does not always
ensure success. The great majority *are* in earnest.
What I ask you to do is to express it ! To show it !
To go about manifesting what you feel ! It is often
said nowadays not to be ' good form ' to be put
about, to be enthusiastic and demonstrative about
anything. A detached, unresponsive, formal manner
and the suppression of all sign of emotion is the
fashion, especially when you come to religion. Now
this is as far from the manifestation of earnestness for
which I plead as the east is from the west. What can
the fashion of this world matter to us ? As a matter of
fact, this willingness to live in the arctic regions is
one of the most damnable consequences of that vile
sin—pride and self-conceit. Away with it !

> I want, dear Lord, a soul on fire for Thee,
> A soul baptized with heavenly energy ;
>   A willing mind, a ready hand
>   To do whate'er I know,
> To spread Thy light wherever I may go.

Holy men of God spake as they were moved by the Holy Ghost.—2 Peter 1 : 21.

Paul **said unto them, Ye know, from the first day that I came . . , after what manner I have been with you at all seasons, . . . and how I kept back nothing that was profitable unto you, but have shewed you, and have taught you publicly, and from house to house.**—Acts 20 : 18, 20.

That instruction on the things of God, which is a necessity for every true child of God, comes almost invariably by the agency or through the experiences of others. The joys and consolation of fellowship can only be the result of communion with the saints. And though it is true that God can, and often does, wonderfully teach and inspire His people without the direct aid of any human agent, it is equally true that He generally does so by the employment of His word, which He has revealed to men. Nor does this in the least detract from our absolute dependence upon Him. The man who crosses the Atlantic in a steamship is no less dependent on the sea because he employs the vessel for his journey. And so we are no less dependent upon God because He has been pleased to employ various humble and simple instruments to save and teach and guide us. After full allowance has been made for the power and influence of intervening agencies, it is in Him we really live and move and have our being.

Jesus hath God raised up, whereof we all are witnesses . . . and having received . . . the promise of the Holy Ghost, He hath shed forth this, which ye now see and hear.—Acts 2 : 32, 33.

Victory for you will mean victory for others. Jesus will reveal Himself through you. Men shall see your smile and hear your testimony and note the witness of your humility and faith and patience and kindness—your gentleness in trial, your long-suffering in provocation, your joy in sorrow, your peace in the storm—and they will say just as men said to one another in Jerusalem when they saw the exultant looks and triumphant steps of the disciples after the Resurrection, ' Why, Jesus must be risen again—this is none other than the power of His Resurrection—it is like life from the dead ! '

To you it is given, by the life and power of Jesus, to show forth the Impossible accomplished.

> Only as I truly know Thee
>   Can I make Thee truly known ;
> Only bring the power to others
>   Which in my own life is shown.

Christ sent me . . . to preach the gospel : not in wisdom of words. . . . For the word of the cross is to them that are perishing foolishness ; but unto us which are being saved it is the power of God.
—1 Corinthians 1 : 17, 18 ; R.V.

The fact is, that Revelation not only declares principles and discloses facts, but it claims at the same time that men must bring themselves into harmony with those principles and build upon those facts. If they do not do this, they cannot see them ; they cannot understand their character ; they cannot discern their origin ; they cannot discover their place in God's plan.

This is eminently the case with the Cross of Christ and all that it means. No research, no erudition, no wisdom, as we understand wisdom, can, without a personal experience of its power, explain its glories or apprehend its mysterious truth. Indeed, this very thing—the strange incapableness of the wise of this world to comprehend the purposes and principles of God's scheme—is expressly foretold by the Prophets of old, by Christ Himself and by His Apostles.

> Come, Jesus, Lord, with holy fire,
> Come, and my quickened heart inspire,
>   Cleansed in Thy precious Blood ;
> Now to my soul Thyself reveal,
> Thy mighty working let me feel,
>   Since I am born of God.

Keep the sabbath day to sanctify it, as the Lord thy God hath commanded thee . . . that thy manservant and thy maidservant may rest as well as thou.—Deuteronomy 5 : 12, 14.

The whole trend of modern life is in the direction of wiping out the distinction between the Sabbath and the other days of the week. In course of time, unless His people are very careful, this provision God has made for the cultivation of the spiritual life of the race, by the setting aside of one day in seven for rest and worship, will be entirely swept away. Now we must set our face like a flint against this tendency, and teach our young people to have due regard for the Sabbath. They need to be given correct ideas as to how to make the best of the day. We do not want them to become narrow, fanatical ' Sabbatarians,' but to train them to make it a day of worship, spiritual refreshment and happy spiritual service.

> Give us a day of wonders,
>   Jehovah, bare Thine arm ;
> Pour out Thy Holy Spirit,
>   Make known Thy healing balm ;
> Give blessings without number,
>   Supply us from Thy store ;
> Dear Saviour, richly bless us,
>   Baptize us more and more.

Let not sin therefore reign . . . : but yield yourselves unto God, . . . as instruments of righteousness unto God. For sin shall not have dominion
over you : for ye are not under the law, but under
grace.—Romans 6 : 12 14.

What a *destroyer* sin is ! What fine, true, sincere
natures we see brought down by it ! What kindly,
sympathetic, loving hearts are changed to be cold and
selfish and cruel under its influences. What powers
of fidelity and courage never get a real chance in many
men—sin stabs them at the very beginning and they
die. What generous young hearts we often know
about—ready to believe all the good they can, and
to give and to forget themselves—and how sin just
kills it all, and they grow selfish and mean and
suspicious as the years come and go ! Yes, sin is the
great destroyer.

> Ah ! give me, Lord, the tender heart
>   That trembles at the approach of sin ;
> A godly fear of sin impart,
>   Implant, and root it deep within,
> That I may dread Thy gracious power,
> And never dare offend Thee more.

Who His own self bare our sins in His own body on the tree.—1 Peter 2 : 24.

He was wounded for our transgressions, He was bruised for our iniquities : the chastisement of our peace was upon Him ; . . . the Lord hath laid on Him the iniquity of us all.—Isaiah 53 : 5, 6.

Let us make men see the meaning of the agony which broke the dying Saviour's heart. He was wrestling with evil, He was standing in the breach for us, fighting single-handed the cruel fight with our murderous foe, and taking upon Himself the horrid and crushing guilt of our sin. Let us proclaim this uprooting but up-building truth more fearlessly than ever. Let us, I say, make men see and feel this. Tell them that Jesus Christ's message was no goody-goody recipe for covering over the abominations of man's evil nature. Tell them His work was no effort to make a little sect of those who should look down on their fellows from the heights of some imaginary holiness. No, Jesus in His heart agony, His loneliness, His bloody sweat, His hideous torture on the cross, His dying cry, His shameful death, speaks to us of a tremendous conflict to conquer sin, to break its bonds, to wash out—oh, thanks be to God !—to wash out its stains.

> Was it for sins that I have done
>   He suffered on the tree ?
> Amazing pity, grace unknown,
>   And love beyond degree !

The Lord make you to increase and abound in
love one toward another, and toward all men.
—1 Thessalonians 3 : 12.

Forgiving one another . . . even as Christ forgave you, so also do ye.—Colossians 3 : 13.

In nothing is it more demanded of us to approve
ourselves the ministers of God than in this. Indeed,
the condition of our own forgiveness is that we
forgive. Let us do it quickly. There is never an hour
to lose. Man is such a poor, passing creature ; if we
miss the moment for saying the word of forgiving
kindness, it may never return. Forgive and forget at
once ; let not the sun go down upon an unforgiven
wrong :

    ' Be swift in kindness, a long delay
      In kindness takes the kindness all away.'

This is the spirit of kindness ; and what men sow
they reap. People who go about ' scattering seeds of
kindness,' often come to the reaping of a rich harvest
much sooner than they expect. Just as one selfish and
unkind act begets another, so every kind deed done,
and kind word spoken, call forth other kind things
which come with blessing in their train.

Not as though I had already attained, either were already perfect : but I follow after . . . Christ Jesus. Brethren, I count not myself to have apprehended : but this one thing I do, forgetting those things which are behind, and reaching forth unto those things which are before, I press toward the mark for the prize of the high calling of God in Christ Jesus.—Philippians 3 : 12–14.

Let us take that lesson to our hearts, in this superficial, painted, rushing generation. Let us beware of resting our hope to satisfying the eternal claims of God upon some great event in our spiritual history of long ago. It is not enough to have been converted. It is not enough to have had the adoption of the Father. It is not enough to have entered the spiritual family of Christ. It is not enough that even Jesus revealed Himself in us. Thousands of false hopes are built on these past events, which, divinely wrought as they may have been, have ceased to possess any vital connection with the life and character of to-day. Such a religion is a religion of memory, destined to be turned in the presence of the Throne to unmixed remorse.

> My soul, be on thy guard !
> Ten thousand foes arise,
> The hosts of sin are pressing hard
> To draw thee from the Skies.
>
> Oh, watch, and fight, and pray ;
> The battle ne'er give o'er !
> Renew it boldly every day,
> And help Divine implore.

Be still, and know that I am God.—Psalm 46 : 10.
**Thou wilt keep him in perfect peace, whose mind
is stayed on Thee : because he trusteth in Thee.**
—Isaiah 26 : 3.

If we look closely at Christ's daily life, we can see
He was patient in the small trials. He showed the
same quiet, passive, waiting spirit when the petty
vexations swept up against Him, in Galilee, in
Jerusalem, in Samaria. A sacred patience holds Him.
His will is joined to His Father's. He can wait till
the clouds pass over, and be still when the small
storms go raging round. His own temper, the spirit
which surged up within Him when He saw the evil
that He abominated, was sanctified and controlled
and became wholly and absolutely still when the
small contradictions and oppositions met Him.

Can we learn this lesson ? How many people we
know who can rise up to the heights of spiritual
grandeur and power when called upon to do or suffer
some great thing for God, and yet are brought down
to defeat and discouragement by the little things,
just because they have not this power to be still !

> Only thy restless heart keep still,
>   And wait in cheerful hope, content
> To take whate'er His gracious will,
>   His all-discerning love, hath sent ;
> Nor doubt : our inmost wants are known
> To Him who chose us for His own.

And [Jesus] **spake . . , that men ought always
to pray, and not to faint.**—Luke 18 : 1.
Be ye therefore sober, and watch unto prayer.
—1 Peter 4 : 7.

Prayer is a guardian of the soul, nay, of the whole
man. The life of prayer, the spirit of prayer, the love
of prayer, the act of prayer. When travellers by
night would rest in safety in the depths of forests that
are frequented by beasts of prey, they light fires
around the little camp, and the wild animals do not
approach. The fire keeps them off. Even so the
fire of prayer ascending from a cleansed heart is the
surest protection against the creatures of darkness
that assail both body and soul.

> Sweet hour of prayer, sweet hour of prayer,
> That calls me from a world of care,
> And bids me at my Father's throne
> Make all my wants and wishes known :
> In seasons of distress and grief
> My soul has often found relief,
> And oft escaped the Tempter's snare
> By thy return, sweet hour of prayer.

I am not ashamed of the gospel of Christ : for it is the power of God unto salvation to every one that believeth.—Romans 1 : 16.

Ye know that ye were . . . redeemed . . . with the precious blood of Christ, as of a lamb without blemish and without spot.—1 Peter 1 : 18, 19.

The central, illuminating, mastering fact of all is the Divinity of Christ's nature. The blood and sacrifice of a man could never put away sin and repair the wrong that man has done to God. It is the Divine Man—the God-man—whose Precious Blood, shed for us, alone can wash away our stain.

Here many stumble. It is not to be surprised at. They will not have the Blood. They do not mind the lofty moral standards and the gentle counsels of the New Testament. They are quite pleased to note the progress of mankind in all that pertains to Jesus Christ's teaching about peace and mercy and charity. They even allow that His example in character and conduct was the noblest the world has seen. But when they come to His shame, His condemnation, His sacrifice, His death on the tree, they deny His testimony and refuse His offer of mercy. They say that the modern ideas resent the notion of one dying for another, and that to talk of the ' Blood of the Lamb ' is ' out of date ' and revolting to ' their highest sense.' Without this the whole message we have to proclaim is little more than a lifeless fable. Once more ' the blood is the life.'

**Lot dwelled in the . . . plain, and pitched his
tent toward Sodom. But the men of Sodom were
wicked and sinners before the Lord exceedingly.**
—Genesis 13 : 12.
Jesus said : **Ye cannot serve God and mammon.**
—Luke 16 : 13.

Lot's history, in spite of the difference between
then and now, appears to me to be a very instructive
study for these days. Among other lessons, this
story shows that no man can serve two masters, and
that in the end, though saved by ' the skin of his
teeth,' half and half loses all.

Compromise with the world will not make it any
better ! Lot threw away his life, his family, and his
fortune, all to no purpose, for he did no good in Sodom.
He made no convert to Jehovah there. So it ever is—
compromise with the world always fails. It pulls down
the man who proposes it and never raises up any one
else. Beware ! It often seems very reasonable to
make concessions—for the sake of peace. It was
Lot's wish to avoid the quarrelling of his servants
with those of Abraham that led him first to think of
Sodom—' I am not called,' Lot would say, ' for the
sake of the flocks, to sacrifice everything for Abraham
and his servants ' ; and you are not called, the Devil
will say, to do so for the sake of The Army. But
concessions to the world spell ruin and death.

> Take the world, but give me Jesus ;
>   He alone can satisfy :
> Take the world, but give me Jesus ;
>   'Neath His Cross I'll live and die.

**Jesus knowing that all things were now accom-
plished, that the scripture might be fulfilled, saith,
I thirst. . . . When Jesus therefore had received
the vinegar, He said, It is finished.**—John 19 : 28, 30.

Thus in His last, ever-wonderful words Jesus
pronounces Himself the sentence of His own heart
upon His own work. It is completed. Every barrier
is broken down. Every battle is fought, every hellish
dart has flown, every wilderness is past, every drop
of the cup of anguish has been drunk up, and with a
note of victorious confidence He cries out, ' It is
finished ! ' Looking back from the cross on all His
life in the light of these words, we see how He regarded
it as a great opportunity for accomplishing a great
duty and for the fulfilment of a mission. Now, He
says, ' The duty is done—the mission is fulfilled ; the
work is finished ! ' Truly it is a lofty, a noble, yea, a
godlike view of life !

Is it ours ? Death will come to us. ' The living
know that they shall die.' The waters will overflow
and the foundations will be broken up, and every
precious thing will grow dim, and our life, also, will
have passed. We shall then have to say of something,
' It is finished ! ' It will be too late to alter it.
' There is no man that hath power in the day of
death.'

Tribulation worketh patience ; and patience, experience ; and experience, hope ; and hope maketh not ashamed ; because the love of God is shed abroad in our hearts by the Holy Ghost which is given unto us.—Romans 5 : 3–5.

The dark valleys of bitterness and loneliness are often better for us than the land of Beulah. A queen, sitting for her portrait, commanded that it should be painted without shadows. ' Without shadows ! ' said the astonished artist. ' I fear your Majesty is not acquainted with the laws of light and beauty. There can be no good portrait without shading.' No more can there be a good Salvationist without trial, sorrow and storm. There might, perhaps, remain a stunted and unfruitful infancy life—but a *man* in Christ Jesus, a *Soldier* of the Cross, a *leader* of God's people, without tribulation *there can never be*. Patience, experience, faith, hope, love, if they do not actually grow from tribulations, are helped by them in their growth.

Since all that I meet shall work for my good,
The bitter is sweet, the medicine is food ;
Though painful at present, 'twill cease before long,
And then, oh, how pleasant the conqueror's song !

Mary Magdalene came and told the disciples that she had seen the Lord, and that He had spoken . . . unto her.—John 20 : 18.

Well done, Mary! Your simple witness did accomplish a mighty work in those two doubters' souls! It shook them to the very foundations! It put new life into the bit of real good left in them! It was the right word! It was a word of life! Ah! there are tens of thousands of men and women around us to-day who would come back to the Saviour they have left if only some one would call and tell them that there is still hope ; that the grave is empty—that their crucified Lord is alive and seeking for them.

Oh, tell them! Tell them! No matter who you are, inside or outside The Salvation Army, if you know anything at all about His love, tell them, and tell them now : for the grave is empty—the Crucified is alive!

> Glory to Jesus! Praise to His name,
>   For He of praise is worthy !
> He frees the captives, breaks every chain,
>   Pardoning the rebels freely.
> Glad are the tidings I have to bear,
> Sinners around me of Christ shall hear,
>   As I proclaim the grace of my Lord
> To whom each soul is dear.

90

I set my face unto the Lord God, to seek by prayer and supplications, . . . and I prayed unto the Lord my God.—Daniel 9 : 3, 4.

Some of the most wonderful answers to prayer have, no doubt, been answers to long-considered and thoughtful praying spread over an extended period. But I do not think any one can give a general ruling as to the time we should spend in prayer any more than any one can say how much food is necessary to keep up the strength of others. That must depend upon a hundred circumstances, past and present, that differ in each case. Neither can any of us say what is necessary to keep any individual soul awake and keenly alive to God. It cannot be determined by law, or by the example of others, but must be discovered by each for himself.

I would urge every one to find out what are those things and occasions which are most favourable to his intercessions, which break up the ground of desire, and touch and move the best parts of his nature ; and having found them to make the utmost use of them. That, above all, is for him the time to pray, to cry out to God for what he needs and desires.

The Lord God omnipotent reigneth. Let us be glad and rejoice, and give honour to Him. —Revelation 19 : 6, 7.
Submit yourselves therefore to God.—James 4 : 7.

The Lord Christ shall reign in us ! And because He reigns, we reign also, as the Apostle says : ' Much more they which receive abundance of grace . . . shall reign in life by one, Jesus Christ.' How will this be brought about ? *There must be complete submission.* Everything, down to the least thing, opposed to God must go. That is the moment of our crowning. The moment of our absolute submission to the King is the beginning of our own kingship. Just when we go down, He raises us up ! When self is dethroned, His life triumphs ! Do you know those precious lines :
' Above the blatant tongues of doubt,
We hear the still small voice of love
Which sends its simple message out ;
And dearer, sweeter, day by day,
Its mandate echoes from the skies :
" Go, roll the stone of self away,
And let the Christ in you arise ! " '
But this will not be done all at once. Submission and life—they are an act of man and an act of God ; they are done like a flash ! But then comes progress ; then begins the evolution of spiritual things in the soul ; then we go onward, being cleansed from sin, to cultivate the plants our Heavenly Father will plant and bring forth fruits worthy of His power and to His glory. This is the true evolution, the true growth : ' First the blade, then the ear, after that the full corn in the ear.'

Put on the new man, which is renewed in knowledge after the image of Him that created him.
—Colossians 3 : 10.

God's great work is the making of men, in His own image—the restoration of the dismantled temple to the likeness of its Maker. What does it all mean ? I cannot tell ! I can only see dimly some of the beginnings of His purposes.

To be in the likeness of God must mean to have the everlasting approval of God. You cannot even think of God as though He did not approve Himself. His acts are good—' as for God, His ways are perfect.' From everlasting to everlasting He has the unwavering approval of His own nature, and to be restored to His image means that, sooner or later, by His grace, men shall be restored also to His favour, to His entire approval, without which there is neither real happiness, true progress nor moral power.

You do not need me to point out the alternative to the everlasting approval of God. It is His everlasting disapproval ; the eternal darkness of those who will not come unto Him, that they might be renewed by the Holy Ghost.

> Renew my will from day to day ;
> Blend it with Thine, and take away
> All that now makes it hard to say :
> Thy will be done !

Confess your faults one to another, and pray one for another. . . . The effectual fervent prayer of a righteous man availeth much. Elias was a man subject to like passions as we are, and he prayed. —James 5 : 16, 17.

Real prayer is one of the great secrets of real power. In fact, I am not sure that there ever can be a really powerful life, or a really powerful spiritual experience, without constant, earnest prayer. Moreover, I believe that the secret of the feebleness in some souls who give us so much anxiety by their weakness and inconsistency lies just there—they do not pray. They do not seek after God. They do not wait on the Lord. They do not inquire of Him His will. They do not ask Him for what they need.

Now, this makes me say : Let us pray. Let us all pray. Let the people pray. Let the Soldiers pray. Let the young Converts pray. Let the children pray. Let us have praying Soldiers, praying Corps, praying Bands. Let The Army be an Army of Prayer.

> Hear me ! hear me,
> Saviour, hear me while I pray !
> As before Thy Cross I kneel,
> Saviour, hear me while I pray !

To the Lord our God belong mercies and forgive-
nesses.—Daniel 9 : 9.
. . . Jesus, whom ye slew and hanged on a tree,
Him hath God exalted . . . to be a Prince and a
Saviour, for to give . . . forgiveness of sins.
—Acts 5 : 30, 31.

The desire for forgiveness is indeed an instinct of
the human heart everywhere. The soul, even in the
lowest depths of numbness to all that is good, has still
the perception that it would be a desirable thing to
get the past put right. The prodigal who is sick of
the wanderings and want of the far country, and longs
to get home again to the plenty of former days, asks
first of all, ' Can I be forgiven ? Home and abundance, and the old ways, and the old faces, will be
unbearable without forgiveness and oblivion for the
past.' Thank God, we have a pardon to offer—on
certain terms, of course ; but, thank God, a pardon,
which carries with it the assurance of its own
continuing reality.

> I have long in sin been sleeping,
>   Long been slighting, grieving Thee ;
> Long the world my heart's been keeping.
>   Oh, forgive and rescue me—even me !
>
> Love of God—so pure and changeless,
>   Blood of Christ—so rich and free,
> Grace of God—so strong and boundless,
>   Magnify it all in me—even me !

**Thus speaketh the Lord . . , saying, Execute
true judgment, and shew mercy and compassions
every man to his brother : . . . and let none of you
imagine evil against his brother in your heart.
But they refused to hearken. . . . Yea, they made
their hearts as an adamant stone.**—Zechariah 7 :
9–12.
Jesus had compassion on them.—Matthew 20 : 34.

If it is only by His continual compassion that our
Master obtains and maintains His rule, will it not be by
a similar means that we may hope to bless and influence the souls of men ? Yes ; that has already
been the great lesson of The Salvation Army. It is
founded on sympathy, on a universal compassion.

The moment we turn from that, and rely merely on
our systems, or on methods, or our teaching, we
cease just in that proportion to be true Salvationists.
We aspire to rule men's hearts by seeking souls in
their sorrows and sins ; by making them feel our true
heart-hunger over them, our true love, our entire
union with the Christ in His compassion for them.

Except I be moved with compassion,
How dwelleth Thy Spirit in me ?
　　In word and in deed,
　　Burning love is my need ;
I know I can find this in Thee.

Paul, a servant of Jesus Christ, . . . separated unto the gospel of God, . . . concerning His Son Jesus Christ our Lord, which was . . . declared to be the Son of God with power, according to the spirit of holiness, by the resurrection from the dead.—Romans 1 : 1, 3, 4.

Just as one of the great proofs, if not *the* great proof, of the truth of Christianity is the vast fact of the world's need for it, so one grand proof of the Resurrection lies in the fact that no interpretation of Christ's teaching or Christ's life would be worth a brass farthing—so far as the actual life of suffering man is concerned—without His Death and Resurrection. That teaching might be illuminating—convincing—exalting ; yea, even morally perfect ; and yet, if He did not die, it would be little more than a superior book of proverbs or a collection of highly-polished copybook maxims. That wonderful life might be the supremest example of all that is or could be good and great and lovely in human experience ; and yet, if He did not rise again from the tomb, it would, after all, be only a dead thing—like a splendid specimen of carved marble in some grand museum : exquisite to look upon, and of priceless value, but cold and cheerless, lifeless and dead.

For it is a Living Person men need to be their Friend and Saviour and Guide.

Salvation is of the Lord.—Jonah 2 : 9.
**Our Saviour Jesus Christ ; who gave Himself
for us, that He might redeem us from all iniquity,
and purify unto Himself a peculiar people.**
—Titus 2 : 13, 14.

Salvation is of the Lord, or not at all ! It is a touch ;
a revelation ; an inspiration ; the life of God in the
soul. It is not of man only, nor of that greatest of
human forces—the will of man, but of God and the
will of God. It is not mere will-work, a sort of ' self-
raising ' power—it is a redemption brought home by
a personal Redeemer ; made visible, tangible, know-
able to the soul redeemed in a definite transaction with
the Lord. It brings forth its own fruits, carries with
it the assurance of its own accomplishments, and is its
own reward. It is impossible to declare too often or
too plainly that *Salvation is of the Lord*.

> Jesus, transporting sound,
>   The joy of earth and heaven !
> No other help is found,
>   No other name is given
> By which we can Salvation have ;
> But Jesus came the world to save.

Jesus said : **When He, the Spirit of truth, is come, He will guide you into all truth.**—John 16 : 13.
Jesus answered, . . . Every one that is of the truth heareth My voice.—John 18 : 37.

How often do some people stumble into doubt as to what God wants in their lives ! For example : As to uniform wearing ; or taking up some duty in the Corps ; or seeking the Salvation of others at work or at home ; or as to offering for Officership, and so on. They are in a strait betwixt two, being of one mind at one time and later of another. Then more light comes. They begin to see what they ought to do, but are afraid. There is unrest, fear, gloom, sometimes condemnation. They suddenly feel like one who realizes some one else's displeasure or suspicion, though no human soul may know of their conflicts. What does this mean ? Why this—it takes two to make a controversy ! It means that God is within them, guiding them, trying to bring them into His will, and making them feel that He is at hand.

And then when they say, ' Very well, Lord ; not my will, but Thine be done ! ' great calm follows the turmoil, and rest takes the place of the perplexity and doubt. Why is this ? It is because God was really near, watching for His chance to deliver and bless and save.

Not mine, not mine the choice
  In things or great or small ;
Be Thou my Guide, my Guard, my Strength,
  My Wisdom and my All.

**Then said Jesus . . . I am the good shepherd
. . . : and I lay down My life for the sheep. . . .
No man taketh it from Me, but I lay it down of
Myself. I have power to lay it down.**—John 10 :
7, 14, 15, 18.

**Then Jesus beholding him loved him, and said
unto him, . . . Come, take up the cross, and
follow Me.**—Mark 10 : 21.

Our Saviour raised His bruised and bleeding head
for the last time, and cried in token of His triumph,
' It is finished ! ' Up to that concluding hour it was
always possible for Him to draw back. His was, in the
very highest and widest sense of the word, a voluntary
death. Up to the very last, therefore, He could have
stepped down from the cross. But the moment
came when this would be no longer possible ; when,
even for Him, the possibility ' to save Himself ' was
ended.

Is there not something that should answer to this
in the lives of many of His disciples ? Is there not an
appointed Calvary somewhere at which we can settle
the questions that have been so long unsettled, and,
in the strength of God, at last declare that, as for
controversy of any kind with Him, ' it is finished ' ?
Is there not at this very same cross of our dying
Saviour a place where doubt and shame may perish
together—crucified with Him, and finished for ever ?
This would be, indeed, a blessed conformity to His
death.

I ordained thee a prophet unto the nations.
Jeremiah 1 : 5.
General Bramwell Booth's Journal, 10.4.21 :

' Our dear old General's Birthday. How wonderful he seems ! Many things connected with the sea* recall him to me to-day. To begin with—there is a great deal of it ! And so there was of him ! What largeness of purpose—what breadth of mind—what heights and depths of love—were in him ! Surely from beginning to end there was nothing mean or small about him ! Another thing—the ocean's freedom and surprise. How great was his liberty ! How wonderful a surprise he was in himself—going out on to the stormy waters of suffering and woe and making a pathway " where no keel ever ploughed before " !

' Again, the service of the sea is on all the shores. Praise God, there was nothing in my dear Father's life that was allowed to close him in—not even his wonderful humanity could do that. He had the vision to see and the courage to declare that all nations were within the embrace of God's loving plans, and as for himself, every people came as near to his own heart as his own people.'

> To make our weak hearts strong and brave,
> > Send the Fire !
> To live a dying world to save,
> > Send the Fire !
> Oh, see us on Thy altar lay
> Our lives, our all, this very day ;
> To crown the offering now we pray,
> > Send the Fire !

WILLIAM BOOTH.

*Written on an Atlantic voyage.

The fear of the Lord is the beginning of wisdom.
—Proverbs 9 : 10.

God, who commanded the light to shine out of darkness, hath shined in our hearts, to give the light of the knowledge of the glory of God in the face of Jesus Christ.—2 Corinthians 4 : 6.

Knowledge without God is like a man learned in all the great mysteries of light and heat who has never seen the sun. He may understand perfectly the laws which govern them, the results which follow them, the secrets which control their action on each other—all that is possible, and yet he will be in the dark.

So, too, knowledge, learning, human education and wisdom are all possible to man ; he may even excel in them so as to be a wonder to his fellows by reason of his vast stores of knowledge, and yet know nothing of that light within the mind by which he apprehends them. Nay, more ! He may even be a marvellous adept in the theory of religion, and yet, alas ! alas ! may never have seen its *Sun*—may still be in the blackness of gross darkness, because he knows not Jesus, the Light of the world, whom to know is life eternal.

> Farewell, mortality ! Jesus is mine !
> Welcome, eternity ! Jesus is mine !
> He my redemption is,
> Wisdom and righteousness,
> Life, light and holiness ; Jesus is mine !

He said unto Jesus, Lord, remember me. . . .
And Jesus said unto him, . . . I say unto thee,
To-day shalt thou be with Me in paradise.
—Luke 23 : 42, 43.

The crucifixion of the two robbers with Jesus was a
sort of topstone of obloquy and disgrace contrived by
His murderers with the double object of further
humiliating Him in the eyes of the people, and of
adding poignancy to His own agony. And yet, in
the presence of this extremity of human wickedness
and cruelty, Jesus found an opportunity of working
a wondrous work of God ; a work which reveals Him
as the Saviour, strong to save, both by His infinite
mercy and by His infinite confidence in the efficacy
of His own sacrifice. No word of resentment ; no
sense of distance or separation between the spotless-
ness and perfection of His character and this poor
lonely convict—but a strange and wonderful nearness,
now and to come. 'With Me,' He says—'With Me
in Paradise.' Ah ! this is the secret of much in the
life of the Son of God—this intimate, constant, conscious nearness to sinners and to sin ! He had sounded
the depth of evil and, knowing it, He pitied, with an
infinite compassion, its victims ; He got as near as
He could to them in their misery, and died to save
them from it.

With great power gave the apostles witness of the resurrection of the Lord Jesus : and great grace was upon them all.—Acts 4 : 33.

It is the life of Jesus and the evidences of that life in us that are really all-important. No extent of worldly wisdom or historical testimony can finally establish for us the fact and power of Christ's Resurrection, unless we have proof in ourselves of His presence there as a Living Spirit. That is the knowledge that cleanses the heart, destroys the strength of evil and brings in that true righteousness which is the power to do right. That is the greatest proof of the Resurrection.

No books, not even the Bible itself ; no testimony, not even the testimony of those who were present on that first Easter Day, can be so good as this, the experimental proof. It is the most fitting and grateful, and adapts itself to every type of human experience. And it is beyond contradiction ! What avail is it to contradict those who can answer, ' We know that we dwell in Him, and He in us, because He hath given us of His Spirit ' ?

> I find Him in secret, I find Him in prayer,
> In sweet meditation He always is there ;
> My constant Companion, we never will part ;
> All glory to Jesus who reigns in my heart !

Lord, Thou hast heard the desire of the humble : Thou wilt prepare their heart, Thou wilt cause Thine ear to hear.—Psalm 10 : 17.

Let us therefore come boldly unto the throne of grace, that we may obtain mercy, and find grace to help in time of need.—Hebrews 4 : 16.

When I say, ' Let us pray for the living,' I mean let us have real prayer—prayer that rises from the great deeps of desire—prayer that ascends on the wings of love for what we pray for—prayer that climbs to the heart of the Great Father—prayer that appears on the very steps of His Throne and pleads with Him direct until it prevails.

God is Himself ever on the watch for the approach of man. I think it is evident that He is not merely willing to hear men who cry to Him ; not merely ready to be attentive when His attention has been called by our earnestness or importunity, but He is really waiting for us, as one who expects a visitor, or as one who would not miss a word spoken by those He loves. It is, as some one says :—

> ' I cannot ope mine eyes,
>   But Thou art there to catch
> My morning cry and sacrifice.'

Joseph . . . went to Pilate, and begged the body of Jesus . . . and laid it in his own new tomb, which he had hewn out in the rock : and he rolled a great stone to the door of the sepulchre, and departed.—Matthew 27 : 57–60.

Our Lord Jesus Christ . . . died for us, that . . . we should live together with Him.—1 Thessalonians 5 : 9, 10.

For a little time they lost Him. The grave opened her gloomy portals ; they laid Him down, and the gates were closed—for a little time. And yet He was just as really there, as really alive for evermore, as really theirs and ours.

Is not that the lesson of His burial for every one who sorrows for the loss of loved ones called up higher ? Are they not buried with Him ? Are they not gone on before ? Are they not ours still ? Are we not theirs as really as ever ? He passed through that brief path of darkness and death out into the everlasting light of the Resurrection glory. Do you think, then, that He will leave them behind ? The grave could not contain Him. Do you think it has strength to hold them ? You cannot think of Him as lying long in the garden of Joseph of Arimathea ; why, then, should you think of your dear ones as in the chilly clay of that poor garden in which you have laid them ? No—no ! they are alive—alive for evermore ; because He lives, they live also.

> Give me the wings of faith to rise
> Within the veil, and see
> The saints above—how great their joys,
> How bright their glories be.

When the Lord saw her, He had compassion on her, and said unto her, Weep not.—Luke 7 : 13.

The kindness of the minister of God will find expression in consideration for all who are around us. It will especially lead to a tender compassion for all who are in sorrow, or want, or suffering. It was thus that Jesus felt—He had compassion on the multitude.

Nothing so closes people's hearts as going about amongst them without feeling ; while nothing so opens their hearts as allowing them to see that you are touched, that you feel, that you are in sympathy. This tenderness of spirit in the presence of human suffering is more than money—it is more than all else that man can do.

> Help us to help each other, Lord,
>   Each other's cross to bear ;
> Let each his friendly aid afford,
>   And feel his brother's care.

The wicked, through the pride of his countenance, will not seek after God : God is not in all his thoughts.—Psalm 10 : 4.

The pride of life, is not of the Father, but is of the world. And the world passeth away, . . . but he that doeth the will of God abideth for ever. —1 John 2 : 16, 17.

See how sin makes men try to be *independent of God*, their rightful sovereign. It sets up that self exaggeration which we call pride, and which leads to envy and jealousy, to malice and hate toward others We were made to love God and lean upon Him and set Him up on high in our lives. But sin brought in this plague of the human spirit—pride, and we know how it destroys the very best of people. The most attractive children, how horrid pride can make them ! The people who have a beautiful form, or countenance, or voice, or other outward charm, how pride can and often does make them hateful instead of lovable ; and those with special ability or gifts, how, when pride gets in, it separates us from them and them from us and from God.

> From Thee I would not hide
> My sin, because of fear
> What men may think ; I hate my pride,
> And as I am appear—
> Just as I am, O Lord,
> Not what I'm thought to be,
> Just as I am, a struggling soul
> For life and liberty.

Never man spake like this man.—John 7 : 46.
**Jesus . . . said unto them, . . . the words that
I speak unto you, they are spirit, and they are life.**
—John 6 : 61, 63.

The words of the dying Christ on His cross are a
true and wonderful revelation of His character and
His spirit. As it is only by the light of the sun that
we see the sun, so it is by Jesus that Jesus is best
revealed. Never one spake like He spake ; and yet,
in this respect, so real was His humanity, He spake
like us all. The Truth must, above all, and before all,
make manifest what is true of Himself.

Jesus, in His depth of midnight darkness, *sees* His
mother standing by the cross. Bless Him, oh, ye that
weep and mourn in this vale of tears ! Bless Him for
ever ! His eyes are eyes for the sorrowful. He sees
them. Surely, there never was sorrow like unto His
sorrow, and yet in its darkest crisis He has eyes and
heart for His mother's sorrow.

What a lesson of love it is ! What a message,
especially to those who are called to suffer with Him
for the souls of men. The burden of the people's
needs, the care of the Church, the awful responsibility
of ministering to souls—these things, sacred as they
may be, cannot excuse us in neglecting the hungry
hearts of our own flesh and blood, or in forgetting
the claims of those of our own household.

These words, which I command thee this day, shall be in thine heart : and thou shalt teach them diligently unto thy children, and shalt talk of them when thou sittest in thine house.—Deuteronomy 6 : 6, 7.

The children will need our love, our guidance. They will need our encouragement to pray and to trust for themselves, and our patient leading to know God in working and suffering for Him and His Kingdom.

Especially would I urge on all the importance of making the converted children pray. None can be too young, or too old, for this. Guide them to take their cares and troubles to the Throne, and lead them to pray for all they feel they need. The habit of prayer once formed is a mighty power in any life.

Yet still to His footstool in prayer I may go,
　　And ask for a share of His love ;
And if I now earnestly seek Him below,
　　I shall see Him and hear Him above,
In that beautiful place He has gone to prepare
　　For all who are washed and forgiven ;
And many dear children are gathering there,
　　' For of such is the Kingdom of Heaven.'

Jesus Himself stood in the midst of them, and saith unto them, Peace be unto you. . . . And while they yet believed not for joy, . . . He said unto them, . . . All things must be fulfilled, which were written . . . concerning Me . . . ye are witnesses of these things.—Luke 24 : 36, 41, 44, 48.

Peter, in his address on the day of Pentecost, referred to David's tomb as still there, and to death as still holding David in its grip. Why did not—why could not—those who denied the Resurrection appeal to Jesus Christ's tomb ? It was there, in a public situation, well known and easily accessible. There can only be one reason for their silence in the face of Peter's challenge. *They knew that tomb was empty.* And more, no one dared so much as to say that it was empty because the Body had been stolen. There, within a few weeks of the death, close to the very spot where it had all happened, before the eyes of thousands of men who knew the whole story, that myth was already exploded.

But, powerful as all this must have been, it was really the returned disciples' own conscious personal knowledge of their risen Master, and the joy that His presence gave them, which slew their doubts and charmed away their fears.

> The melting story of the Lamb
>   Tell with that voice of thine,
> Till others, with the glad new song,
>   Go singing all the time.

Our Saviour Jesus Christ . . . hath abolished death, and hath brought life and immortality to light.—2 Timothy 1 : 10.

But for the hope and promise of resurrection, the world would become little more than a mortuary ; a dark and dreary dead-house ; a temple of the dead. We should lapse again into the worst forms of barbarism, amidst which, like savage peoples, death would be our constant horror and life one long futile flight from its approach. It is only too evident, however, that we must all ' go down to the bars of the pit, and rest together in the dust,' and that the journey of life, so far as this world is concerned, will conclude at last in the silent nothingness of the tomb. If that is to end all, we are, as Paul said, the ' most miserable.' Nay, if that is to be the end, one may almost exclaim that beginning and ending seem alike a deplorable catastrophe, if not an unmitigated wrong. How awful, how hideous, is the mere thought of such a barren universe. Jesus Christ saw this. He made evident the truth about the world to come. He declared that part of His own work was to put His foot on the neck of the cruel skeleton, and to conquer death by rising from the dead Himself. *He did it.*

> He arose ! He arose !
> Hallelujah ! Christ arose !

Above all . . . put on love, which is the bond of perfectness.—Colossians 3 : 14 ; R.V.

Love never faileth : . . . now abideth faith, hope, love, these three ; and the greatest of these is love.
—1 Corinthians 13 : 8, 13 ; R.V.

My comrades, let us keep this banner in the breeze, even in the days of hate and fear. Hold it up. Fight for love. Give for love. Sacrifice for love. The love of man for all the things of a true mannood that we can still see in him, and for all the likeness of God that we can also still see in him. Let us witness to this—that love is more than all ! More than learning or riches, or beauty or strength or freedom, more than empires or armies or fleets, more than thrones or principalities or powers, or things present, or things to come ! Love is above them all—and will surely conquer at last. We must not doubt it—we will not !

So we'll lift up the Banner on high,
  The Salvation Banner of Love !
We'll fight beneath its colours till we die,
  Then go to our Home above.

The virgin's name was Mary. And the angel
. . . said, Hail, thou that art highly favoured, the
Lord is with thee ; blessed art thou among women.
. . . Fear not, Mary : . . . thou shalt . . . bring
forth a son, . . . He shall be great, and shall be
called the Son of the Highest.—Luke 1 : 27, 28, 30–32.

Jesus . . . saith unto His mother, Woman,
behold thy son !—John 19 : 26.

When Jesus had spoken these words to His mother,
He addressed the disciple He had chosen, and indi-
cated by a word that henceforth Mary was to be cared
for as his own mother. Great as was the work He had
in hand for the world, great as was His increasing
agony, He remembered Mary. He knew the meaning
of sorrow and loneliness, and He planned to afford
His mother such future comfort and consolations as
were for her good.

This tender care for His own is a rebuke, for all
time, to those who will work for others while those
they love are left uncared for !

And what a word of infinite strength and joy it was
that Jesus said to Mary—looking forward to the
coming victory. He knew that nothing could so fill
her soul with holy exultation as this. And so He
makes it quite plain, speaks the word to her Himself
in the ears of others, sends it ringing down the
corridors of time, and on to the waiting heralds of the
eternal world, that He, the dying Saviour, was Mary's
Son.

The angel answered and said . . , Fear not ye : for I know that ye seek Jesus, which was crucified. He is not here : for He is risen, as He said. —Matthew 28 : 5, 6.

To us Salvationists, the hope of the world and the strength of our hard and long struggle for the souls of men centre in this glorious truth. He is risen, and is alive for evermore ; and because He lives, we live also ! All around us are the valleys of death, filled with bones—very many and very dry. Love lies there, dead. Hope is dead. Faith is dead. Honour is dead. Truth is dead. Purity is dead. Liberty is dead. Humility is dead. Fidelity is dead. Decency is dead. It is the blight of humanity. Death—moral and spiritual death in all her hideous and ghastly power —reigns around us. Men are indeed dead—' dead in trespasses and sins.' What do we need ? What is the secret longing of our hearts ? What is the crying agony of our prayers ? Is it for any human thing we seek ? No. God knows—a thousand times, no ! We have but one hope or desire, and that is ' life from the dead.'

> Oh, joyful sound ! oh, glorious hour,
> When Christ by His almighty power
>   Arose and left the grave !
> Now let our songs His triumph tell
> Who broke the chains of death and Hell,
>   And ever lives to save.

As for me, my prayer is unto Thee, O Lord, in an acceptable time : O God, in the multitude of Thy mercy hear me, . . . And hide not Thy face from Thy servant ; for I am in trouble : hear me speedily. Draw nigh unto my soul, and redeem it. —Psalm 69 : 13, 17, 18.

Prayer is to lead us to God, no matter what our particular feelings may be. Prayer is to unite us with Him not only in the intense moments of our lives and in the great excitements, but to draw us near Him in calm confidence, in firm dependence on His goodness, and in settled conviction that He is always there working for us. Prayer is to aid us to subordinate everything in our being to His holy will, and to reveal in our minds day by day what that will is.

We ought not, therefore, to suppose that it is necessary to be in this or that state of feeling in order successfully to draw near to God. Nor that when we lack agreeable feelings we should neglect drawing near to Him. Indeed, in many cases I think that when our feelings prompt us least to seek Him that very fact is an indication that we need most to seek Him. There is no condition of our feelings laid down in that most wonderful command and promise of the Apostle : ' Draw nigh to God, and He will draw nigh to you.'

Great is the mystery . . : God was manifest in the flesh, justified in the Spirit, seen of angels, . . . believed on in the world, received up into glory. —1 Timothy 3 : 16.

We have a great high priest . . , Jesus the Son of God, . . . touched with the feeling of our infirmities.—Hebrews 4 : 14, 15.

We to whom the Living Christ has spoken the word of life and liberty, although we may not now fully comprehend this great wonder of all wonders—God manifest in the flesh—cannot doubt its central truth, *that God dwelt with man.*

Here was, indeed, a perfect union of two spirits. There was the suffering and obedient spirit of the true man ; there was the unchanging and Holy Spirit of the true God. It was a union—it was a unity. It was God in man—it was man in God. A Being of infinite might and perfect moral beauty, sent forth from the bosom of the Father ; and yet a being of lowly and sensitive tenderness, having roots in our poor human nature, tempted in all points like as we are, and touched with the feeling of all our infirmities.

> Christians, awake ! salute the happy morn
> Whereon the Saviour of mankind was born ;
> Rise to adore the mystery of love
> Which hosts of angels chanted from above ;
> With them the joyful tidings first begun
> Of God Incarnate and the Virgin's Son.

This is the message that ye heard from the beginning, that we should love one another. —1 John 3 : 11.

God saw that all His wonderful world would have been incomplete without love. Even Eden itself with all its beauty could not be perfect without it. And as with God's work for man, so it is with our work for God. No matter how clever we are, no matter how well we arrange and lead the people and push the Meetings and raise the money and keep up the advance, it will all be incomplete without love— unfinished and unfruitful without the presence of that God-made gift—' the greatest thing in the world,' as it has been called. But love makes glad all the rest. How are you to get it ? From God. As it was in the beginning, so it is now and ever shall be—love is the gift of God. It is His great gift—it is, above all things, His great gift to Salvationists. Oh, seek it— you shall not seek in vain ! The rest of a sanctified heart is really the rest of love.

> Let love be first, let love be last,
> Its light o'er all my life be cast ;
> Come now, my Saviour, from above
> And deluge all my soul with love,
> So that wherever I may go
> Thy love shall conquer every foe.

He that dwelleth in the secret place of the most High shall abide under the shadow of the Almighty. I will say of the Lord, He is my refuge and my fortress : my God : in Him will I trust.—Psalm 91 : 1, 2.

The Lord shall give thee rest.—Isaiah 14 : 3.

Now, I do not mean to suggest that all along our pathway we shall have unalloyed happiness, overflowing joy, unbroken peace. This world is not a place of rewards, but of trials. I think John Bunyan was about right when he said, ' Children, the milk and honey is beyond this wilderness.' Nevertheless, God does give peace of mind and rest of heart, in spite of all outward care, to those who make their Home—who abide—in Him, who grow in faith and love, and increase in union of purpose with Him—to those who dwell in Him and He in them.

Something of the same thought must have been in the mind of David. It is often referred to in the Psalms as an actual experience of his daily life, as when he said : ' I will say of the Lord, He is my refuge and my fortress. Return unto thy rest, O my soul.' Does this sound unreal to you ? I hope not, for it is a great reality !

> Oh, spread Thy covering wings around,
> Till all our wanderings cease,
> And at our Father's loved abode
> Our souls arrive in peace !

Hear the words of the wise, and apply thine heart unto my knowledge . . . keep them within thee ; they shall withal be fitted in thy lips. That thy trust may be in the Lord, . . ; that thou mightest answer the words of truth to them that send unto thee.—Proverbs 22 : 17–19, 21.

Casting down imaginations, . . . and bringing into captivity every thought to the obedience of Christ.—2 Corinthians 10 : 5.

People should be taught the necessity of mastering and training their thoughts. This is an immensely important matter, if only because of the fact that all responsible action begins in the mind. The time that elapses between thought and action may be as slight as between the flash of the lightning and the instant crash of the thunder—the one seeming to be almost simultaneous with the other ; all the same, the act has its origin in the thought. Here is the true wisdom which underlies Paul's words as to ' bringing into captivity every thought to the obedience of Christ.'

Now this can only be reached by disciplining and training the mind. Before they were saved, the minds of most people were uncontrolled. They allowed their thoughts to wander. Just as Satan is said to find mischief for idle hands to do, so he leads an idle, wandering, unoccupied mind into temptation. People need to be taught to call in their wandering thoughts, and to train their minds to dwell on the true, the best, the highest things.

> My mind upon Thee, Lord, is stayed,
> My all upon Thy altar laid ;
>   Oh, hear my prayer !

The glorious gospel of the blessed God, which was committed to my trust. . . . And the grace of our Lord was exceeding abundant with faith and love which is in Christ Jesus. This is a faithful saying, . . . that Christ Jesus came into the world to save sinners.—1 Timothy 1 : 11, 14, 15.

The Spirit-given Love is everlasting. Even Faith and Hope—glorious sisters of God's mercy—will pass away at last. But Love will never die. Faith and Hope may not be strong enough to reach out of our own little circle, or city, or country, and take in all souls—but Love, the Love of God's Great Heart, the Love of Pentecost, compasses All ! All ! *All !*

Oh, has the Holy Spirit visited you after this fashion ? This was the great result of the first Pentecost which we commemorate at Whitsuntide. After the Baptism, the revelation and the rejoicing, those disciples, each one of them, men and women alike, went out of the Upper Room, and then and there began to love and bless and save the people all around them. And it was the all-important thing. *They poured out their love.* They testified and declared and fought for Jesus. Nothing satisfied them but that multitudes should be saved. They were filled with holy Love.

> Love Divine, all loves excelling,
>   Joy of Heaven, to earth come down ;
> Fix in us Thy humble dwelling,
>   All Thy faithful mercies crown.
> Jesus, Thou art all compassion,
>   Pure, unbounded love Thou art ;
> Visit us with Thy Salvation,
>   Enter every longing heart.

They that wait upon the Lord shall renew their strength ; they shall mount up with wings as eagles ; they shall run, and not be weary ; and they shall walk, and not faint.—Isaiah 40 : 31.

Commit thy way unto the Lord ; trust also in Him ; and He shall bring it to pass. . . . Rest in the Lord, and wait patiently for Him : fret not thyself.—Psalm 37 : 5, 7.

I am sure much prayer is wasted just because it is lacking in persistence. People give up so easily. They take for granted that, because God does not open the door the first time they pull the bell, He will not hear. They forget Abraham praying for Sodom, Elijah praying for rain and Daniel praying for his people ; they forget the words of Jesus Christ about the importunate widow.

And this persistence, this waiting patiently for the Lord, is the way to His secret places of joy and communion. It lifts the soul up to the heights where, by His love, the arrows of fear and envy cannot strike us, where sin loses its power to weigh down our spirits and where the Devil himself cannot disturb our peace. Is not this exactly what so many people need ?

I believe that the spirit of prayer in us is like a lamp which loses nothing of its own brightness by setting other lamps aflame.

Give me Thy strength, O God of power !
Then winds may blow, or thunders roar ;
Thy faithful witness will I be—
'Tis fixed : I can do all through Thee.

Beloved, if God so loved us, we ought also to love one another. . . . If we love one another, God dwelleth in us, and His love is perfected in us.
—I John 4 : II, I2.

The Army's 'high ideal'! Is it not completely defined in the one word Love ? Is it not the sum and substance of all that impels The Salvation Army, whether in its finest service or in its highest aims ? Nay, may I not go further and say that love—to God and man—is not only the root from which The Army itself, together with all its activities, has sprung, but is also the choicest fruit which it has bestowed upon the world ? Cause and effect have never been seen to bear a more intimate relation than here. Love the living seed—and love the precious flower. Love the original planting—and a holy love the glorious harvest.

> Love I ask for, love I claim,
>   A dying love, like Thine :
> A love that feels for all the world ;
>   Saviour, give me a love like Thine.

What doth it profit, . . . though a man say he hath faith, and have not works ? can faith save him ? . . . Thou believest that there is one God ; thou doest well : the devils also believe, and tremble.—James 2 : 14, 19.

Jesus said : Not every one that saith unto Me, Lord, Lord, shall enter into the kingdom of heaven ; but he that doeth the will of My Father which is in heaven.—Matthew 7 : 21.

Like so many other things in our lives, the triumph over temptation depends upon co-operation between man and God.

Over and over again, the Scriptures insist, in one form or another,—by example, by precept, by entreaty, by warning—that God and man must both work, and must work together, and must work to the end, to accomplish man's Salvation.

To believe on Christ, and then to rest in that faith alone, without giving heed to obedience to the Divine Law, is a hollow imitation of true religion, alike useless to those who practise it and dishonouring to the God it pretends to serve. 'Ye are My friends,' said Jesus, 'if ye do whatsoever I command you.' It is difficult to repeat too often that the continued favour of God depends just as much upon holy living as upon fully trusting, upon obedience as upon faith.

Have Thy way, Lord, have Thy way !
This with all my heart I say :
I'll obey Thee, come what may :
Dear Lord, have Thy way !

He that hath not the Son of God hath not life.
—1 John 5 : 12.
You hath He quickened, who were dead in trespasses and sins.—Ephesians 2 : 1.

All the attention given to education, to refinement
and culture, to the development of gifts—for instance,
such as music or inventive science—to the practice of
self-restraint and the pursuit of morality, is so much
attention to the casket that will perish, to the neglect
of the eternal jewel that is enclosed. It may be
possible to present a kindly, honest, law-abiding,
agreeable life to our neighbours ; to go through
business and family life without finding much of
great moment with which to condemn ourselves ; to
be thought, even by those nearest to us, to be living
up to a high standard of morality, and yet—for all
this has to do with the casket—to be dead all the
while in trespasses and sins.

> Thou hidden Source of calm repose,
>   Thou all-sufficient Love Divine,
> My Help and Refuge from my foes,
>   Secure I am if Thou art mine :
> And lo ! from sin, and grief, and shame
> I hide me, Jesus, in Thy name.
>
> Jesus, my All-in-all Thou art,
>   My rest in toil, my ease in pain,
> The medicine of my broken heart,
>   In war my peace, in loss my gain,
> In grief my joy unspeakable,
> My life in death, my All-in-all.

Open Thou mine eyes, that I may behold wondrous things out of Thy law.—Psalm 119 : 18.

Behold, God exalteth by His power : who teacheth like Him ? . . . Remember that thou magnify His work, which men behold. Every man may see it.—Job 36 : 22, 24, 25.

The sight of the eye must become the servant of the soul, trained, like the thoughts of the mind and the words of the lips, to serve the highest interests. And, you know, it is a striking fact that in a very beautiful and wonderful way when the bodily eyes have been trained thus ' to see and yet not see ' that which is injurious, or unprofitable, then the soul develops an inner vision, and learns ' to see what worldly eyes cannot behold.' Then we can discern everywhere marks of the goodness of God. We see His power and beauty reflected in the daisy of the field—in the fruit on the table—in the worlds that star the heavens. Then we can discern His hand in the trials and deprivations of life, no less than in its love and mercies and benefits and joys.

Give me the faith that clearly sees
    What worldly eyes cannot behold,
That knows the way the Lord to please,
    That can His secret ways unfold ;
That gives up greatness for the good,
That wins the fight with Fire and Blood.

126

The dead in Christ shall rise first.—1 Thessalonians 4 : 16.
Many of them that sleep in the dust of the earth shall awake, some to everlasting life, and some to shame and everlasting contempt.—Daniel 12 : 2.

Oh, do not let us doubt ! If we begin to doubt the resurrection of the unjust, we shall go on to doubt the resurrection of the just. If we begin to question the resurrection to damnation, we shall go on to question the resurrection to life eternal, and then to doubt any resurrection at all ! That was what Paul foresaw and warned us of when he wrote, ' If there be no resurrection of the dead, then is Christ not risen ; and if Christ be not risen, then is our preaching vain, and your faith is also vain. Yea, and we are found false witnesses of God. . . . Ye are yet in your sins. Then they also which have fallen asleep in Christ are ' —Oh, cruel thought !—' perished.'

Let us look then, on all men as on beings who must certainly live again. How earnest, how faithful, how resolved, how bold this will make us in caring for their souls. Oh, my comrades, look at men's future.

> Where the shadows deepest lie,
>   Carry truth's unsullied ray ;
> Where are crimes of blackest dye,
>   There the saving sign display.
>
> To the weary and the worn
>   Tell of realms where sorrows cease
> To the outcast and forlorn
>   Speak of mercy and of peace.

127

Ye shall receive power, after that the Holy Ghost is come upon you : and ye shall be witnesses unto Me . . . unto the uttermost parts of the earth.
—Acts 1 : 8.

Is it not true that you who read these words have often longed for a Pentecost ? Have you not sometimes said to yourself, when you have read about that Upper Room in Jerusalem : ' Oh, if I could only have a filling of my soul with Holy Power like that—then I should conquer temptation and unbelief ; then I should have inward rest ; then I should be able to work for God and the souls of men ' ? Well, *you can* —even *you* can have a Pentecost of your own, and the Holy Spirit shall be poured out upon you, filling all the powers of your nature.

But you must put away the things that now obstruct His work. You must dare to open every part of your life to Him, and lay all you have at His feet. Then His Spirit of power and love will be poured out upon you.

And it will not be a changing, passing affair. His glorious promise was—' I will send you another Comforter, and He shall abide with you *for ever*.'

> Holy Spirit, come, oh, come !
> Let Thy work in me be done !
> All that hinders shall be thrown aside ;
> Make me fit to be Thy dwelling.

Is there no balm in Gilead ; is there no physician
there ? . . . Oh, that my head were waters, and
mine eyes a fountain of tears, that I might weep
day and night for the . . . people ! . . . for they
proceed from evil to evil, and they know not . . .
the Lord.—Jeremiah 8 : 22 ; 9 : 1, 3.

We are not the servants of this cold world ; we
are the servants of the great God of light, ' who
maketh His ministers a flame of fire. Let men know
that you are in earnest ! Do not be afraid to let your
feelings stir you to the depths. Let the longings of
your heart be seen. Let your own anxiety for God's
glory and the rescue of the Blood-bought souls be
felt by all you touch. Let sympathy and pity flow
out of your eyes. Cry to God : ' Open in me that
fountain of tears, give me a flowing heart ! '

> Lord, speak to me, that I may speak
> In living echoes of Thy tone ;
> As Thou hast sought, so let me seek
> Thy erring children lost and lone.
>
> Oh, fill me with Thy fullness, Lord,
> Until my very heart o'erflow
> In kindling thought and glowing word
> Thy love to tell, Thy praise to show.

If Christ be not raised, your faith is vain ; ye are
yet in your sins. . . . If in this life only we have
hope in Christ, we are of all men most miserable.
—1 Corinthians 15 : 17, 19.

Noble and pure as Jesus Christ's example undoubtedly was, it could of itself never satisfy a human
soul or inspire poor, broken human hearts with hope
and love, or wash away from human consciousness
the stains of sin. These things can only be done by a
Living Person. So it is that we are not told to
believe on His teaching or on His Church, but on Him.
He did not say ' Follow My methods, or My disciples,' but ' Follow Me.' If He be not risen from the
dead, and alive for evermore ; if it be a dead man we
are to follow and on whom we are to believe—then
we are, indeed, as Paul says, ' of all men the most
miserable.'

> I know that my Redeemer lives !
> What joy the sweet assurance gives :
> He lives triumphant from the grave,
> He lives omnipotent to save !
>
> He lives, my wise and constant Friend,
> He lives and loves me to the end,
> He lives my mansion to prepare,
> He lives to guide me safely there.

**We preach Christ crucified, unto the Jews a
stumblingblock, and unto the Greeks foolishness ;
but unto them which are called, both Jews and
Greeks, Christ the power of God.**—I Corinthians I :
23, 24.

It is ever so. The Greeks, the renowned of the then
world for learning and intellectual gifts, in their
search for wisdom, found only foolishness in Calvary.
To them the whole story seemed an absurd remainder
of a bygone age of myth, an anachronism, a slap-in-
the-face for all their fine ethical teaching and grand
philosophies.

Just so ! Is not this exactly how many of the wise
of to-day regard that same Cross ? They do not see,
as Paul said, ' The foolishness of God is wiser than
men, and the weakness of God is stronger than men.'
They do not know, as Paul knew, and as we know,
that this very thing which to them spells only emo-
tional weakness or intellectual folly, is to us the power
of God, and the wisdom of God, and the love of God.
It is this which so few of the princes of this world's
learning know ; for did they know it, they would not
deny the Lord of Glory in His crucifixion and resurrection, and in His atoning, pardoning and sanctifying
grace.

> Where'er I go I'll tell the story
>   Of the cross.
> In nothing else my soul shall glory,
>   Save the cross.
> Yes, this my constant theme shall be,
> Through time and in eternity,
> That Jesus tasted death for me
>   On the cross.

The Lord is not slack concerning His promise . . . ; but is longsuffering to us-ward, not willing that any should perish, but that all should come to repentance. But the day of the Lord will come as a thief in the night. . . . Wherefore, beloved, . . . be diligent.—2 Peter 3 : 9, 10, 14.

Are you actually in close daily engagement with the enemy, attacking him, forcing him to realize that you and God, whose servant you are, are bent on bringing him down ? Are you known throughout your town and Corps as a fighter, a determined opponent of evil in men's hearts, an attacker of those who love and practise it ? How often do you attack it ? Above all, what is the range, the scale of your fighting ?

That is the most shocking part of the business ! Some are content with the little crowd of a hundred or two Soldiers and friends and adherents who gather regularly Sunday by Sunday, most of whom are already familiar with all they can say concerning the claims of God ; while outside, in the thronging streets, among the crowded tenements, or in the long rows of cottages, or in the villages, men and women stream along on their way to Hell, many of them unawakened, and therefore careless of their danger.

Call His name JESUS : for He shall save . . . people from their sins.—Matthew 1 : 21.
The Father sent the Son to be the Saviour of the world.—1 John 4 : 14.

It is just here, in the sin of the heart, that we see most clearly the failure of what is called civilization. There might perhaps be some doubt as to whether civilization could meet the outward consequences of evil—or, at any rate, some of them. Increased knowledge, refinements of custom and beauty, elevation of law as between man and man, extension of freedom and wider diffusion of wealth—these may be said to be the elements of civilization, and no doubt they may do something to curtail the woes and soften the miseries which sin produces in human life. But when we come to the heart and moral nature of man, in which sin is established like a disease, civilization is helpless. The fact is, that nothing which is of the material order can do anything with sin. What is wanted there is a Redeemer, a Saviour, a Deliverer.

> So that He for me might die,
> Jesus left His throne on high ;
> To save from woe that lasts eternally
>   He in love became my ransom.
>
> By the Blood my Saviour shed upon the tree
>   He redeemed me, He redeemed me ;
> By the Blood my Saviour shed upon the tree
>   I am now from sin set free.

We preached unto you the gospel of God . . . we exhorted and comforted and charged every one of you, as a father doth his children, that ye would walk worthy of God.—1 Thessalonians 2 : 9, 11, 12.

I have confidence in you through the Lord. —Galatians 5 : 10.

It very often happens that the greatest kindness that you can possibly do a man is to trust him, and let him see that you trust him. Multitudes go through life without once enjoying that sunshine of the heart which comes of being trusted. True kindness will seek out occasions for making those around us of every class feel that we confide in them. The children —ah, what a joy it would be to many of them to feel that in some things they had your confidence ! The weak and unsatisfactory—if you could only find something these could do for you, even if they bungled it, with which they would feel you really trusted them, it might work a revolution in them, accustomed as they are to be mistrusted. The young Convert— how many of the most timid disciples have been strengthened in the first days of their new life by being asked to care for another Recruit. The returning backslider—how often have his shame and fear been helped away by making him feel that some one believed in him, whether others did so or not.

Behold, I send the promise of My Father upon you : but tarry ye . . . until ye be endued with power from on high.—Luke 24 : 49.

Some are never endued with Power from on high. They never realize the peace and rest which the Comforter can give.

Oh ! this is the reason that the word of God so often speaks, not to the unsaved only, but to the children of God, about sin and self-will. Again and again we are called upon to depart from sin, to put away idols, to turn from the world, to renounce sinful affections and fleshly lusts and selfish ends ; to cut off what offends our God and cast it from us, no matter how precious it may be. All this is to make straight the way of the Lord, to enable the Blessed Spirit within us to impart the riches of His grace, to pour out the fullness of His Salvation and baptize us with the Holy Fire sent down from Heaven.

> On the altar now we lay
>   Soul and body, mind and will.
> All the evil passions slay,
>   Come, and every corner fill !
>
> Come, oh, come, Great Spirit, come !
> Let the mighty deed be done.

**Is not God in the height of heaven ? . . .
Acquaint now thyself with Him, and be at peace.**
—Job 22 : 12, 21.
**Let us search and try our ways, and turn again
to the Lord.**—Lamentations 3 : 40.

It is a help to look at our own needs in a practical
way. Take the man who is impulsive, and who finds
himself in difficulties because of his hastiness. Let
him look at himself honestly. Instead of excusing
that which he regrets, let him recognize that it is
more of the Living God he needs in order to correct
this weakness in his character. I am sure that this
sort of reflection would stir the holy desires, would
increase this hunger and thirst, and would make us
resolve, ' Never will I rest until my need for God,
the Living God, is satisfied.'

> None else my soul can satisfy,
>   Or give the rest I seek ;
> Thy voice, O Lord, I wait to hear,
>   Now to Thy servant speak.
>
> Let grace my longing soul supply ;
>   This hunger, Saviour, meet.
> Thy fullness, Lord, to me impart,
>   Whilst waiting at Thy feet.

While Paul waited . . . at Athens, his spirit was stirred in him, when he saw the city wholly given to idolatry. Therefore disputed he in the synagogue with the Jews . . . and in the market daily with them that met him.—Acts 17 : 16, 17.

I used to think that the country, with its wide and peaceful spaces, its calm and ordered life, and the population sprinkled here and there, was more favourable to faith and holiness and love than the cities with their multitudes and their hurry. I am not so certain now ! There is surely much in the town and its throngs which is just as able to carry us to God as the fields and hills and streams. To those who have eyes to see, and ears to hear, does He not look at us and speak to us through the people ? Is not this in harmony with His shedding forth the great Gospel of our Lord Jesus Christ from the very first amidst the tumult of the market and in the crowded places of the great cities ?

> In the slums, 'midst heathen darkness,
>   Who the light of love will show ?
> Saviours, brave and good, are wanted ;
>   Will you to the rescue go ?
>   Are you ready
>   Now, for Jesus' sake, to go ?

We see Jesus, who was made a little lower than the angels for the suffering of death . . . ; that He by the grace of God should taste death for every man.—Hebrews 2 : 9.

Being then made free from sin, ye became the servants of righteousness.—Romans 6 : 18.

Tell men of this. Tell them of it in their selfishness and misery, in their drunkenness and uncleanness and moral helplessness and in their naked poverty as to all that is good. Make them take it in and think about it. Let it be the theme not merely of our platform, whether in the Hall or at the street corner, but of the daily talk from house to house, in the factory and mill and office and shop and home. Jesus, the Son of God, tasted death for every man in order to smash the fetters of individual evil, to deliver the captives of passion and doubt, to give peace and rest to the restless and pardon to the law-breakers.

> Salvation ! Speak Salvation
>   In every sinner's ear ;
> It carries consolation,
>   It stanches sorrow's tear.
> The sad, the sick, the dying
>   In Christ are fully blest ;
> Yea, all on Him relying
>   In Him find perfect rest.

Without faith it is impossible to please Him.
—Hebrews 11 : 6.

What I speak of now is that inner, heart misgiving,
of which perhaps only God knows, which questions
His call in the past and mistrusts His providence in
the present ; which forgets, like Israel of old, the
miracle of the Red Sea, the daily manna, and the
deliverances and blessings of the wilderness march.
Those misgivings confuse past experiences in a dis-
torting mist of doubt, and men ask themselves, ' Was
God in it, after all ? ' As a result of doubting about
the past they become troubled about the future.

All such doubts and fears are a wounding of God.
It is just such denials of His providential love and care,
and of His ordering and over-ruling of our lives—
rather than the denials and insults of publicans and
infidels—which really crucify the Son of God afresh.
It was the doubts and denials of Thomas and Peter,
the treachery of Judas, which broke His heart. I
solemnly believe that many who would hate themselves if ever they wilfully openly sinned against Him,
do not realize what a sin, what a grievous sin, they
constantly commit and what grief they cause Him
by this wretched mistrust.

> I am trusting Thee, Lord Jesus,
>   Never let me fall ;
> I am trusting Thee for ever
>   And for all !

Lift up thy face unto God . . . He shall save the humble person.—Job 22 : 26, 27, 29.

Behold, what . . . love the Father hath bestowed upon us, that we should be called the sons of God : . . . and it doth not yet appear what we shall be : but . . . we shall be like Him.—1 John 3 : 1, 2.

To be weak, to be small, to be sadly unfit for the strifes of time ; to feel weary and unequal to the hard battles of life ; to realize that you are pushed out and away by the crowd, to be contemptuously forgotten by the multitude shouting and singing across the road—all this may be your case, and *yet* you may be God's chosen vessel, intended—framed—' to suffer and triumph with Him.' You, even you, may be destined by His wisdom to fill for Him some great place in action against the hosts of iniquity and unbelief. Above all, you may be appointed by God the Father to be like His Son, with a holy likeness of will, of affection, of character.

> Lord Jesus, Thou dost keep Thy child
> Through sunshine or through tempest wild ;
>   Jesus, I trust in Thee.
> Thine is such wondrous power to save ;
> Thine is the mighty love that gave
>   Its all on Calvary.
>
> Love perfecteth what it begins ;
> Thy power doth save me from my sins :
>   Thy grace upholdeth me.
> This life of trust, how glad, how sweet !
> My need and Thy great fullness meet,
>   And I have all in Thee.

Feed the flock of God which is among you, taking the oversight thereof, not by constraint, but willingly ; . . . neither as being lords over God's heritage, but being ensamples to the flock. —1 Peter 5 : 2, 3.

How wonderful are God's ways ! Man is not only to co-operate with Him in continuing the race, and peopling the earth with his kindred, but is also to share with Him the work of preserving, training and moulding it—to share, in fact, in all that goes to the true making of his own offspring.

God not only honours us by making us partners with Him in begetting the children of the Kingdom, but He also expects us to share in the great work of the Holy Spirit in training and teaching the hearts and fashioning the lives of the babes in Christ—the little ones of the flock of God—and so to work together with Him in building up their characters in the likeness of Christ.

Oh ! are you doing this, the daily work of the makers ? It needs courage, but God will give it. It demands true patience, and God will give it. It needs the spirit of the Cross of Jesus, and God will give that also. If you have failed here in the past, begin right away. Unless we make men of God, all we do is a ghastly failure, and you will fail, we all shall fail, unless we watch and feed, and train and guard, and love and lead them, one by one.

Have ye received the Holy Ghost since ye believed ?—Acts 19 : 2.

Alas ! In some hearts the Holy Spirit meets with opposition and obstruction. It is very sad, but true, that many who let God come into their lives, and hope quite sincerely that they may have peace with Him, still go on hindering His work. They cling to things that darken the light which He brings. They do that which works against the love He is trying to pour out upon them. So that, although the Holy Spirit has come, and brought in His blessed light and love and zeal and joy, these unsanctified spirits stop the pouring out of these blessings upon their souls.

The consequence is that, although they may be very good and well-meaning people, they never get the Baptism of the Holy Ghost. He never falls upon them. They are never filled with the Spirit.

> Hearts are open to receive Thee,
>   Tho' we've grieved Thee o'er and o'er ;
> Holy Ghost, we greatly need Thee,
>   Come, abide for evermore.

**When they saw the boldness of Peter and John,
and perceived that they were unlearned and
ignorant men, they marvelled ; and they took
knowledge of them, that they had been with Jesus.
—Acts 4 : 13.**

**The way of holiness ; . . . the wayfaring men,
though fools, shall not err therein.—Isaiah 35 : 8.**

How very silly and very impertinent is the notion
that only the highly educated and so-called ' intel-
lectuals ' can apprehend Jesus Christ's great revelation ! I see every day proof positive to the contrary.
The common Soldier of The Salvation Army—the
rough-and-tumble workman of the pit, or the forge,
or the mill, or the field—he lives religion with understanding be he ever so far removed from its philo-
sophical systems. He knows quite well what religion
ought to do for him and his mates, if it be religion at
all. And he knows that it is something which must
be worked out in him as an individual. He knows,
difficult as in many cases it would be for him to
explain the theory of it, that religion is a personal
revelation in his own soul—something which comes
from outside himself—comes from above—comes
from God !

> Oh, what a mighty blessing
>   That Jesus made it plain,
> And did not say it was for James
>   Or any other name.
> 'Twas one word, ' Whosoever,'
>   For simple folks to see,
> And even I can understand
>   That that means me.

143

Know ye not that the friendship of the world is enmity with God ? whosoever therefore will be a friend of the world is the enemy of God.—James 4 : 4.
We have peace with God through our Lord Jesus Christ.—Romans 5 : 1.

You cannot have peace between nation and nation or between man and man in the affairs of this world while one party holds on to the enemies of the other. The thing is self-evident. And so with God—peace with Him is impossible without breaking up these evil alliances. It is only possible to those who renounce the world, who dedicate their flesh to be the temples of God and who turn for ever to fight against the Devil and all his works.

One of the great teachers of the past says : ' Do you know what it is that makes man the most suffering of all creatures ? It is that he has one foot in the finite and one foot in the infinite. He is torn asunder between two worlds.' Yes, and there will be no peace till he gives up living for this world only and begins to live for the world to come.

How happy every child of grace
　　Who knows his sins forgiven !
This earth, he cries, is not my place,
　　I seek my home in Heaven !
A country far from mortal sight ;
　　Yet, oh, by faith I see
The Land of Rest, the saints' delight,
　　The Heaven prepared for me.

As . . . ministers of Christ, and stewards of the mysteries of God. . . . It is required in stewards, that a man be found faithful.—1 Corinthians 4 : 1, 2.
A faithful man shall abound with blessings.—Proverbs 28 : 20.

God says quite plainly, ' If the watchman see the sword come, and blow not the trumpet, and the people be not warned ; if the sword come, and take any person from among them . . . his blood will I require at the watchman's hand.' There is no middle course or condition for you or for me : we are either faithful to those whom God has entrusted to us, or unfaithful ; we are either true keepers, or we are Cains !

Above all, remember that it is the voice of God in your soul when conscience compels you to say, ' I am my brother's keeper.'

In the toils and conflicts faithful I will be,
All things I will gladly bear, they'll be good for me ;
To be a saviour of mankind, slaves of sin to bring,
Give me holy courage, mighty, mighty King.

Blessed be the God and Father of our Lord Jesus Christ, which according to His abundant mercy hath begotten us again unto a lively hope by the resurrection of Jesus Christ from the dead, to an inheritance incorruptible, . . . reserved in heaven for you, who are kept by the power of God through faith unto salvation.—1 Peter 1 : 3-5.

This is what we need. Not good laws only, but the power to observe them. Not beautiful and lofty ideals only, but the power to translate them into the daily practice of common lives. Not merely the glorious example of a pure faith, but the actual force which enables men to live by that faith amid the littleness, the depression, the contamination and the conflict of an evil world.

Perfect laws, liberal institutions, patriotic sentiments, though they may elevate, can never rule a people. *Every man must have a king!* Call him what we will, recognize him or not, every man is the subject of some ruler. I say that in Jesus are assembled in the highest perfection all the great qualities which go to make *the King of men!* He is the rightful Sovereign of every human soul.

> Unto Thee, O Saviour King,
> Our allegiance now we bring ;
> Body, soul and spirit—all,
> In obedience to Thy call.
> Naught have we Thou didst not give ;
> By Thy life and grace we live.
> Selfish aims do we forsake,
> Service with our Lord to take.

146

In the multitude of my thoughts within me Thy comforts delight my soul.—Psalm 94 : 19.
Search me, O God, and know my heart : try me, and know my thoughts.—Psalm 139 : 23.

Train your thoughts to dwell on God. And that will help to repel evil and unworthy thoughts. The way to exclude what is profitless is to be engaged with what is profitable. Idle or useless or uncharitable thoughts are very unlikely to find entertainment in the mind which is being trained to dwell upon God— on His almighty Power, His Holiness, His inflexible Justice, His unmeasured Love, His boundless Mercy, the marvels of His Law, the wisdom of His Providence, the truths of His word, the mighty forces of His government, the righteousness of His Judgment. What themes are these !

Oh, yes, it can be done ! ' Thou wilt keep him in perfect peace, whose mind is stayed on Thee.' That was the experience of one of the busiest men of his time. It is possible for each of us so to ' stay ' his mind on God. Just as a spring door, when the pressure of the hand is removed, swings back into its place, so the mind will turn back toward God whenever, throughout the hours of day or night, the pressure of work or business is removed or the mind awakes from the unconsciousness of sleep. Do not we all know something of this blessed experience ?

**We give thanks to God . . . ; remembering
without ceasing your . . . labour of love.**—1 Thessalonians 1 : 2, 3.

By love serve.—Galatians 5 : 13.

Love is known by what it does. That is exactly
what we say about God's love for souls. In reality it
is only known and felt and understood by the work it
has done and the sacrifice it has made. Here is the
very inward truth that makes Jesus Christ's coming,
and His life and His death, so important. They were
the proof of God's love. They were the pledge—the
sign—the grand act of love. Love is what it does, and
God's love can be seen by all the world in what it did.

Just so—and in no other way—love for souls
burning in the heart will be known and felt and
understood by what we do. For us, as truly as for
God, love is what it does.

> Gracious Spirit, dwell with me !
> I myself would gracious be ;
> And with words that help and heal
> Would Thy life in mine reveal ;
> And with actions bold and meek
> Would for Christ, my Saviour, speak.

Jesus saith unto him, . . . he that hath seen Me
hath seen the Father. . . . Verily, verily, I say
unto you, He that believeth on Me, the works that
I do shall he do also ; and greater works than
these shall he do ; because I go unto My Father.
—John 14 : 9, 12.

I have often heard dear saints wishing that they
had lived in the time of Moses, or Joshua, or David,
that they might have seen the arm of the Lord made
bare in some of the mighty works He wrought by
those men and have been enabled better to trust in
Him. And yet all the time, before their very eyes,
were wonders, if anything greater than any that He
performed in the days of old. Do not let us make the
mistake of looking for Jesus in the empty sepulchre,
and missing Him in the common earth-marked garb
of the gardener. These moral miracles are, in reality,
far grander than any which have happened in the
world of nature. To convert a sinner from the error
of his way is a higher wonder than to bring down
fire from heaven ; to loose the slave of lust from his
bondage is a greater triumph than to change the
water into wine ; to save the three thousand in one
day at Pentecost was a miracle of far higher moment
in every way than to slay all the first-born in Egypt.

> Lord, we believe to us and ours
>   Thy precious promises were given ;
> We wait the Pentecostal powers,
>   The Holy Ghost sent down from Heaven.

As it was in the days of Lot ; they did eat, they drank, they bought, they sold, they planted, they builded ; but the same day . . . it rained fire and brimstone from heaven, and destroyed them all. Even thus shall it be in the day when the Son of Man is revealed.—Luke 17 : 28–30.

Where is Lot's faith in God ? Where is his courage ? Where is his manhood ? All are gone ; sold to the world for the sake of a house and a living ! Ah, do we not know some modern Lots ? All their daring and faith gone—dwelling in the plains of business prosperity, within comfortable homes or good situations, holding popular positions or drawing big salaries ; but who, with all that these well-watered lands can give them, are poor, miserably lonely, ease-loving, unfruitful Lots all the same ! For some doubtful gain they forsook Abraham and the highway of faith, and compromised ; and now they have become but shadows of their former selves ; and, alas, alas, Sodom is Sodom still, and the fire is coming !

Oh, my comrades, would to God that we could learn this lesson ! Have you anything to do with Sodom ? Escape for thy life, from it and its treasures; look not back ; tarry not in the plain ; lest thou be consumed, or be tempted into some half-way house like Zoar, some accursed place, though it be a little one. Little sins have long stings.

They were all amazed, insomuch that they questioned among themselves, saying, What thing is this ? what new doctrine is this ? for with authority commandeth He even the unclean spirits, and they do obey Him.—Mark 1 : 27.

Look to yourselves . . . Whosoever transgresseth, and abideth not in the doctrine of Christ, hath not God. He that abideth in the doctrine of Christ, he hath both the Father and the Son. —2 John 8, 9.

The doctrine of Jesus is the spirit of a new life. It is a transforming power. A man may believe that the American Republic is the purest and noblest form of government on the earth, and may give himself up to live and fight and die for it, and yet be the same man in every respect as he was before ; but if he believes with his heart that Jesus is the Christ, the Son of God, and gives himself up to live and fight and die for Him, he will become a new man, he will be a new creature. The acceptance of the truth, and acting upon it, in the one case, will make a great change in his manner of life—his conduct ; the acceptance of the truth, and acting upon it, in the *other*, will make a great change *in the man himself*—in his tastes and motives, in his very nature.

> Thy nature, gracious Lord, impart,
>   Come quickly from above ;
> Write Thy new name upon my heart,
>   Thy new best name of Love.

Go ye into all the world, and preach the gospel to every creature.—Mark 16 : 15.

The great message of The Army of the past to The Army of the future is this : That The Salvation Army exists for *the whole world*. It therefore follows that we must make it our own purpose to bless and serve and save mankind. How shall we do that ?

I do not think we shall do it merely by improvements in the human conditions of society, no matter how desirable such improvements may be. No doubt changes could be effected in many of the laws of the different nations, from China to Peru, with great advantage. Though as I get older I am more and more of the opinion expressed in the old couplet :

' How small the part that human hearts endure,
    Is that which kings or laws can cause or cure ! '

But until the will be changed and the heart set on what is good, nothing of any real moment is done in any man's life. There has been the great error of all the plans or human reform, from the philosophies of ancient Egypt down to the socialism of to-day ! They have all had in mind, in some degree, the improvement of man, but they have sought to accomplish it by changing his surroundings without changing him. They have acted as though to provide him with clean linen was the same thing as to make him clean !

I determined not to know any thing among you,
save Jesus Christ, and Him crucified . . . not the
wisdom of this world, nor of the princes of this
world . . , but . . . the wisdom of God.—1 Corinthians 2 : 2, 6, 7.

Christ . . . appeared to put away sin by the
sacrifice of Himself.—Hebrews 9 : 24, 26.

This is the great test, alike for time and eternity :
How far do we know and love and live Jesus Christ ?
The religions, at any rate of the Western world, are
going off on any number of side questions, and letting
this stand back. They openly say they are for culture
and civilization, and education and social service, and
better housing and higher wages, and democratic
influences.

But what Jesus Christ was after was to get the
people saved from sin and made citizens of the
Kingdom of God. What Paul strove for was Salvation
by faith ; what he said he was determined to do was
to know nothing among men save Jesus Christ and
Him crucified. What John defined as God's will was
to ' know the Father, and Jesus Christ whom He hath
sent.' *This, this, this* is what The Salvation Army is
for, to spread this—and all our thousand agencies and
schemes and departments and activities in all lands
are for this, *or they are nothing*.

> Ye servants of God ! your Master proclaim,
> And publish abroad His wonderful name ;
> The name all-victorious of Jesus extol ;
> His Kingdom is glorious and rules over all.

Do good to them that hate you, . . . that ye may
be the children of your Father which is in heaven :
for He maketh His sun to rise on the evil and on
the good, and sendeth rain on the just and on the
unjust. For if ye love them which love you, what
reward have ye ? Do not even the publicans the
same ?—Matthew 5 : 44–46.

Now, here is one of the foundation principles of our
Social Work. From the beginning we have said openly
that our love and labour are for all. It is not necessary to have a good character to secure our compassion and help. We do not make it a condition of
being blessed and comforted that a man should belong
to a Union or go to Church or join The Salvation
Army. We make, so far as we can, our sun, like our
Father's, to shine on what are called the ' undeserv-
ing,' the ' worthless ' poor as well as on the others ;
and our rain to descend on the bad and idle, as well
as on the good and industrious.

Why ? Because it is not those who are well, but
those who are sick, that need the physician. Because
if we can only make them see that we care, and that
Christ cares about their darkened future, some, at
least, will wake up to care for themselves. Because
Christ has redeemed them for time as well as for
eternity.

We go forth not to fight 'gainst the sinner, but sin :
    The lost and the outcast we love ;
While the claims of our King unto all we will bring,
    As we call them His mercy to prove.

154

**My days are like a shadow that declineth ; and I
am withered like grass. But Thou, O Lord, shalt
endure for ever.**—Psalm 102 : 11, 12.
**The Father . . , with whom is no variableness,
neither shadow of turning.**—James 1 : 17.

How great are the changes wrought in us by the
curbing influences of time ! How much that in youth
and early manhood we meant to do, and could do,
and did do, has to be laid down or left to others as our
years approach the limit of their pilgrimage ! I
have known some who, for this reason alone, did not
desire to live beyond the years of strength and vigour
—they preferred ' to cease at once to work and live.'
But, no matter what the cause, certain it is that within
and without all seems to change. . . .

High above all your changes ; high above all the
storms and disappointments that belong to them ;
high above all the wretched failure and doubting of
the ' do-the-best-I-can ' life you are living, He lives
to bless, to save, to uplift, to keep. Unnumbered
multitudes, fighting their way to Him in spite of the
timidities and wobblings, the ' couldn'ts ' and
' wouldn'ts ' of their own nature, have proved Him the
faithful and unchanging God. Will not you ?

**Examine yourselves, whether ye be in the faith ;
prove your own selves. Know ye not your own
selves, how that Jesus Christ is in you, except ye
be reprobates ?**—2 Corinthians 13 : 5.

The love our Lord Jesus Christ gives us in ex-
change for our love-consecration to Him is the same
kind of love as His own ; and the kind of love
which governs His Being is self-sacrificing love. Not
only are we to ' love thy neighbour as thyself,' or to
love as brothers, we are to love *as He loved*. *This* is
the love He bestows on us, setting its holy currents
flowing through every power in our being, so that we
actually see and know in ourselves a love similar to
that which we see and know in Him.

' He teaches to yield up the love of life
For the sake of the life of love ! '

Surely this must be the meaning of the Apostle's
words, ' until Christ be formed in you.' Not the
bodily Christ, of course, but the Divine Christ—with
the Christ spirit, with the Christ nature, with the
Christ sincerity and patience and sacrifice and
compassion and humility. All this to be formed in
our spirit, in *our* patience, in *our* sympathies and
compassions. It is the re-appearance of Christ ; it
is Christ come again ; *it is Christ formed anew* !

When Ephraim saw his sickness, and Judah saw
his wound, then went Ephraim . . . and sent to
king Jareb : yet could he not heal you, nor cure
you of your wound.—Hosea 5 : 13.

Saith the Lord : though your sins be as scarlet,
they shall be as white as snow ; . . . if ye be willing and obedient.—Isaiah 1 : 18, 19.

The mere condemnation of sin, no matter how fully
it harmonizes with our sense of what ought to be, does
not satisfy man. The excusing of sin is no better ; it
leaves the sinner who loves his sin, a sinner who loves
it still.

The re-naming of evil which has often been
attempted during the last two or three thousand
years, and again in quite recent days, has little or no
effect either upon its nature or upon those who are
under its mastery. The new label does not change the
poison. Its victim is a victim still. Nor does the
punishment of sin entirely dispose of it, either in the
sufferer or in the consciousness of the onlooker.
Sending a fever patient to hospital is a poor expedient
unless we cure the disease. Sending a thief to prison
is a poor affair if he remains a thief. It is not in
reality a victory over thieving.

Yes—it is a cure we need. And we know it.

> Come and rejoice with me !
> I, once so sick at heart,
> Have met with One who knows my case,
> And knows the healing art.

Brethren, my heart's desire and prayer to God for Israel is, that they might be saved.—Romans 10 : 1.

Fathers, mothers, widows, brothers, sisters, broken-hearted lovers, have all confided in me—have all begged me, in one form or another, to give them some word of hope about their silent dead. And I have so often found that in life and health and safety there was not only little done to warn and save, but that there was little prayer made for them—so very little prayer for their souls.

Ah, my friends, how do we stand in this matter ? How can we answer to ourselves—I am not thinking just now of our responsibility to God—how can we, I say, answer to ourselves for the souls who have, in our sphere of influence, in our own time, lived and died in sin, for whom we have not even offered to God one strong, yearning prayer ? Let us pray for the living ! Let us pray for their souls.

> Daily I will strive to seek
>   To live holy here below ;
> To the dying I will speak,
>   Tell them how Thy Blood does flow.

Then were there brought unto Him little children, that He should put His hands on them, and pray : . . . Jesus said, Suffer little children, and forbid them not, to come unto Me : . . . and He laid His hands on them.—Matthew 19 : 13–15.

The children must be brought to Christ. That is the inner meaning of His own words, ' Suffer them to come unto Me.' Watching them and teaching them, all amount to nothing if they do not come to Him. The real trouble in their lives is—and is going to be— the power of evil. The evil in their nature—the evil in their will—the evil in their feelings and affections. Unless that can be conquered, no matter how much is done, nothing is done. They will be worse in time and worse in eternity for having met The Salvation Army unless that evil is mastered. Only Jesus Christ can do it. Bring them to Him. Bring them to be convicted of their sin, to repent and forsake it and to believe on Him for pardon and for a new heart, just as you bring the older people.

But thousands and thousands who wander and fall
   Never heard of that Heavenly Home ;
I should like them to know there is room for them all,
   And that Jesus has bid them to come.
I long for the joys of that glorious time,
   The sweetest and brightest and best,
When the dear little children of every clime
   Shall crowd to His arms and be blessed.

Behold, I stand at the door and knock : if any man hear My voice, and open the door, I will come in.—Revelation 3 : 20.

This know . . , that . . . perilous times shall come. For men shall be lovers of their own selves, covetous, boasters, proud, blasphemers, disobedient to parents, unthankful, unholy, . . . lovers of pleasures more than lovers of God. —2 Timothy 3 : 1, 2, 4.

Sin ! Look how the hateful thing works its way ! See the *disorder* it brings. Upsetting God's plan for men at the very beginning of their lives—just as a grain of sand falling into the eye upsets the whole arrangement of the eye and its work, leading at last to blindness. Sin disarranges everything in men's souls—the lower nature gets the mastery ! Lies come to look like truth ! Virtue appears foolish and vice seems wise ! Pleasure grows more important than duty ! Self is preferred to God ! Darkness to light ! Time to eternity ! It is a kind of upside-downism of the soul.

Redeemed from the foe, we Jesus proclaim
And triumph to know the power of His name ;
Preservèd from evil through God the Most High,
The world and the Devil and sin we defy.

**A righteous man regardeth the life of his beast :
but the tender mercies of the wicked are cruel.**
—Proverbs 12 : 10.
**Sparrows . . . and one of them shall not fall on
the ground without your Father.**—Matthew 10 : 29.

Remember that your kindness is to extend to the
animal creation. Be kind, therefore, to all living
things—they belong to your God. Never kill, or
allow any one to kill, any animal unless it is necessary
that it should die, and then, even with what are called
vermin—rats and mice and so forth—always do it
mercifully. Be no party to the overloading or over-
driving of horses.

Never, if you can help it, allow a poor woodland
bird to be imprisoned in a cage. Remember that,
like yourself, it was born free, and that every time it
sees the blue sky or hears the sound of day its little
heart is torn with anguish, with hope, with fear,
until its wings grow weary with beating against the
cruel bars. By and by the little captive will droop
and die, but God will notice the wrong suffered—not
a sparrow falls to the ground without His knowledge.

Show a high example, then, and especially among
the young, of quiet, persistent kindness ; it will not
only increase their love for you personally, but it will
help them to understand that ours is a religion of love.

My little children, let us not love in word, neither in tongue ; but in deed and in truth. . . . This is His commandment, That we should believe on the name of His Son Jesus Christ, and love one another, as He gave us commandment.—1 John 3 : 18, 23.

' Love for souls ' embraces so much of the life and work of The Salvation Army that it might almost be said to be an alternative name for the whole Organization. I can imagine some holy being just arrived from another world asking ' What is The Salvation Army ? ' and being answered in terms according to his own understanding, ' The Salvation Army is love for souls.'

Love is the attraction which has brought us together as an Army. It is the uniting principle which, in spite of many differences in race, language, character and temperament, has made us one.

Love is more than this. It is the sustaining force of the Movement. With love, The Army, no matter how small or poor or despised, is a living Branch in the True Vine of the Kingdom of God on earth.

> From my soul break every fetter,
>   Thee to know is all my cry ;
> Saviour, I am Thine for ever,
>   Thine I'll live and Thine I'll die,
>   Only asking
>   More and more of Love's supply.

As for me, I will call upon God ; and the Lord shall save me. Evening, and morning, and at noon, will I pray, and cry aloud : and He shall hear my voice.—Psalm 55 : 16, 17.

We must regard prayer as a regular duty as well as a privilege and a help. I am sure that regular habits of prayer are exceedingly helpful, even though they are not absolutely necessary, in maintaining the spirit of prayer. Both my observation and my own experience go to show that if we leave prayer for any hour, or even claim that we leave it to all hours, it will often come to this—that we shall leave it to none.

One of the great dangers of all spiritual work lies in doing it by fits and starts. And it is just because the Devil knows that regular and fixed times of meeting with God will more and more reduce his power over us and free us from temptation, that he makes it specially difficult for us to get those settled times. Business seems so pressing. Other works appear so important. The claims of those around us look so urgent. And using all this, the Devil hopes to chase away the plan of regular meeting with our God.

> Oh, guide us with Thy inward light,
>   With softest breathings deeply stir
> And thrill our waiting souls with life,
>   Spirit of God, the Comforter.

Herein is love, not that we loved God, but that He loved us.—1 John 4 : 10.

The Lord hath appeared . . . unto me, saying, Yea, I have loved thee with an everlasting love.—Jeremiah 31 : 3.

How few people there are, after all, who really act as though they knew God loves them and wants to use them to spread that love to others ! Even for us who can say we are His by faith, and who know we love God, there is something more important still— a thousand times more important : God loves us ! He gave Himself for us. Behind the changing circumstances of life and the cold, irresponsive conditions to which many of us seem bound by invisible chains, there is the world of Love prepared, and prepared for us—the world of Light and Rest and Peace and Joy unspeakable—the Kingdom of God.

Our War is against selfishness. No weapon is of much use in that conflict but love. Love and faith —love from God, faith in God. Love towards man, faith for man, Love and faith—these are our high explosives, our engines for the conquest of souls and for the destruction of that great enemy of righteousness—Sin.

> The faith that conquers all,
>   And doth the mountain move, .
> And saves whoe'er on Jesus call,
>   And perfects them in love.

Surely He hath borne our griefs, and carried our sorrows.—Isaiah 53 : 4.

Jesus . . . said . . . Ye now . . . have sorrow : but I will see you again, and your heart shall rejoice, and your joy no man taketh from you. —John 16 : 19, 22.

Sorrow is the most common of all human experiences. There are no homes without it, and there are very few hearts which have not tasted its cup, and to millions of men Christ has appeared in their affliction and taken possession of their lives.

What was the secret of His influence over them ? Was it His dominion from sea to sea ? Was it even His victory over death and His kingly conquest of the grave ? Was it His sovereign throne of power ? No, I do not think it was thus He won them ; but as ' the Man of Sorrows, and acquainted with grief,' who could compassionate with them in their sorrows also.

Let the human heart once realize that in its deepest depths of sorrow it may have for helper One who has been deeper still ; and it is in the nature of things that it should fly to that One for succour, for sympathy, for strength. And when that One out of His riches gives of His own might and of His own sweet, unfathomed consolations, then His government is assured, His rule is established.

Though He slay me, yet will I trust in Him.
—Job 13 : 15.

God has His own appointed methods of securing
victory for His people, though we do not always
perceive them. The connection between the plan
that He will have us adopt, and the results which are
attained, is often hidden, like a river which flows in
fertilizing beauty for miles and suddenly disappears
into the earth, coming forth again later as a mighty
torrent on its way to the sea. We cannot see the
connection, but we know quite well that it is there.

There is much about God's ways with us as individuals which seems to be planned upon this
principle. He leads and guides and directs us for a
time openly and plainly ; we can easily trace His
hand in all we receive and accomplish. Then all at
once cross-currents and opposing influences come in :
and suddenly we cannot see Him ; we cannot hear
His voice ; and though we search for Him we do not
find Him. Then is the hour for faith to look up, and
to say, ' Not as I will, but as Thou wilt.' This is what
Job meant when, in spite of the disasters, and disease,
and degradation which overtook him, he said, ' But
He knoweth the way that I take ; when He hath
tried me, I shall come forth as gold.' ' I know that
my Redeemer liveth.'

For this cause we also . . . do not cease to pray for you, and to desire that ye might be filled with the knowledge of His will in all wisdom and spiritual understanding ; that ye might walk worthy of the Lord . . , being fruitful in every good work, and increasing in the knowledge of God.—Colossians 1 : 9, 10.

I am sure that there ought to be a great deal more prayer for one another amongst us. We are all leaves upon the same tree of life. Every one of us is influenced by the others, and we draw our strength from the same source. I am convinced that great blessings would come down on many if we could secure a little more pleading with God for one another. I feel an absolute conviction that such intercession would have a mighty influence. . . . Observe, I am here thinking of *prayer for others*—that personal believing, persistent supplicating of the Throne which moves the heart of God.

> In me Thy Spirit dwell,
>   In me Thy mercies move,
> So shall the fervour of my zeal
>   Be the pure flame of love.

My presence shall go with thee, and I will give thee rest.—Exodus 33 : 14.

The God of love . . . shall be with you.—2 Corinthians 13 : 11.

Let . . . love continue.—Hebrews 13 : 1.

Love becomes the rule of our lives, whether we live or die, work or rest, suffer or rejoice. In injury or misunderstanding, when suffering from slander or weakness, as well as in victory and prosperity, and even in the common things of daily life and toil— often so meaningless without this—love fills, surrounds, crowns us, and flows out of a heart in which God abides and rules ; and God is love.

Oh, is it so with you ? In the burden and worry, amid the humble duties, and especially in the little things that try your patience and harass you, and seem so useless a part of your discipline : *is love the answer of your heart*, both for yourself and for others ?

It was that it might be so that He created us at first. Love is the goal to which He desires to bring the whole creation. He made us in His own image ; we are the work of His hands ; *His will for us is the rest of His presence* ; the rest of His will done in us and by us ; the rest of always going forward and never going backward ; the rest of victory, the rest of love.

Shall not the Judge of all the earth do right?
—Genesis 18 : 25.
**Ascribe ye greatness unto our God. . . . His
work is perfect : for all His ways are judgment : a
God of truth . . , just and right is He.**—Deuteronomy 32 : 3, 4.

Peace is impossible without the recognition that
God is right. That His purposes are right and will be
right. That His dealings with man are rooted in everlasting righteousness. How can a man have peace
with his Maker if in his heart of hearts he thinks his
Maker unjust, unreasonable, or unkind ? Ridiculous ?
Impossible ! Why, you could not have peace in a
nursery on that principle ; no, nor in the Heaven of
Heavens itself ! The heart that cries for peace with
sincerity will cry in full acknowledgment that God is
right, and will say with the wise man of old, ' God
giveth to a man that is good in His sight wisdom, and
knowledge, and joy '——and *that He is right when
He gives them*—' but to the sinner He giveth travail,
to gather and to heap up '—*and He is right when He
gives it*.

Let all men praise the Lord,
    In worship lowly bending ;
On His most holy word,
    Redeemed from woe, depending.
He gracious is and just ;
    From childhood doth He lead ;
In Him we place our trust
    And hope in time of need.

The sufferings of this present time are not worthy to be compared with the glory which shall be revealed in us.—Romans 8 : 18.

Unnumbered multitudes have realized in suffering a gift of priceless value, renewing the soul-refining character of its baser qualities and developing the noble and the true—sympathy, humility, patience, strength—and bringing with it, hand in hand, a revelation of God and His grace and power which had before seemed impossible.

More than this, suffering, if only it be accepted with meekness, is a mighty enemy for routing the great enemy—selfishness. And more still, it is the great agent by which God works for our perfection in the service of others. This is the meaning of the Apostle's words about the endurance and perfecting of our Lord Jesus Christ—' It became Him, for whom are all things, and by whom are all things, in bringing many sons unto glory, to make the captain of their salvation perfect through sufferings.'

> Our sufferings, Lord, to Thee are known,
>   For Thou wast tempted once like us ;
> Regard our grief, regard Thine own,
>   When hanging bleeding on the cross.
>
> Thou wilt not break a bruisèd reed,
>   Nor quench the smallest spark of grace ;
> Thou wilt affliction's painful seed
>   Mature, in fruits of righteousness.

Whither shall I go from Thy Spirit ? or whither shall I flee from Thy presence ? If I ascend up into heaven, Thou art there ; if I make my bed in hell, behold, Thou art there. If I take the wings of the morning, and dwell in the uttermost parts of the sea ; even there shall Thy hand lead me, and Thy right hand shall hold me.—Psalm 139 : 7–10.

The fact of the presence of God has no relation to this place or that. No doubt the place we are in does influence us—that is one of the reasons for not ' standing in the way of sinners, nor sitting in the seat of the scornful.' But it does not alter the fact of God's presence—for, as David shows us, He is everywhere—though it may affect our sense of His presence.

But the other side of the truth is also to be taught ; that God is no respecter of places. Wherever duty or devotion calls us we shall find God at hand. If we are right with Him we may be just as conscious and just as sure of His Presence in the little cottage kitchen as in the great assembly of saints ; in the palace as in the prison ; that His Presence is to be realized as truly at the bottom of a coal-pit as in the sunny forest glade. We may, in fact, look for Him with the same confidence in the factory, working with a thousand others who know nothing of His love, as in the death chamber of some saintly soul going forth from the body with songs of joy to meet the Lord. The place is nothing to Him ; the person He comes to meet and to live with is everything.

I say unto you, What things soever ye desire, when ye pray, believe that ye receive them, and ye shall have them.—Mark 11 : 24.

But there is one important thing that must precede prayer if prayer is to succeed, and that is : *desire*. Desire is to prayer what soil is to a plant—the bed out of which it grows. Desire varies as soils do. On the one hand you may have a soil that is warm, genial and conducive to growth ; on the other hand, there are soils that are cold, stony and inhospitable. So prayer is influenced by the character of desire.

And I think that probably many persons are as blessed when, by an act of determination, they say : ' I will go up to the house of the Lord, though my feet are heavy and my heart is not inclined that way,' as when they can say with David : ' I was glad when they said unto me, Let us go into the house of the Lord.'

> Me with a quenchless thirst inspire,
> A longing, infinite desire,
>   And fill my craving heart.
> Less than Thyself, oh, do not give ;
> In might Thyself within me live ;
>   Come, all Thou hast and art.

**Hold fast the . . . love which is in Christ Jesus.
That good thing which was committed unto thee
keep by the Holy Ghost which dwelleth in us.**
—2 Timothy 1 : 13, 14.

All can understand love. All have had some kind
of experience of it. The great and small, the self-
righteous and the self-condemned, the proud and the
selfish, no matter of what race or nation, are all
subject to its attraction.

> '. . . Pity and need
> Make all flesh kin. There is no caste in blood
> Which runneth of one hue ; nor caste in tears
> Which trickle salt with all . . .'

The heart-broken and the despairing and the most
degraded, the most sad alike with the most glad—
they all know love when they see it ! They may not
know God—they may never have known any one
whom they thought good—they may not understand
anything about the Bible or religion or churches or
Heaven or Hell—but they all understand love. That
is why we say the great weapon to use for their salvation, the great means to win them, is just this one
simple, beautiful, Godlike thing, a holy love—love
for them—love for their souls.

Unto you that fear My name shall the Sun of righteousness arise with healing.—Malachi 4 : 2.
God is light, and in Him is no darkness at all. If we say that we have fellowship with Him, and walk in darkness, we lie, and do not the truth.—1 John 1 : 5, 6.

I see that the astronomers say that the light of the sun is five hundred thousand times greater than the light of the moon, and yet the moon is able to cut off into darkness and shadow that wonderful world of light. How often I have seen this. Men and women walking in the light of God, rejoicing in the glory of the Lord, and then something not evil in itself, but *separating* in its effect, has intercepted the light and cut off the joy. It may be money, position, wife, husband, children, lover, friend. There may be nothing wrong with them, any more than the dear old moon ! But if they get between us and the Sun of Righteousness, they become an obstruction, yes, even an abomination !

An eclipse is a kind of outrage on the sun. And ought we not to view everything which comes between the soul and God as an outrage upon Him ? We are apt to think of evil only as it affects ourselves, injures our own future and imperils our own safety. But it is all an outrage on Him, an offence against His Majesty, a wounding of His love. Oh, come away from darkness ! *Let us be one with the Light !*

God is my King . . , working salvation in the midst of the earth.—Psalm 74 : 12.

They went forth, and preached everywhere, the Lord working with them, and confirming the word.—Mark 16 : 20.

God is not only in His Heaven ; God is not only amidst the golden candlesticks in His Temple ; God is not only enshrined in the hearts of those who love and trust and serve Him ; God is not only in the mighty forces of the natural world around us, in the bursting life of the universe—God is in the souls of wicked men. He is present with the worldlings in their vain pursuits ; He is in the very midst of the backsliders and the betrayers of His Son. And being there He is ready to unite with us in our great offensive for the capture of men's wills—the great deciding factor.

He will work with us. Let us see to it that we work with Him—that we ' play into His hands '—so that the great result in the recovery of what He has lost may be attained in the best—that is, in the quickest —way. In our great hunt for souls, I claim that we may say, ' The best of all is that God is with us ! '

> We are with Thee 'neath the Cross,
> Henceforth earthly things are dross ;
> Thine, resigned to mortal ill,
> Thine to die if Thou shouldst will.
> Thou who hast the winepress trod,
> Reconciling us to God,
> Help us each returning day,
> Be Thou with us all the way.

175

Jesus said : **Let not your heart be troubled : ye believe in God, believe also in Me. . . . I go to prepare a place for you . . . that where I am, there ye may be also.**—John 14 : 1-3.

Jesus passed this same way before you. He wore a shroud. He lay in a grave. The last resting place is henceforth for us fragrant with immortality. The very horrors, shadows and mysteries of the death chamber have become signs that death is vanquished. The tomb is but the porch of a temple in which we shall surely stand, the doorway to the place of an abiding rest. 'In my Father's house are many mansions ; if it were not so, I would have told you.'

Living or dying—but especiallly when dying— we have a right to cry with Stephen, the first to witness for Christ in this horror of death : 'Lord Jesus, receive my spirit.' To Him we commit all. He passed this way before with a worn and bruised body in weakness and contempt, and on Him we dare to cast ourselves—on Him and Him alone. On His merits, on His Blood, on His body dead and buried for us. He will be with us even to the end, *He has passed this way before us.*

> Speak to me by name, O Master,
>   Let me know it is for me.
> Speak, that I may follow faster,
>   With a step more firm and free,
> Where the Shepherd leads the flock
> In the shadow of the rock.

God saw every thing that He had made, and behold, it was very good. . . . Thus the heavens and the earth were finished, and all the host of them. And . . . God . . . rested on the seventh day from all His work which He had made. And God blessed the seventh day, and sanctified it. —Genesis 1 : 31 ; 2 : 1–3.
Return unto thy rest, O my soul : for the Lord hath dealt bountifully with thee. . . . I will walk before the Lord in the land of the living.—Psalm 116 : 7, 9.

But the law of that Sabbath was the law of life and service—of action, not of idleness. There was indeed rest, but there was no standing still. The inner life of the new world which had just been called into being went forward. The sun, the stars, the wind, the sea, the dew, the herbs, the trees, the moving creatures, the man—yes, even God Himself—all fulfilled their life, hour by hour. Nothing stopped growing, nothing stopped yielding of its fruits. There was the rest of a perfect harmony, but there was no stagnation.

So with us ; the rest of full Salvation—of the indwelling God—does not imply that we shall grow no more, or know no more. No, no, prayer and faith and the Bible are just as necessary and just as precious, and communion with God is just as beautiful and helpful, the lessons of His providence are just as fruitful, while dependence upon Him for strength and life and guidance are just as real as ever.

' Rest is not quitting the busy career ;
    Rest is the fitting of self to its sphere.'

Be strong in the Lord, and in the power of His might . . . that ye may be able to stand against the wiles of the devil.—Ephesians 6 : 10, 11.

Jesus treats the Devil as the tempter all the way through. He calls him Satan. It is one of the strong advantages that Jesus had in the conflict, that He *recognized His enemy*. It will be a great strength to you, my comrades, to attribute to the Devil at once the temptations which assail you. When the evil thought comes to you, say to yourself, ' That is of the Devil.' Do not on any account listen to the twaddle which would make it appear that evil is nothing but an influence around you—a sort of disagreeable gas ! It may be an influence, perhaps, but it proceeds direct from that old serpent, the Devil ! When you listen to the suggestions of evil you are really listening to him ; when you yield to that influence you are yielding to the great destroyer himself.

If one temptation fails, the enemy will try another. Do not be surprised at anything ! The Devil will stick at nothing !

> Jesus, the name high over all,
> In Hell or earth or sky !
> Angels and men before Him fall,
> And devils fear and fly.

**The Lord said, . . . behold, Satan hath desired
to have you, . . . but I have prayed for thee, that
thy faith fail not.**—Luke 22 : 31, 32.
**That their hearts might be comforted, being knit
together in love. . . . For though I be absent in
the flesh, yet am I with you in the spirit, joying
and beholding your order, and the stedfastness of
your faith in Christ.**—Colossians 2 : 2, 5.

When I speak of giving, I am not thinking about
material possessions only. I am thinking also about
other things.

I am thinking about kindness. What wealth every
one of us may place in the hands and hearts of those
who are around us by kind words and kind looks and
kind deeds !

I am thinking of faith. What a wonderful gift we
can bestow upon others by our confidence, to their
great enrichment ! How many people are there in
some way connected with every one who will read
these words, who could be made richer and happier,
yes, and a great many of them holier, too, if some one
near would only say to them, 'I trust you ; I believe
in you ; I have confidence in you ! '

> Oh, touch our lips, that we may speak
> To guard the tempted, help the weak,
> And guide the wandering to retrace
> Their steps, and seek a Father's face.

The just shall live by faith.—Hebrews 10 : 38.
Faith is . . . the evidence of things not seen.
—Hebrews 11 : 1.

How can we hope to prevail without faith ? I am
all for prayer, I believe in it ! Looking back over my
life, I see how repeatedly God has worked miracles
in answer to prayer ; how He has made His people
stronger than all the forces of the world, the flesh and
the Devil ; and how really and truly prayer is a kind
of secret, for those who know God, by which they live.

But we must pray in faith. Remember believing is
not merely saying, ' I believe ' ; faith is not merely
talking about faith, even though we talk about it in
our prayers ! Faith is a definite attitude of the moral
nature, a putting of ourselves in the place of trust
where we can see and hear God. I call to mind the
lines :

> ' The things unknown to feeble sense,
>   Unseen by reason's glimmering ray,
> With strong commanding evidence
>   Their heavenly origin display.
> Faith lends its realizing light ;
>   The clouds disperse, the shadows fly ;
> The Invisible appears in sight,
>   And God is seen by mortal eye ! '

Now this is the faith we want !

Jesus said : **If God so clothe the grass of the field, which to-day is, and to-morrow is cast into the oven, shall He not much more clothe you, O ye of little faith ? Therefore take no thought, saying, What shall we eat ? or, What shall we drink ? or, Wherewithal shall we be clothed ? . . . for your heavenly Father knoweth that ye have need of all these things.**—Matthew 6 : 30–32.

To doubt God's providence, is an old and ever new difficulty. ' How can my tiny needs and claims come up before Him who must rule and govern a thousand worlds ? ' Well, did not Jesus Christ take infinite pains to meet this very problem by the illustrations He used ?

Now, nearly all those illustrations have to do with what are very small things. The sparrows—how many must fall, yet He says not one could fall to the ground without your Father's knowledge ; and are not ye more than many sparrows ? ' Consider the lilies of the field, how they grow.' *And the grass.* The myriad blades of green grass, which to-day is and to-morrow is cast into the oven, it is all the object of His care ! How small are these things in themselves ! How infinitely small beside the life and will of the human spirit. How small, small beyond the power of words to tell, by the side of Him who cares for them—for us—for all ! If, then, God so clothe the grass, which is to-day in the field, and to-morrow is cast into the oven, how much more *you* ? Trust Him ! *His providence is a loving providence.*

Jesus . . . said unto her, . . . Whosoever drinketh of this water shall thirst again : but whosoever drinketh of the water that I shall give him shall never thirst ; but the water that I shall give him shall be in him a well of water springing up into everlasting life.—John 4 : 10, 13, 14.

One of the most remarkable features of the present time is the extraordinary thirst for knowledge in every quarter of the world. It is not confined to this continent or that. It is not peculiar to any special class or age. It is universal. One aspect of it, and a very significant one, is the desire for knowledge about life and its origin, about the beginning of things, about the earth and its creation, about the work which we say God did, which He alone could do. Oh, how man searches and explores ; seeking to know what will make life longer for him and his ; and, above all, what can make it happier.

And here, again, I say that Jesus is the Man for the Century. He has knowledge to give which none other can provide. I do not doubt that universities and schools and governments and a great press can and will do much to impart knowledge of all sorts to the world. But when it comes to knowledge that can serve the great end for which the very power to acquire knowledge was created—namely, the true happiness of man—then I say that Jesus is the source of that knowledge ; that without Him it cannot be found or imparted ; and that with Him it comes in its liberating and enlightening glory.

Blessed be the Lord my strength, which teacheth
my hands to war, and my fingers to fight.—Psalm
144 : 1.
We wrestle not against flesh and blood, but
against principalities, against powers, against the
rulers of the darkness of this world, against
spiritual wickedness.—Ephesians 6 : 12.

Our very title, Salvation Army, is an expression of
the fact that *we are fighting men and women* ! If it be
true—as, thank God, it is for most of us—that we
received a Divine call to this work, then we may truly
say that God brought us into the world to fight !

But, I ask, who or what is our foe ? Against what
do we fight ? We may say with truth that we are in
conflict with the spirit of evil in its every manifestation in the world. We are against the tyranny
and injustice, the selfishness, the worldliness, the
drunkenness, impurity and lasciviousness all around
us.

In actual practice, that resolves itself into this,
that we have to fight these things *in individual lives*.
It is individual men and women whose hearts are
contaminated and possessed by the different forms
of evil—the worldling, the pleasure hunter, the
gambler, the profligate and the men and women who,
while they may be none of these things, yet have no
place in their hearts for God or Christ—it is these
we have to attack and capture.

In the garden a new sepulchre. . . . There laid they Jesus.—John 19 : 41, 42.

He also Himself likewise took part of the same ; that through death He might destroy him that had the power of death, that is, the devil ; and deliver them who through fear of death were all their lifetime subject to bondage.—Hebrews 2 : 14, 15.

Death has many voices. This death and burial speak aloud in tones of triumph. It was a death that made an end of death, and a burial that buried the grave. And yet it was also a very humble and painful and sad affair.

To many, even among those who have been freed from guilty fear, mortality itself still has terrors. By Divine grace they can lift up their hearts in sure and certain hope of a glorious resurrection, and yet they shrink with painful apprehension at the thought of the change which alone can make that resurrection possible. There is probably no instinct of the whole human family more frequently in evidence than this repulsion for the grave. Death is such an uncouth and hideous thing. Now, in the presence of such shrinkings—has not this vision of the dead body of our Lord something in it to charm away our fears ?

> No more we tremble at the grave,
> For He who died our souls to save
>   Will raise our bodies too ;
> What though this earthly house shall fail ?
> The Saviour's power will yet prevail,
>   And build it up anew.

Jesus said : **The lord said unto the servant, Go out into the highways and hedges, and compel them to come in, that my house may be filled.** —Luke 14 : 23.

Never must we lose sight of the fact that the *spirit of attack* is one of the distinctive features of The Salvation Army. Was it not, in fact, this that brought The Army into existence ? There were already churches and chapels and mission halls. There was probably more religious observance than now, an abundance of preaching, any amount of the routine business of what is called Christian service. That which was lacking—that which gave birth to The Army—was desperate unflinching *assaults on the strongholds of evil outside.* Without waiting until the ungodly chose to come to listen to the offer of Salvation by Christ, but going after them, compelling them to heed us, forcing ourselves with our great message on their attention. We made it impossible for the people to ignore us.

To the war ! to the war ! loud and long sounds the cry ;
To the war ! every Soldier who fears not to die ;
See the millions who're drifting to Hell's endless woe—
Oh, who in the name of Jehovah will go ?

> Fighting on, fighting on !
> With the Blood and Fire we will never tire,
> We'll fight until the Master calls.

Love worketh no ill to his neighbour : therefore love is the fulfilling of the law.—Romans 13 : 10.

Of what value is freedom without love ? I suppose that something which answers to liberty may be said to attach to all that is desirable in human life. So that we have freedom from the monstrous bondage called slavery, freedom of opinion, freedom of speech, freedom to labour or not to labour, freedom to come and go without let or hindrance in the lawful pursuits of life, and freedom of thought and religion. All good, all very desirable, all, I dare say, more or less needed for human happiness, and yet all perfectly powerless to make that happiness without one thing more—and that thing is love. One moment's thought will convince the most untutored mind that none of the freedoms I have mentioned can of themselves be of much real worth to any human being without—love.

> Love Divine, from Jesus flowing,
> Living waters, rich and free,
> Wondrous love, without a limit,
> Flowing from eternity ;
> Boundless Ocean,
> I would cast myself on Thee !

Seek ye first the kingdom of God, and His righteousness.—Matthew 6 : 33.

This is the great lesson of our history. Are we learning it ? Nothing less than the lesson of Calvary ! To give is greater than to get !

What has been the cause of the weakness and decay of so many of the religious movements of the world—movements which, no doubt, originated in true love for God and men ? Is it not here—that a time came when they began to think too much of preserving themselves—of the happiness of their own people—of the prosperity of their own children—of the grandeur of their own sacred edifices—of the beauty and refinement of their own services—of the safety of their own reputation ?

Well, let us stand clear of all that ! Let us hearken to the voice of our own past and go on as an Army of Sacrifice.

Thine was a life from self-seeking apart ;
' Offered for others ' was burned on Thy heart.
Not my own ends, but Thy Kingdom to aid,
Cost what it will, Lord, the price shall be paid.

I am the Lord, I change not.—Malachi 3 : 6.

We, ourselves, change. As the years fly past, the most notable fact about us, perhaps, is the changes that are going on in our experiences, our habits, our thoughts, our hopes, our conduct, our character. How much there was about us only a few years ago, which has changed in the interval. Indeed, might we not say of a great deal in us, which to-day is, that to-morrow it will be cast away for ever ?

Have you, my friend, not had to mourn over some strange changes ? Has not your joy been often so quickly turned to sorrow that you have wondered how you yourself could be the same person ? Is it not, then, a joy unspeakable that, amidst all this, whether we are or are not fully alive to the weakness, and variableness, and deceitfulness of our own hearts, we can look up to the *Rock* that changeth *not* ?

> Cast care aside, lean on thy Guide,
> His boundless mercy will provide ;
> Lean, and the trusting soul shall prove
> Christ is its life and Christ its love.
>
> Faint not, nor fear, His arms are near,
> He changeth not, and thou art dear ;
> Only believe, and thou shalt see
> That Christ is all in all to thee.

In Christ Jesus ye who sometimes were far off
are made nigh by the blood of C irist. For He is
our peace.—Ephesians 2 : 13, 14.
  Jesus said . . , Follow Me.—Luke 9 : 58, 59.

Conformity to Christ's example is only possible by
the re-formation in you of His life, and the growth
again in you of His person ; the mind of Christ in
your mind, the presence of Christ in your flesh and
blood ; the motive power of Christ, the Father's will,
prompting your every thought and word and deed,
and thereby transforming your body into a temple
of the Son of God.

And, because the Christ of Glory stooped, thinking
no humiliation of our nature too deep for His love to
tread, so He will condescend to the lowest depths of
weakness and want revealed in your heart and life.
He will meet you where you are. He will deal with
you just where you are weakest and worst. This is
indeed the keynote of all that God has to show you.
It is your own link in the long chain of patient and
ever-new revelations of God to man.

> I seek the blessing from the Lord,
>   That humble saints receive,
> And righteousness, His own reward
>   To all who dare believe.
>
> Oh, let me now Thy hill ascend
>   Made worthy by Thy grace,
> There in Thy strength to stand and serve
>   Within the holy place.

This charge I commit unto thee, . . . war a good warfare ; holding faith, and a good conscience.—1 Timothy 1 : 18, 19.

What are our Soldiers for if not to fight ? And how can they fight if they never come up with the enemy and force him to stand, and see their leader strike home with the truth ? The fact is that some Corps—and fine bodies of men and women they are— make little or no impression on the great mass of people in their district, or outside the comparatively small circle of their own people and their families and a fringe of regular hangers-on outdoors and in, just because they do not stand up to the enemy and provoke a proper *battle*.

If you are a fighter, if you are determined to attack the people and force them to give up their sin, you will go after them and *make* them listen to the claims of God. God has called you to be a man of war. You have been trained from your youth up to fight for Him. Think of all He has done to make you a warrior !

> I have read of men of faith
> Who have bravely fought till death,
>   Who now the crown of life are wearing ;
> Then the thought comes back to me :
> Can I not a Soldier be
>   Like to those martyrs bold and daring ?
>
> I'll gird on the armour and rush to the field,
> Determined to conquer, and never to yield ;
>   So the enemy shall know
>   Wheresoever I may go,
> That I am fighting for Jehovah.

190

Sing praises to God, . . . sing praises unto our King, sing praises. For God is the King of all the earth : . . . God sitteth upon the throne of His holiness.—Psalm 47 : 6–8.

The Lord is the true God, He is the living God, and an everlasting king. . . . He hath made the earth by His power, He hath established the world by His wisdom, and hath stretched out the heavens by His discretion.—Jeremiah 10 : 10, 12.

Call His name JESUS. . . . He shall reign over the house of Jacob for ever ; and of His kingdom there shall be no end.—Luke 1 : 31, 33.

Unless the Lord is king, all must be confusion, dissonance, and disaster. The supreme fact in human life after all is, that our God is ' the creator, preserver, and governor of all things.''

And here it must be remembered that He aspires to rule men's hearts. His kingdom is moral and spiritual first, and then physical and material. That is why it will endure for ever. It is in the region of motive and affection, of reason and emotion, of preference and choice, that He designs to be Ruler. It is to reign in men's hearts that Christ laid aside His heavenly crown and throne. If He cannot be a Ruler there, then He will account little of His Kingship in the skies.

> Reign over me, Lord Jesus !
>   Oh, make my heart Thy throne !
> It shall be Thine, dear Saviour,
>   It shall be Thine alone.

Jesus went about all the cities and villages, . . .
preaching . . , and healing every sickness and
every disease among the people. But when He
saw the multitudes, He was moved with compassion on them, because they fainted, and were
scattered abroad, as sheep having no shepherd.
—Matthew 9 : 35, 36.

Christ cared about the poor because they were poor.
Poverty itself had a kind of attraction for Him.
Suffering drew Him. All His heart was set toward
relieving the ocean of misery in the world, because it
was misery. When, therefore, He saw the blind, He
immediately wanted to open their eyes. When He
met the lepers, He hasted to cleanse them, just because
they were lepers, and then preached to them afterward. When the multitude was hungry, He fed
them. When He met the widow's dead boy at the
gateway to Nain, He raised him then and there without asking a question or laying down a single condition. All He said was, ' Weep not ! ' He really
wanted to heal the world of its woes. So far as He
could He showered His blessings upon all, just and
unjust. His heart was moved to pity when He looked
on the people, because He saw them as sheep without
a shepherd.

> Thou Shepherd of Israel and mine,
> > The joy and desire of my heart,
> For closer communion I pine,
> > I long to reside where Thou art.
> Thy love for a sinner declare,
> > Thy passion and death on the tree ;
> My spirit to Calvary bear,
> > To suffer and triumph with Thee.

Jesus said : **Watch and pray, that ye enter not into temptation ; . . . And He came and found them asleep again.**—Matthew 26 : 41, 43.
I have given you an example, that ye should do as I have done to you.—John 13 : 15.

After all, the failure of the disciples was very human. Their eyes were heavy. They were weary and sore tired. This, too, is typical of many of the losses we Salvationists are called upon to suffer. Some on whom we have relied and trusted grow weary in well-doing. The strain is so great ! The tax on brain and heart and hand is so constant ! Life becomes so burdened with watchings and prayings and sufferings for and with others, that there is little, if any, time or strength left for oneself ! And so they cannot keep up, but seek rest and quiet for themselves elsewhere. They are heavy, and no longer feel the need to watch with us.

Dear comrade, in your like trial do not doubt that the Lord Jesus is with you. Suffering of this kind will help to liken you to Him—it is a very real bearing of the cross of Christ. Pitiful followers of Him should we be, if we wished to have only joy when He had only suffering.

> Jesus, Saviour, I will follow,
>   Follow just where Thou shalt lead ;
> Though the path bring pain and sorrow,
>   Yet supply my every need.
>
>   Walk with me !
>   All the way from earth to Heaven,
>   Blessèd Master, walk with me !

Jesus saith to Simon Peter, . . . lovest thou Me ? He saith unto Him, Yea, Lord ; Thou knowest that I love Thee. He saith unto him, Feed My sheep.—John 21 : 15, 16.

Take heed . . . to all the flock, over the which the Holy Ghost hath made you overseers.—Acts 20 : 28.

As my beloved sons I warn you.—1 Corinthians 4 : 14.

It seems to me that there are special dangers attached to neglecting God's voice in matters which concern the Salvation of others. Some beautiful spirits amongst us fail here. They do all the Lord has commanded in other matters. They love and labour and endure and sacrifice at His word. They walk, or try to walk, as becometh the Gospel of Jesus Christ in everything but this. Some even lay upon the altars of God a ceaseless toil for His glory in their own localities. But much of the power of it—and sometimes all its power and all its joy—is lost because they do not go further and offer their lives at His command.

Dear Lord, I do surrender
    Myself, my all, to Thee,
My time, my store, my talents,
    So long withheld by me.
I've heard the call for workers,
    The world's great need I see ;
Oh, send me to the rescue,
    I'm here, my Lord ; send me !

Thus saith the Lord, Let not the wise man glory
in his wisdom, neither the mighty man glory in
his might, let not the rich man glory in his riches :
but let him that glorieth glory in this, that he
understandeth and knoweth Me, . . . which exercise lovingkindness, judgment, and righteousness,
in the earth : for in these things I delight, saith the
Lord.—Jeremiah 9 : 23, 24.

' Learn to show kindness at home,' says the
Apostle. That is a capital training-ground for kindness. In fact, it is doubtful whether you will show
it much anywhere if it is absent there. And yet how
often it is absent ! When I visit some people's homes,
I miss the little kindnesses that I expected to find in
profusion. The children are rough to one another.
The husband sits still, and allows the tired wife to
stand unnoticed ; or he goes on eating while she
answers the knock at the door ; or he helps himself
to the food before he asks her to take some. Many of
the kind words and the little trifles of gentleness which
brightened the days gone by are no longer thought of.
He would break his heart if she were to die, but from
want of thought he is unmindful of that which is her
very life.

Learn, or, as one might say, remember to show
kindness at home. Do not forget, because every one
there is so familiar to you, that your Saviour once
lived in a humble little cottage at Nazareth ; and
strive to be kind in your home, as He was in His.

Let the weak say, I am strong.—Joel 3 : 10.

Are you among those foolish persons who are waiting for some great change to take place in you which will enable you to show yourself strong because you are strong ? Are you looking for some far-off event—which, although you get older, does not seem to get much nearer—that will give you the victory always, because no trial will be able to try you and no temptation to disturb your peace ? Or are you living like our dear Paul, day by day conscious of your own weakness, dependent every hour upon God, and humbly crying to Him in the midst of the fight against evil and from amidst the struggles with your common trials, ' Master, I trust in Thee that out of this my weakness Thou wilt make me strong ' ?

> O Lord, I dare to trust in Thee
>   Who maketh all things new,
> My sins to slay, my tears to stay,
>   My sorrows to subdue ;
> And in the battle's blazing heat,
>   When flesh and blood would quail,
> I'll fight and trust, and still repeat
>   That Jesus cannot fail.

The Comforter, which is the Holy Ghost, whom the Father will send in My name, He shall teach you all things, and bring all things to your remembrance, whatsoever I have said unto you.—John 14 : 26.

The Holy Ghost is the great Teacher and Helper in the matter of how to pray. He knows the deep things of God. He shows us what God will give us, and then prompts us as to the form in which to present our petitions, and in what words to ask ; and the words He gives, no matter how simple, will prove the best words. As Paul says, ' Which things also we speak, not in the words which man's wisdom teacheth, but which the Holy Ghost teacheth.'

Prayer may be a mere cry. It may be a groaning without words. It may be a few sentences wrung from the heart that knows not how to utter them. It may be a thought or a desire lifted on the melody of song. Or it may be an ordered and reasoned appeal by the mind of man to the mind of God. But whatever form it takes, if only the soul comes into the presence of God and really addresses itself to Him, then it is true prayer and prayer that is acceptable to Him, acceptable and pleasing even when in His wisdom He does not grant our petition.

Behold . . . my beloved, in whom my soul is
well pleased : . . . A bruised reed shall he not
break, and smoking flax shall he not quench, till
he send forth judgment unto victory.—Matthew 12 :
18, 20.

Our war is a contest between selfishness in all its
forms and all that is pure and good and God-like.
In the very truest sense it is a war between the Son of
God and that old Serpent the Devil ; between the
Lamb that was slain and the Beast and all beastly
things. Some people doubt the issue and wonder
who will win. But they do not know our Lord.
They do not realize that He will never lay down His
sword till every knee has bowed and every tongue
confessed that His Name is above every name, to the
glory of God the Father. Yes, He will win.

If it were not so, what an unending night of death
and Hell the future would be for those who believe in
the soul of man and the government of God ! What
a sordid thing human life itself would become for us
who believe in both ! What a welter of shame and
slime would time represent ! No, thank God, we have
a better outlook than that ! The promise of the Father
is Victory for His Son.

The day of victory's coming, 'tis coming by and by,
When to the Cross of Calvary all nations they will fly.
O comrades in The Army, we'll fight until we die,
For the day of victory's coming by and by.

There remaineth . . . a rest to the people of God. For he that is entered into his rest . . . hath ceased from his own works. . . . Let us labour therefore to enter into that rest, lest any man fall after the same example of unbelief.—Hebrews 4 : 9–11.

There cannot be rest if two wills are contending—if you are pulling one way, and God is calling another ; nor can there be rest if you are seeking to work out your own plans while God is working out His. That will but bring back the old confusion and the old darkness, as at the beginning, and you will go back to the sinning and repenting as at the first. The real rest is in His, not in our will ; in His and never in our plan. When we are really abandoned to do and suffer all His will we shall take pleasure in Him, and He will find pleasure in us.

> Leave God to order all thy ways,
>   And hope in Him, whate'er betide ;
> Thou'lt find Him in the evil days
>   Thy all-sufficient strength and guide :
> Who trusts in God's unchanging love
> Builds on the Rock that naught can move.

Then spake Jesus again unto them, saying, I am the light of the world : he that followeth Me shall not walk in darkness, but shall have the light of life.—John 8 : 12.

If we walk in the light, as He is in the light, we have fellowship one with another, and the blood of Jesus Christ His Son cleanseth us from all sin. —1 John 1 : 7.

What a chilly thing is the eclipse of the sun ! I remember the last. I went out to watch it and instantly I was chilled and, looking at the thermometer as I returned, I was amazed to see that it had dropped seventeen degrees !

Is not this just what happens when we are separated from the Light of the world ? Is not this the secret of the coldness in many souls and lives ? Cold testimonies, cold singing, cold prayers, cold love ? Sometimes I hear people talking as though cold and heat were matters of their own manufacture. No ! The secret is in the Sun ! If His way is clear to reach us, if there are no obstructions, if there are no hindrances to His will, if we are in the right relation to the Sun, then we shall be warmed ; then the spiritual temperature will be right and, in place of the cold things named, there will be fiery testimonies and hot singing, hot prayers and burning love !

It is the obstructions that make the winter. This going about rubbing our cold powers, striving to catch a little heat from our comrades and working up some warm feelings in our hearts, will come to very little. *What we need is the Sun !*

I will maintain mine own ways before Him. He also shall be my salvation.—Job 13 : 15, 16.

He that trusteth in the Lord, mercy shall compass him about.—Psalm 32 : 10.

Job believed in a Saviour ! And, though tried to the very verge of death and Hell, he still believes, he still hopes, he still pursues his God ! Indeed, the whole book is stamped by evidences of Job's vivid realization and confidence that he is dealing with God, and that God is dealing with him—that his afflictions come by the hand of God and that, bewildering as it all seems, God keeps him ever in view.

The very emptiness of life, its fleeting, shifting scenes, its disappointing pleasures, its fading joys, the unsubstantial objects on which it gazes—all lead him to look away from the material, to look up, to look on, to look to God ; ' I know that my Redeemer liveth.' Yes, confidence that we are in His care—that He is not indifferent to our poor little lives—and that though we seem to come and go ' like insects of a summer breeze ' we are in His thoughts and in the infinite wisdom of His plan and in the boundless love of His mighty heart !

> Oh, how sweet is this assurance
>   Midst the conflict and the strife,
> Although sorrows past endurance
>   Follow me through life ;
> Home in prospect still can cheer me,
>   Yes, and give me sweet repose,
> While I feel His presence near me,
>   For my Heavenly Father knows.

**Like as a father . . , so the Lord pitieth . . .
For He knoweth our frame.**—Psalm 103 : 13, 14.
I had fainted, unless I had believed.—Psalm 27 : 13.

The religion of The Army has ever been characterized by a joyful confidence. Nothing has more contributed to the extension of our influence than the assurance and faith in God which our people have manifested. Perhaps for this very reason it is just their faith in God which the Devil has most bitterly attacked in some. He knows well that if he can *shake their trust* they will be shaken altogether. To some temperaments the temptation to distrust God becomes peculiarly powerful inasmuch as it finds in them the natural soil prepared for the seeds of questioning and misgiving. In their experience of trial and sorrow, and in times of disappointment and failure, such spirits are assailed with fierce and persistent cruelty by the great enemy. . . .

But doubts will not be dispersed by bringing the standard down to the doubters ! None of us can really trust in the over-seeing, over-ruling fact of the Heavenly Father's personal interest without being helped. I watched from the deck of my ship the other day a little waterfowl, alone amid the vast spaces of the Pacific Ocean, and its passage across the waste recalled these precious lines :

' He who from zone to zone
Guides through the boundless sky thy certain
flight
In the long way that I must tread alone
Will lead my steps aright.'

Know ye that the Lord He is God : it is He that hath made us, and not we ourselves ; we are His people, and the sheep of His pasture . . . be thankful unto Him, and bless His name. For the Lord is good ; His mercy is everlasting.—Psalm 100 : 3–5.

This is the work of God, *the making of men*. As it was in the beginning, so it still remains the great central fact of creation. The unmeasured greatness, the marvellous beauty, the abundant plenty, the continuing life of this mighty universe, do not satisfy Him without man. It was all the work of His hands. He blessed it all, and pronounced it good. It has not ceased to praise Him since the hour when the morning stars broke the silence of the ages, and sang together in adoration, and it will praise Him to the end. But without man all is only a vanishing cloud before Him. He longs for the love of men ; He waits for their praise ; He takes a supreme interest in them, and is still in the same purpose as when He spoke before the onlooking hosts of celestial beings, saying, ' Let Us make man in Our image, after Our likeness.'

And can it be that I should gain
   An interest in the Saviour's Blood ?
Died He for me who caused His pain ?
   For me who Him to death pursued ?
Amazing love ! How can it be,
That Thou, my God, shouldst die for me ?

Oh, how great is Thy goodness, which Thou hast laid up for them that fear Thee ; which Thou hast wrought for them that trust in Thee before the sons of men ! Thou shalt hide them in the secret of Thy presence . . . : Thou shalt keep them secretly in a pavilion from the strife of tongues.
—Psalm 31 : 19, 20.

I remember with what delight, one day in Manchester when walking to my billet after a Meeting, I came suddenly upon a carter with a wagon and horses, his one hand on the horses' bridle, while in the other he held before him a New Testament.

' I am pleased to see you reading that,' I said. ' Oh, sir,' he replied, ' I was just thinking of the wonderful goodness of God ! ' There in the crowded street of the great city, with the rush and roar of its surging traffic around him, this man had fenced off a little space in his thoughts and was dwelling upon the marvel of the goodness of God to men ! With David, he might have exclaimed : ' How precious are Thy thoughts to me, O God ; how great is the sum of them ! '

> Now, in a song of grateful praise,
> To my dear Lord my voice I'll raise ;
> With all His saints I'll join to tell :
> My Jesus has done all things well.

Look unto Me, and be ye saved, all the ends of the earth : for I am God, and there is none else . . . the word is gone out of My mouth in righteousness, and shall not return, That unto Me every knee shall bow.—Isaiah 45 : 22, 23.

Peace without victory ! Yes, that is an old story. Men have always wanted it. I mean, that they have wanted peace with God without letting Him have the victory, and without bending their proud necks to His yoke. But the thing is full of impossibilities !

Peace is impossible without submission. Man is in rebellion against his Maker, and rebellions can only be brought to an end by the surrender of the rebels. And they who would have peace with God must cease the rebels' thought as well as the rebels' strife, and own that He is King. There is no other way. Sooner or later it is bound to come, for to His Name every knee shall bow.

> Before Jehovah's awful Throne
>   Ye peoples bow with sacred joy ;
> Know that the Lord is God alone ;
>   He can create, and He destroy.
>
> Wide as the world is Thy command,
>   Vast as eternity Thy Love ;
> Firm as a rock Thy truth shall stand
>   When rolling years shall cease to move.

Then saith Jesus unto him, Get thee hence, Satan : for it is written, Thou shalt worship the Lord thy God, and Him only shalt thou serve. Then the devil leaveth Him.—Matthew 4 : 10, 11.

No matter how near the soul may dwell to the very source of Holiness, or how intimate its union with God, it will not escape the fiery darts of the wicked one, nor elude the attacks of his malicious hate. If purity could be a preventive, or holiness could avert temptation, then assuredly Jesus would not have been the subject of this awful visitation ; whereas we see here the Son of God Himself assaulted by the basest forms of evil.

This is a wonderful and helpful fact. Christ was tempted, tempted in all points, tempted like as we are, suffered being tempted, and yet without sin. He conquered the Devil !

To him that o'ercometh God giveth a crown ;
Through faith we shall conquer, though often cast down.
He who is our Saviour our strength will renew ;
Look ever to Jesus, He will carry you through.

O Lord, truly I am Thy servant ; . . . I will pay my vows.—Psalm 116 : 16, 18.

The Bible says a great deal about being servants of God, but the word that has been translated ' servant ' might more correctly have been translated ' slave.' The underlying idea in all such references to servants is the idea of being mastered, that God's people are not their own, that they are under the will of another, and that they have submitted wholly to the claims of their Master.

Some of us have been brought to submission by His providence ; some by His afflictions, those which He bore Himself and those which He laid upon us ; some by the attractions of His wonderful love ; but, by whatever means, the great fact is that we have been bowed down, we have said, ' *Not my will, but Thine, be done.*'

> Not my own ! To Christ, my Saviour,
>   I, believing, trust my soul,
> Everything to Him committed
>   While eternal ages roll.
>
> Not my own, oh, no !
>   Saviour, I belong to Thee ;
> All I have and all I hope for,
>   Thine for all eternity.

As He walked by the sea . . , He saw Simon and Andrew his brother casting a net into the sea : for they were fishers. And Jesus said unto them, Come ye after Me, and I will make you to become fishers of men.—Mark 1 : 16, 17.

The days of fishermen and gardeners, who were also disciples and apostles and evangelists, are not passed ! Sometimes I think they are only just beginning ! Glory be to God ! Only call the fishermen in the name of the Lord Jesus Christ, and they will come ! Only get them baptized with the Fire sent down from Heaven, and they will go forth and win ! Nothing can prevent it !

Salvation is our motto,
  Salvation is our song,
And round the wide, wide world
  We'll send the cry along.
Yes, Jesus is the sinners' Friend,
  The Bible tells us so ;
Their many sins He will forgive,
  And wash them white as snow.

Steadily forward march ! To Jesus we will bring
Sinners of every kind, and He will take them in ;
Rich and poor as well, it does not matter who :
Bring them in with all their sin, He'll wash them white
  as snow.

This poor man cried, and the Lord heard him, and saved him out of all his troubles. . . : O taste and see that the Lord is good : blessed is the man that trusteth in Him.—Psalm 34 : 6, 8.

I feel, more and more, that God *does* meet the soul that is hungering for Him, and that the reason He so seldom meets some people is simply this—they do not truly seek Him. They fail to find the joy of His presence, not because they do not need it, but because they do not *seek it*. If only that joy were with them everything would be different.

' My soul thirsteth for the living God.' That is what David meant. I feel, especially in these days, that it is this thirsting, desiring, aspiring after God Himself, that makes so much difference in life and work. And it is equally precious in every type of character and every stage of experience. The tiny gnat floating in the summer sunshine can be just as really a hungry and thirsty creature as the leviathan sporting in the ocean. So that we who feel we are the weakest of the weak, who are so conscious of our unworthiness that sometimes it oppresses us to the ground, and we hardly have the courage to pray— even we, who have failed so often—we who have been so easily discouraged, so easily offended—we who have almost yielded to the temptation to let everything go—even we, if only because of our *hunger* and *thirst*, may taste and see that the Lord is gracious.

Wherefore, my beloved, . . . work out your own salvation with fear and trembling. For it is God which worketh in you.—Philippians 2 : 12, 13.

We are, God expressly says, ' workers together with Him.' We are to have a share in the toil and struggle, and therefore a share in the glory and rewards of making men.

Ours it is to gather up the ruins of blasted lives and broken hearts and disordered characters, and bring them to Him. Ours it is to warn and persuade and entreat the shipwrecked souls around us that they may be willing to return to God, and that they may be made anew.

And if we are to work together with Him for others, how much more for the renewing of ourselves. Without Him we can do nothing ; and without us—I say it in reverent love—He too can do nothing. He must work in us according to His Divine power ; but we must also work out our own Salvation. Are you, my comrade, thus working with Him till the new creation is complete in you ?

> Teach me how to fight and win
> Perfect victory over sin ;
> Give me a compassion deep,
> That will for lost sinners weep ;
> That henceforth my life may prove
> That I serve Thee out of love.

Beloved, think it not strange concerning the fiery trial which is to try you, as though some strange thing happened unto you.—1 Peter 4 : 12.

Fiery trial came upon our Saviour immediately after a remarkable manifestation of the Divine favour. Just before He went into the wilderness to be tempted, the heavens had been opened, and those around Him saw the Spirit of God descending like a dove and lighting upon Him ; and lo ! a voice from Heaven, saying, This is My beloved Son, in whom I am well pleased.

And if the Father's love appointed so sharp a contrast to the Son Himself, you need not, then, be surprised or cast down if your fiery trial assails you. The moments of our exaltation are often followed by those of our deepest heaviness and humiliation. *After a great blessing will often come a great testing.* After a wonderful deliverance will, perhaps, come the bitterest disappointment, the most cruel blows of personal rebuff, bringing with them distressing apprehensions and misgiving. After the open and acknowledged bestowal of some precious gift, the Devil may be permitted to bring you to the most distressing trial of your faith and love. Be neither afraid nor ashamed when such trials befal you. This is a lesson writ large in your Lord and Master's experience for your comfort and for your strengthening.

God, who is rich in mercy, for His great love wherewith He loved us, even when we were dead in sins, hath quickened us together with Christ. —Ephesians 2 : 4, 5.

God hath not given us the spirit of fear ; but of power, and of love.—2 Timothy 1 : 7.

When I speak of giving I am thinking of love. I do not mean the sentimental, maudlin thing which often passes by the name of love ; I am thinking of love in the sense of goodwill, of service, of willingness to sacrifice for the good of the object loved. What a wealth is here ! What riches God has bestowed upon us in giving us the power to love our fellows ! What wealth we can impart to those around us—not only those within our immediate circle, who are often the most needy of all, but to the outsiders around us ; the ungodly around us, if we can only make them feel that we love them !

Yes, love was the very instrument the Holy Spirit employed to shed abroad the Love of God in us ! Well, we also are to use love as the instrument to spread abroad that Love. We are to employ it in the same way—whether by sanctified emotion, or by fiery words, or by holy deeds, or by overflowing sympathy. We are to go about as those who have been endued by this Spirit of Love.

**The Lord said unto Moses, . . . speak unto the
children of Israel, that they go forward.**—Exodus
14 : 15.

The Salvation Army exists not so much for the
Salvationist as for the whole world. So that the
safety and continued life of The Army depend not
upon our guarding and shepherding what we have
won, but upon our uttermost devotion of it all to
help and bless and save mankind. This is the grand
message of The Army of the past to The Army of the
present.

Oh, my comrades, whether your Corps or Institu-
tion is large or small—whether yours is a hard fight or
a winning campaign—this is the secret of future
progress : Sacrifice—Sacrifice—Sacrifice ! Don't hold
back ! Don't be happy merely to hold your own !
Don't be content to give only as you gave before !
Don't be satisfied with the victories of yesterday !

> Onward ! Upward ! Blood-washed Soldier,
>   Turn not back, nor sheathe thy sword ;
> Let its blade be sharp for conquest
>   In the battle for the Lord.
>
> Onward ! till thy course is finished ;
>   Like the ransomed ones before,
> Keep the faith through persecution,
>   Never give the battle o'er.

In Thee, O Lord, do I put my trust : . . . Be Thou my strong habitation, whereunto I may continually resort.—Psalm 71 : 1, 3.

There is a wonderful sense in which *God is our Home.* You know how some people, when they are distressed or in misfortune or torn with anxiety, take refuge in their families and find in the peace and seclusion of home a gracious comfort and freedom from care. This is, indeed, one of the things which make many men and women so greatly desire a home of their own. Well, *He is our Home.* ' He hath raised us up together ' in The Army ' and made us sit together in heavenly places in Christ Jesus.' That is, He has made the heavenly place, the Kingdom of Heaven, to come down to us by Jesus Christ, that we may dwell there and find the rest, the peace, the safety of a true Home.

> Where'er I dwell, I'll dwell with Thee,
> In Heaven, or earth, or on the sea ;
> All scenes alike engaging prove,
> My soul impressed with sacred love.
>
> To me remains no place nor time,
> My homeland is in every clime ;
> I can be calm and free from care
> On any shore, since God is there.

As free, . . . but as the servants of God. Honour all men. Love the brotherhood. Fear God. Honour the king.—1 Peter 2 : 16, 17.

Without love freedom may actually help men to their own destruction. Look at some of the results of liberty, which can be seen around us, where there has been no love to rule and sanctify it. The freedom of the sensual and indulgent is the very thing which brings their ruin upon them. The freedom of the proud and self-willed—they are destroyed just because they do as they like, and neither love to God nor man restrains them. As for what is called political freedom, remember Rome, the greatest of all free States, with the proudest of all free citizens, and how by thirst for power she came to be destroyed. And the freedom of thought and opinion of which this age boasts so loudly is the sure way, without love to guide it, to the folly which says there is no God, or to the greater folly which acts as though—if there be one—He is of no account.

> Let me love Thee, Saviour,
> Take my heart for ever !
> Nothing but Thy favour
> My soul can satisfy.

Pilate . . . brought Jesus forth, . . . : and he saith unto the Jews, Behold your King ! But they cried out, Away with Him, away with Him, crucify Him.—John 19 : 13–15.

Thou shalt say unto them, Thus saith the Lord God. And they, whether they will hear, or whether they will forbear, . . . yet shall know that there hath been a prophet among them.—Ezekiel 2 : 4, 5.

Knowing full well that He was not wanted—Christ came. Knowing all along that He would be rejected —He still loved and suffered, and taught and died. Knowing that the very greatness of His sacrifice would be turned against Him—He just went forward and made it without wavering. The fact that He was not wanted by men did not blind Him to that other greater fact that they needed Him ; and so, in His faithful love, He made the glorious provision of Salvation, whether they would claim it or whether they would refuse.

In all this He set before His people a notable example. We are not only to profit by His work for our own Salvation, but we are to enter upon the business of representing Him to those whom we can influence in order to lead them to trust their souls to His keeping.

We are to do this not merely when we are welcomed and believed in, but when we are unwelcomed and unadmired, and when it is only too plain, both in the spirit and in the words of those we seek to save, that they do not want our warnings and that, indeed, they do not want anything whatever to do with us, or our Message, or our Master.

Blessed are they which do hunger and thirst after righteousness : for they shall be filled.—Matthew 5 : 6.
Great peace have they which love Thy law : and nothing shall offend them.—Psalm 119 : 165.

What God requires of men is not merely the doing of righteousness, but the love and choice of it, the soul's preference for it—the experience expressed in the prayer of the Psalmist : ' Incline my heart unto Thy testimonies.'

That love and, to the new nature, natural preference for good is the greatest triumph of God in the human heart. It is nothing less than the reproduction of His own nature in us—so that just as He loves righteousness with all the strength of His being, He enables us to love it with all the strength of ours.

> Thee will I love, my Strength, my Tower ;
>   Thee will I love, my Joy, my Crown :
> Thee will I love with all my power,
>   In all Thy works, and Thee alone ;
> Thee will I love till the pure fire
> Fills my whole soul with chaste desire.

217

Seek the Lord, and ye shall live ; . . . seek Him
that maketh the seven stars and Orion, and turneth
the shadow of death into the morning. . . . The
Lord is His name.—Amos 5 : 6, 8.
This is the covenant that I will make with the
house of Israel . . , saith the Lord ; I will put my
laws into their mind, and write them in their
hearts.—Hebrews 8 : 10.

Interesting talk at end of morning Meeting with a
very intelligent ' unbeliever '—hope I helped him.
He could not say why it should be more difficult, or
more unreasonable, to believe in a Divine consciousness than in the consciousness of another human
personality, of, for example, some unknown person
or some historical person. Much of the trouble of
those who ' doubt ' really arises from their own lack
of clear and courageous thinking, and from a very
foolish clinging to preconceived notions. Very often
this comes from pride, or from a kind of pigheadedness,
which will not allow those notions to be abandoned
till long after it is seen they will not fit ! But the
notion that it is the brain, the mere matter that acts
upon us instead of we ourselves—the personal energy
which *is us*, that acts upon the brain—is an amazing
blunder.

> I thank Thee, uncreated Sun,
>   That Thy bright beams on me have shined ;
> I thank Thee, who hast overthrown
>   My foes and healed my wounded mind ;
> I thank Thee, whose enlivening voice
> Bids my freed heart in Thee rejoice.

Render therefore to all their dues. . . . Owe no man any thing, but to love one another.—Romans 13 : 7, 8.

Look not every man on his own things, but every man also on the things of others.—Philippians 2 : 4.

Moses' hands were heavy ; . . . and Aaron and Hur stayed up his hands . . . until the going down of the sun.—Exodus 17 : 12.

It is the duty of leaders to give full credit to all those who labour with them. The service rendered by Aaron and Hur on that day will be an everlasting memorial of honour to them. From generation to generation the story will be told of how they helped to avert a frightful catastophe ; and it was Moses himself who placed it upon record. He wrote the report, as we read it in Exodus, in the splendid simplicity of truth. It is said that one of the greatest marks of leadership is the ability to attract the services and devotion of other noble hearts and able minds. But is not this because nearly all true leadership—at any rate in the service of God—is largely inspired by a generosity which disdains to withhold from any man the credit, and every bit of the credit, of any service which he has rendered to God and His Kingdom ?

O Lord, consider my meditation. Hearken unto the voice of my cry, my King, and my God : for unto Thee will I pray. My voice shalt Thou hear in the morning, O Lord ; in the morning will I direct my prayer unto Thee, and will look up. —Psalm 5 : 1-3.

Prayer pleases God also because He knows its wonderful benefits to those who offer it. This is often, if not always true, even where our prayers are not answered to the full ; yes, and even when they do not seem to be answered at all. Prayer to God is in itself a help to all that is highest in man. It is the guide toward the spiritual and eternal. It is the strength of all that is unselfish. It is the very life of humility, courage and love. God who loves us sees all this, and rejoices to find us seeking Him in prayer.

And more than this, prayer fortifies men against evil. That is one reason which makes it such a touchstone of spiritual experience. ' Prayer,' says one of the saints of former times, ' will either make a man leave off sinning, or sin will make him leave off praying.'

> Sweet hour of prayer, sweet hour of prayer,
> Thy wings shall my petition bear
> To Him whose truth and faithfulness
> Engage the waiting soul to bless ;
> And since He bids me seek His face,
> Believe His word and trust His grace,
> I'll cast on Him my every care,
> And wait for thee, sweet hour of prayer !

Put ye on the Lord Jesus Christ.—Romans 13 : 14.

The spirit of many of those with whom the youth of to-day have to mix tends to increase their self-confidence and self-will. The talk prevalent in the schools and workshops, the influence of many of the newspapers and of other things, tends in the same direction.

Now all this calls for teaching and guidance of a very careful and definite nature if our young people are to be trained in the likeness of Christ and made into conquerors of the world, the flesh and the Devil. It is clear to us all that our Lord Jesus Christ was at once the bravest and strongest soul who ever breathed. And yet He was the most humble and gentle—the most kind and considerate—the most unassuming and simple—the most forgiving man who ever walked this earth. By the side of this Example, how unkind and rough and thoughtless many of the young people are—how lacking in humility and simple child-like love !

> Teach me, Lord, Thy steps to know,
> By the way which Thou didst go,
> Ever keeping close to Thee,
> Loving Him who first loved me.

Faithful in all things.—1 Timothy 3 : 11.

Let us lay aside every . . . sin which doth so easily beset us, and let us run with patience the race that is set before us, looking unto Jesus the author and finisher of our faith.—Hebrews 12 : 1, 2.

What havoc sin works with *faithfulness* !. We see it every day. How men and women change from faithful to unfaithful, and then break their promises and vows ! Look at the children who promised to care for their parents, and don't ! Look at the men and women who vowed to be faithful to one another, but have broken their vows and let in floods of sorrow !

And what of unfaithfulness to God ? How sin inclines the heart to mistrust Him ! Faith is one of the natural powers of the soul ; perhaps nearly, if not quite, its most wonderful capacity. There is, in fact, nothing in us, except love, which comes near to it in power and influence. Sin attacks and weakens that capacity till it becomes more natural to doubt God than to trust Him.

> Jesus, Shepherd of the sheep,
> Pity my unsettled soul.
> Guide and nourish me, and keep,
> Till Thy love shall make me whole ;
> Give me perfect soundness, give,
> Make me steadfastly believe.

Jesus said . . . : can ye drink of the cup that I drink of ? and be baptized with the baptism that I am baptized with ?—Mark 10 : 38.

I am distressed sometimes by the absence of compassion in some comrades. They go about this poor world so unmoved amidst its grief, its misery, its sin. They view the people, day after day, and month after month, with so little pity. Sometimes in the Prayer Meetings, when souls are crying aloud for mercy and while some of their comrades are in an agony of desire, they seem almost without true feeling. Their very presence is a chill upon the loving souls around. It is a sign of coming and terrible backsliding.

> Tender Spirit, dwell with me !
> I myself would tender be ;
> Tender in my love for men,
> Wooing them to God again ;
> With compassion pure and sweet
> Lead the lost to Jesus' feet.

Beloved, believe not every spirit, but try the spirits whether they are of God . . . Hereby know ye the Spirit of God : Every spirit that confesseth that Jesus Christ is come in the flesh is of God . . . Hereby know we that we dwell in Him, and He in us, because He hath given us of His Spirit.—1 John 4 : 1, 2, 13.

The great principle of redemption has found expression in The Salvation Army. We are of those who see in every human being the ruins of the Temple of God ; but ruins which can be repaired and reconstructed, that He may fit them for His own possession and then return and make them His abode.

Never listen to that fateful lie, that to be a man means of necessity to be always a sinner ; that humanity is only another word for irreclaimable desert or irreparable despair. When the enemy of your soul whispers to you out of his lying heart that, because sin has found one of its strongholds in the appetites and propensities of your body, or in the original perversity of a rebellious spirit, you cannot be expected to triumph over that evil nature because it is your nature—answer him with the promise of God, ' I will dwell in you, and walk in you.' It was because He purposed to cleanse, wholly, body and soul and spirit, that He came, taking the body, soul and spirit of a man, and that He will come again, taking your body, soul and spirit as His dwelling place.

Jesus saith . . . God is a Spirit : and they that worship Him must worship Him in spirit and in truth.—John 4 : 21, 24.

Jesus . . . saith . . . When ye stand praying, forgive, if ye have ought against any : that your Father also which is in heaven may forgive you your trespasses. But if ye do not forgive, neither will your Father which is in heaven forgive your trespasses.—Mark 11 : 22, 25, 26.

I am quite sure that for God's people successful praying, the praying which prevails, is not only dependent upon faith but upon two other matters. Indeed, faith will not be exercised unless we are right in these.

First of all, *sincerity*. To be honest and true toward God in our thoughts and purposes is necessary if He is to hear us. Oh, let us teach the people they must be truthful before God—seeking to view their lives in His presence as neither better than they are nor worse than they are.

And then there is another condition of prayer that is to prevail—the *spirit of forgiveness*. I believe the secret of a good deal of the unanswered prayer in the world to-day is that men go to God seeking His favour or pardon or help, when they withhold from their fellows *their* pardon, *their* help.

The worship, the adoration, the prayer God loves is that which rises from a sincere and forgiving heart. Yes—' the Father seeketh such to worship Him.'

Jesus said : **When the Comforter is come, . . . the Spirit of truth, which proceedeth from the Father, . . . He will reprove the world of sin, and of righteousness, and of judgment.**—John 15 : 26 ; 16 : 8.

Here is one of the great, perhaps the greatest, encouragements for all who are seeking after the Salvation of souls. No matter whom it is we strive to influence, God is there before we are. He is our never-failing support in the struggle to turn men from the power of Satan. He is our grand Ally. In a wonderful way He is still in possession of part of the citadel we are trying to capture. Bad and selfish as men are, God has not entirely deserted them. In the very centre of their beings He holds fast to some remnants of His original possession. When we assault from without, He attacks from within. To every righteous claim we make He compels the assent of reason or conscience, or both. He stirs up the few remaining forces of goodness, calls in the aid of memory, revives the dying embers of hope and *fights with us for the soul He loves.*

The Lord thy God, . . . He will not fail thee.
—Deuteronomy 31 : 6.
Jesus said : **I said unto you, I go away, and come again unto you. . . . And now I have told you before it come to pass, that, when it is come to pass, ye might believe.**—John 14 : 28, 29.

Christ left them when they most needed Him. His face was hidden. Darkness veiled the sky. Providence seemed to join with Herod and Jerusalem in frowning upon them. They could almost take up their dying Master's cry and say, ' My God, my God, why hast Thou forsaken us ? ' And when they cried there was no answer.

Do we not know what that is also ? Have we not times in which prayer fails and hope dies down to a poor flicker, and we can do nothing and think nothing, and we feel as dead men that cumber the ground ? Such times will come. They also are for the fulfilling of His purpose. Nothing is by chance in our lives ; if we trust Him, all is by love.

> Blessèd Lord, in Thee is refuge,
> Safety for my trembling soul,
> Power to lift my head when drooping
> 'Midst the angry billows roll.
> I will trust Thee,
> All my life Thou shalt control.

The word of the Lord was made a reproach unto me, . . . daily. Then I said, I will not make mention of Him, nor speak any more in His name. . . . For I heard the defaming of many, . . . Report, say they, and we will report it.—Jeremiah 20 : 8–10.

The best and greatest of God's servants are tempted sore in such times of disappointment and hardship to give up the work and abandon their high vocation. There can be no mistake about the severity of Jeremiah's temptation. He was almost overwhelmed. Listen to his sad words : O Lord, Thou hast deceived me—that is, I trusted in Thy protection and approval, and here I am left to the mercy of cruel circumstances.

And have you not had similar trials ? If Satan whispered such suggestions of unfaithfulness and despair to this grand old prophet, is it any wonder that he says something like it to you ? Have you not also cried out in your haste, ' The Lord has failed me ; I trusted in Him, I obeyed His call, I delivered His message, and here I am, left to help myself, rejected by the people, misunderstood by my superiors and forgotten by God ' ? Have you not, in your heart, if not with your lips, sometimes even crossed over the line, as Jeremiah crossed it, and said, I will not speak any more in His name ?

> Keep on believing, Jesus is near ;
> Keep on believing, there's nothing to fear !
> Keep on believing, this is the way :
> Faith in the night as well as the day.

Jesus Christ, . . . the first begotten of the dead, . . . that loved us, and washed us from our sins in His own blood, and hath made us kings and priests unto God and His Father ; to Him be glory and dominion for ever and ever.—Revelation 1 : 5, 6.

It is the Spirit that beareth witness.—1 John 5 : 6.

He which . . . hath anointed us, is God : who hath also sealed us, and given the earnest of the Spirit in our hearts.—2 Corinthians 1 : 21, 22.

Your merely human Salvationist, no matter how pure, how strong, how thoughtful, how clever, how industrious, will fail, and ever fail. And even so the man who is lost in visionary seeking after the Divine alone, to the neglect of action, of duty, of law, of self-denial, of the common conflicts and contracts of the man, will equally fail, and always fail. It is the man we want. The man—but the man born of the *Spirit*. The man—but the man full of the *Holy Ghost*. The man—but the man with *Pentecost* blazing in his head and heart and soul.

Comrades, what are you ? Are you striving to be a prophet without possessing the spirit of the prophets ? Are you trying to be a priest without the priestly baptism ? Are you labouring to be a king without the Divine anointing ?

> Come, Holy Ghost, our hearts inspire,
>   Let us Thine influence prove,
> Source of the old prophetic fire,
>   Fountain of life and love.

Daniel . . . went into his house ; and his windows being open in his chamber toward Jerusalem, he kneeled upon his knees three times a day, and prayed, and gave thanks before his God, as he did aforetime.—Daniel 6 : 10.

Undoubtedly, the habit of prayer begets the love of prayer. Habits of soul are acquired just as are habits of the mind and body. He who accustoms himself day by day to wait on the Lord, to learn His mind, will undoubtedly come to love prayer, to delight in it, to find in it not only strength and guidance, but increasing joy.

I have always advocated that a man should set apart a regular time and place for private prayer— have, in fact, a daily appointment with God which he should keep as one of the most sacred obligations of his life. But I have equally insisted that prayer can be offered anywhere—especially prayer which relates to some matter of absorbing interest to the soul.

But I do not think there is any reason why one should prevail at this or that hour more than at any other. Christ has taught explicitly : ' Men ought always to pray.'

There is no peace, saith the Lord, unto the wicked.—Isaiah 48 : 22.

Thus saith the Lord, . . . I will cure them, and will reveal unto them the abundance of peace and truth. . . . I will cleanse them from all their iniquity, whereby they have sinned against Me ; and I will pardon all their iniquities.—Jeremiah 33 : 4, 6, 8.

Peace is impossible without forgiveness. Every sinner knows it. Every backslider knows it. We all know it. Even if Almighty God sent an angel to proclaim peace to every guilty soul of man, it would make very little difference unless at the same time the angel could whisper to our sin-stricken spirits, ' Thy sins which are many are all forgiven.' Nothing less than this could give peace. No Bibles, no prayers, no happy fellowship, no good times, nor all of them together can bring peace without forgiveness. It was not the new clothes and the grand feasting and music which brought peace to the prodigal, it was the father's forgiving love—the kiss which sealed his pardon.

Soon as my all I ventured on the atoning Blood,
The Holy Spirit entered, and I was born of God ;
My sins are all forgiven, I feel His Blood applied,
And I shall go to Heaven if I in Christ abide.

The mystery that hath been hid from ages and from generations, . . . is made manifest to His saints : . . . which is Christ in you, the hope of glory : . . . Whereunto I also labour, striving according to His working, which worketh in me mightily.—Colossians 1 : 26, 27, 29.

The key to holiness, the secret of happiness, the power of victory, are all to be found in the union of God and man. Neither can effect the high purpose of the one or the true interest of the other. These can only be reached by a partnership of both. Salvation depends upon co-operation. ' I can do all things,' says Paul, ' through Christ which strengtheneth me.'

And what is true of our life in God is true of the acts and experiences which go to make it up. How large a part temptation plays among these experiences, every true child of God knows. And if we are to resist temptation, it must be by that same co-operation. It is we who are to struggle and fight and conquer ; and yet it is God Himself who is to fight and struggle and conquer in us.

> We are with Thee 'gainst Thy foe,
> Fighting for his overthrow ;
> Though the fight be doubly fierce,
> Though the venomed dart should pierce,
> Satan never shall prevail ;
> Thou, O Christ, shalt never fail !
> We who fight with Thee shall win,
> Conquer over Hell and sin.

Though ye have ten thousand instructors in Christ, yet have ye not many fathers : for in Christ Jesus I have begotten you through the gospel. Wherefore I beseech you, be ye followers of me. —1 Corinthians 4 : 15, 16.

By our union with Christ we are to beget children unto the Spirit. So St. Paul, when writing to the Corinthians, said, ' For in Christ Jesus I have begotten you through the gospel ' ; and of another of his converts he wrote, ' whom I have begotten in my bonds.'

Yes, that is it ; that is what the world needs, mothers and fathers in God—men and women who will co-operate with Him in the production of a race of holy men, who will die rather than remain sterile and barren in the service of their Lord, who will stand forth in spite of every difficulty and devil as the makers of men.

> Go, labour on, spend and be spent,
>   Thy joy to do the Father's will ;
> It is the way the Master went :
>   Should not the servant tread it still ?
>
> Toil on, faint not, keep watch and pray ;
>   Be wise the sinning soul to win ;
> Go forth into the world's highway,
>   Compel the wanderer to come in.

That Christ may dwell in your hearts by faith ; that ye, being rooted and grounded in love, may be able to comprehend with all saints what is the breadth, and length, and depth, and height ; and to know the love of Christ.—Ephesians 3 : 17–19.

Let us remember that there is a splendid power of development in the human heart—especially when it has been consecrated and cleansed. To love at large ; to live for all as Jesus Christ died for all ; to believe for great achievements by mercy as well as for great mercies toward ourselves—all this disciplines us and sustains and enlarges the soul. By this men grow to be Great Hearts ; by this they rise above the petty and selfish and narrow. So let us up to the hills and, hearkening there to the voices of those who have gone before, trust in the Living God and hope on for a world still hopeless without Him.

> Father, on me the grace bestow,
>   And make me blameless in Thy sight,
> Whence all the streams of mercy flow ;
>   Mercy, Thine own supreme delight,
> To me, for Jesus' sake, impart,
> And root Thy nature in my heart.

Jesus said : **I am the vine, ye are the branches :
He that abideth in Me, and I in him, the same
bringeth forth much fruit.**—John 15 : 5.

Holiness is something more than an act—or
surrender on our part and of cleansing on the part of
the Holy Spirit—*it is life*. It is true that it begins
in an act, but it necessitates also a continual progress.
Purity should lead to maturity.

Now the lives of some show few marks of this
progress toward spiritual manhood, few signs of
growth in Holiness. They are still in the infancy of
a holy life, when they should be progressing toward
the full stature of men in Christ Jesus. They show
comparatively little knowledge of the deeper things
of the life of Love. Every one should be led beyond
the gaining of a clean heart—which one may describe
as the removal of the weeds and stones and natural
impurities of the soil of the soul—and be helped to
the blossoming forth into beauty and fragrance of
the flowers of a holy character and the bearing of the
fruits of the Spirit.

> Make us like Thee in meekness, love,
>   And every beauteous grace ;
> From glory unto glory changed,
>   Till we behold Thy face.

Every man according as he purposeth in his heart, so let him give ; not grudgingly, or of necessity : for God loveth a cheerful giver.
—2 Corinthians 9 : 7.

Ah ! I fancy sometimes that the selfishness of the human heart can be manifested as truly in religious things as in anything else, and that the spirit of ' grab ' can be shown even amidst the holiest surroundings and influences. Does it not seem as if some people say, ' Let me get all I can out of Christ ; let me have all I can out of The Salvation Army ; let me rejoice and enrich myself with the happiness which flows from its services, from the prayers and attentions of its Officers, from its music and song and from its comradeship and sympathy ; but I am not going to give anything very much back again.'

How far, oh, how very far is all that from the Spirit of the great Giver who, though He was rich, yet for our sakes became poor ! Friend, comrade, stranger, do not be a ' grabber '—be a giver !

> Hark, Soldier ! Jesus speaks to thee ;
> Oh, heed His word divinely plain :
> ' Wouldst thou in earnest follow Me ?
> Deny thyself, e'en unto pain ! '
> That great example Jesus set,
> For us His all surrendering ;
> His passion shall in us beget
> The high resolve our best to bring.

Other foundation can no man lay than that is laid, which is Jesus Christ.—1 Corinthians 3 : 11.

To restore them to the image of God means to bring men to will what He wills. Thus restored they will do His will on earth as it is done in Heaven. Then, instead of separation and contention between men and God, there will be submission and harmony and union.

Is this the pattern by which, and toward which, you are working in the souls of men ? Or are you working to some other design, and building upon some other foundation ? Are you trying to make men happy without making them good ; or trying to make them good without first making them true to God ; or trying to make them love Him supremely, without their first giving up this present world ?

> My hope is built on nothing less
> Than Jesus' Blood and righteousness ;
> I dare not trust the sweetest frame,
> But wholly lean on Jesus' name.
>> On Christ, the solid Rock, I stand
>> All other ground is sinking sand.

The fear of the Lord is the beginning of knowledge : . . . My son, hear the instruction of thy father, and forsake not the law of thy mother.
—Proverbs 1 : 7, 8.

Do not suppose that all is well with the children because they are being better educated than in days gone by. Do not be deceived because so many of the children seem happier in their play, or are better dressed, or are better fed than they were fifty or sixty years ago. Do not suppose that because our advancing civilization has, in most countries, corrected some of the horrors of the old cruel trades in which children toiled and moiled their way down to the grave, all is well. Remember that there is something more than this world even for the children.

Come and help us win them for Christ ! Come and help us, I say, to save the children ! Do not let them die without God while you are waiting for them to grow up. Begin with them where God begins, at the very earliest dawn of intelligence, and point them not merely to an historical Christ, but to a living, present Jesus, who can save them from their sins.

Jesus loves the children just as much to-day
As when on earth He stopped them in their play,
Called them unto Him and a blessing to each gave ;
Just the same to-day He wants each little one to save.

The Lord said, . . . Abraham shall surely become a great and mighty nation, . . . For I know him, that he will command his children and his household after him, and they shall keep the way of the Lord.—Genesis 18 : 17–19.

Train up a child in the way he should go. —Proverbs 22 : 6.

Do not let the children learn to lie and cheat, and to quarrel and hate one another, and hate God and His laws, before they have grown to man's estate. Let us take hold of them when their hearts are tender and their minds are open to the impression of truth, and cultivate what is noble and unselfish in them ; and show them how their young lives may, even now, be laid as an acceptable offering at the feet of Him who gave His life for them.

Do not let them learn to depend upon the labour of others, or to covet the fruits of other men's toil, or to sponge on those who happen to be better off than they are. Teach them the nobility of work and the glory of honest labour and the true beauty and happiness of self-reliance and goodness. Teach them the contempt Jesus Christ had for merely ' getting on ' and being better off than their parents or those around them. Show them the old and often forgotten lesson that ' a man's life consisteth not in the . . . things which he possesseth.'

Herod . . . was exceeding wroth, and sent forth, and slew all the children that were in Bethlehem . . . from two years old and under.
—Matthew 2 : 16.

Ye shall be hated of all men for My name's sake : but he that endureth to the end shall be saved.
—Matthew 10 : 22.

Herod the king sought to kill the Child. So it is even now. Don't be deceived ; where Christ comes, storms come. The world of selfishness and power and wealth will kill the Divine Thing in you, if it can. Between the prince of this world and the Prince of the world to come no truce was possible long ago in quiet Judea, and no truce is possible now. The spirit of the world is still the spirit of murder. It is called by other names to-day, and, under its influence, men will tell you that the life of God in you is not to take those forms of violent opposition to wrong, of passionate devotion to right and of burning zeal and self-denial for the lost, which they took in Jesus. The real meaning of their tale is that they are seeking to kill the Child.

> Soldiers of the Cross, arise,
> Gird you with your armour bright !
> Mighty are your enemies,
> Hard the battle ye must fight.

**The peace of God, which passeth all under-
standing, shall keep your hearts and minds
through Christ Jesus. Finally, brethren, whatsoever things are true, whatsoever things are
honest, whatsoever things are just, whatsoever
things are pure, whatsoever things are lovely . . .
think on these things.**—Philippians 4 : 7, 8.

Before they were saved, the minds of some delighted
in impurity. Imagination became polluted, and their
thoughts ran riot on the least provocation. Though
now they are justified and sanctified, they have still
to live in the same world, with the same invitations
about them to dwell on the low, the base, the unclean.
We should teach them, then, that the mind must be
disciplined as well as cleansed. It must be mastered
and not allowed to wander without restraint, or the
old temptations will enter and the old results will
follow. Uncontrolled thought will lead to unsanctified
desire, and thence to unholy action. There can be
little doubt that some who have been truly sanctified
have lost the priceless blessing, just because they
have not been instructed in this very truth.

Love's resistless current sweeping
  All the regions deep within ;
Thought and wish and senses keeping
  Now, and every moment, clean ;
    Full Salvation
  From the guilt and power of sin.

Jesus said, Are ye also yet without understanding ? . . . Out of the heart proceed evil thoughts, murders, adulteries, fornications, thefts, false witness, blasphemies : these are the things which defile a man.—Matthew 15 : 16, 19, 20.

But for sin there would be no daily peril for the innocent children, no blight in the young people, no God-forgetters, no ruined womanhood, no drink-ridden souls, no corrupt and leprous men. Sin is the curse. Not poverty and want ; not ignorance, not servitude, not loneliness or grief. None of these things are the curse—they are merely its consequences; the real mischief is sin against God.

We see at a glance how hateful it all is when we look at defrauders, murderers, hypocrites and the like. We can see it—the exceeding hatefulness of sin—when we consider the vile schemes by which still viler man destroy the innocent.

But it seems to me that the greatest of all the hatefulness of sin is to be found in the hidden things of the heart. Acts and deeds of wickedness, no matter what sort of wickedness it may be, are only the outcome of what goes on in men's hearts. The root is there from which the shameful and abominable fruits are nourished. There in the higher kingdom of the soul arise the fountains whose filthy waters spread abroad the poisons which blast men's lives, darken the face of Heaven itself and come at last to death and Hell.

God so loved the world, that He gave His only begotten Son.—John 3 : 16.
Then said Jesus . . . I am the good shepherd : the good shepherd giveth his life for the sheep. —John 10 : 7, 11.

Was not love the greatest work of Jesus Christ for the world ? His teaching was only a means to that end. His holy example was only a means to that end. His dying was only a means to that end. His resurrection was only a means to that end. The great thing was to make men believe that He loved them ; that the Father loved them. So it must be with us.

This also applies to our material possessions. ' But whoso, says the Apostle John, ' hath this world's goods, and seeth his brother have need, and shutteth up his bowels of compassion from him, how dwelleth the love of God in him ? ' ' Hereby,' he says, ' perceive we the love of God, because He laid down His life for us ; and we ought to lay down our lives '— that is the most precious thing we have—' for the brethren.' That would be giving indeed ! How then can a man really be united with God and not be a giver also ?

> And is it so ? A gift from me
>   Dost Thou, dear Lord, request ?
> Then speak Thy will, whate'er it be ;
>   Obeying, I am blest.

> I have not much to give Thee, Lord—
>   For that great love which made Thee mine ;
> I have not much to give Thee, Lord,
>   But all I have is Thine.

Hearken, my beloved brethren, Hath not God chosen the poor of this world rich in faith, and heirs of the kingdom which He hath promised to them that love Him ?—James 2 : 5.

Everything associated with the advent of Jesus seems to have been specially ordered to mark His humiliation. Probably none but His mother had, in those early years, any true idea of the mysterious promise which had been given concerning Him. What a contrast it all presents to the years of stress and storm and of victory which were to follow, and to the supreme influence His teaching and example were to exert in the world.

To be of lowly origin or of a mean occupation ; to come out of poverty and want ; to be looked down upon by the rich and powerful ones of earth ; to be treated as of no consequence by governments and rulers, and yet to go on doing and daring, suffering and conquering for God and right ; what is all this but the fulfilment of Paul's words, ' And base things of the world, and things which are despised, hath God chosen, yea, and things which are not, to bring to nought things that are : that no flesh should glory in His presence ' ? Nay, what is it all but to tread in the very steps that the Master trod ?

Holy Father, keep through Thine own name those whom Thou hast given Me, that they may be one, as we are. . . . As Thou hast sent Me into the world, even so have I also sent them into the world.—John 17 : 11, 18.

In the creation of Adam and Eve, God was providing means for making the whole family of men. To our first parents, and through them to their children and their children's children, He gave those powers and instincts both of mind and body which were necessary to the reproduction of their kind. Year by year, as sure as seed-time and harvest, while the world shall stand, one family of men will produce another, and that one another ; one generation will bring into being the next, and so on until the end of time. This was God's plan for the perpetuation of the human race.

And His scheme of a new creation is arranged on a similar plan. He will work to the uttermost for the Salvation of men ; but His energies stand waiting for the action of our faith and love, and come into play only as we work. The command to His sons and daughters of to-day is—' *Go ye into all the world, and preach the Gospel to every creature.*'

> Tell the world, oh, tell the world !
> Make Salvation's story heard
> In the highways, in the byways
>   And in lands beyond the sea ;
> Do some witnessing for Jesus
>   Wheresoever you may be.

In much patience, in afflictions, in necessities, in distresses, in stripes, in imprisonments, in tumults, in labours, . . . by honour and dishonour, by evil report and good report : . . . as poor yet making many rich ; as having nothing, and yet possessing all things,—2 Corinthians 6 : 4, 5, 8, 10.

It is a commonplace of human affairs that many of the successes of life come by its failures, that joy comes out of sorrows, gain by loss, and life by death. And yet it is one of those lessons which many people find very difficult to learn, not only for themselves but as regards the work of God. We of The Army have not been exempt from the problems which can be grouped under the general description, ' Whosoever shall seek to save his life shall lose it ; and whosoever shall lose his life shall preserve it.' But we have again and again proved, especially in the early and formative days of the work, that there are sacrifices which are abundantly worth while, which are, in fact, profitable, which pay well in the fruits which follow them ; and though, in themselves and in the circumstances which surround them, they may be intensely painful, they prove the gateways to increased success and happiness.

They loved the praise of men more than the praise of God.—John 12 : 43.

The Love of Applause. Mark you, I say the love of it, not the thing itself. Like money, it is not an evil in itself. All normally constituted men and women desire some sign that their efforts are approved by those whom they seek to serve ; and a proper appreciation of such marks of approval is perfectly consistent with the most disinterested service on the part of a truly sanctified soul. It is the love of applause, the desire, the secret hunger for it which grows constantly with its indulgence, the having it as an end in view, that makes a temptation which specially besets some people.

Such a motive will soon or later taint the whole of their spirit and service, and they will come at length to be so weak that they cannot go on without it. They should flee it as they flee the Devil. It is the very spirit of the Devil.

> Give me a heart to praise my God,
>   A heart from sin set free,
> A heart that always feels the Blood
>   So freely spilt for me !
>
> A humble, lowly, contrite heart,
>   Believing, true and clean :
> Which neither life nor death can part
>   From Him that dwells within.

Be kindly affectioned one to another . . . ; in honour preferring one another.—Romans 12 : 10.
Be ye . . . followers of God, as dear children ; and walk in love, as Christ also hath loved us. —Ephesians 5 : 1, 2.

' Look not,' says the Apostle, ' every man on his own things, but every man also on the things of others.' That is, even in the exercise of his choicest gifts and graces, let a man forget his own in his desire to employ and bring forward the gifts of others. ' Let nothing be done through strife or vainglory, but in lowliness of mind let each esteem others better than themselves.' That is, in your own mind take a humble view of yourself and your own worthiness, and hold your comrades in higher esteem than you hold yourself, in honour preferring another to yourself. That would be a very real self-denial to some people !

Deny yourself of your own joys, that you may enter into the sorrows of others ; and lay aside your own sorrow and tears, and silence your own breaking heart, when you can help others by entering with joy into their joys.

You will see, beloved, that all this is work which no one can do for you, and that it is in a very true sense high service to God as well as to man. How, then, is it with you ? Are you a self-denying disciple ? If not, beware, lest it should shortly appear that you are not a disciple at all.

We are sure that the judgment of God is according to truth.—Romans 2 : 2.
And now, little children, abide in Him ; that . . . we may have confidence, and not be ashamed before Him at His coming.—1 John 2 : 28.

The Bible fully harmonizes with reason and instinct in this matter. It declares from beginning to end, with a consistency and confidence which are sublime, that just such a thing will happen as men's hearts have from the dawn of time either desired or feared. The first of the prophets, Enoch, only seventh from Adam, foretold it. ' Behold,' he said, ' the Lord cometh with ten thousands of His saints, to execute judgment upon all.' And Paul, almost the latest of the great prophetic voices, with equal definiteness cried aloud in most memorable words that God hath appointed a day, in the which He will judge the world in righteousness, by that Man whom He hath ordained ; whereof He hath given assurance to all men, in that He hath raised Him from the dead. What reason and instinct demand, therefore, revelation has clearly foretold.

> Before me place in dread array
> The scenes of that tremendous day,
>   When Thou with clouds shalt come
> To judge the people at Thy bar ;
> And tell me, Lord, shall I be there
>   To hear Thee say, ' Well done ! ' ?

Thou art a God ready to pardon, gracious and merciful, slow to anger, and of great kindness.
—Nehemiah 9 : 17.
He said unto him, Man, thy sins are forgiven thee.—Luke 5 : 20.

Infinite Love takes full account of sin. Boldly recognizes it. ' O My Father, forgive.' The dying Christ, looking away from His own sufferings, is overflowing with this great thought, with this great fact—that men's first, imperative, overwhelming need is the forgiveness of their sin.

He prays for it. What a transforming thought is the possibility of forgiveness ! How different the vilest, the most loathsome criminal becomes in our eyes the moment we know a pardon is on the way ! How different a view we get of the souls of men, bound and condemned to die, given up to selfishness and godlessness, the moment we stand by the cross of Jesus, and realize, with Him, that a pardon is possible ! The meanest wretch that walks looks different to us. Even the outwardly respectable and very ordinary person who lives next door, to whom we so seldom speak, is at once clothed with a new interest in our minds if we really believe that there is a pardon coming for him from the King of kings.

> Sent by my Lord, on you I call ;
> The invitation is to ALL !
> Come, all the world ; come, sinner, thou !
> All things in Christ are ready now.

Stand in the gate of the Lord's house, and proclaim there this word.—Jeremiah 7 : 2.
That I may open my mouth boldly, to make known the mystery of the gospel.—Ephesians 6 : 19.

Will you come and join in our great world-mission of making Jesus Christ's atonement known ? Will you turn your back on the littleness and selfishness and cowardice of the past, and arise in the strength of the God-Man, to publish to all you can reach, by tongue and pen and example, that there is a sacrifice for men's sins—for the worst, for the most wretched, for the most tortured ? As you set your face with high resolve toward the unknown years, take your stand with *the Man for all the ages* ; and let this be your message, your confidence, your hope for all men—
' Behold the Lamb of God, which taketh away the sin of the world.'

Who is on the Lord's side,
　Who will serve the King ?
Who will be His helpers
　Other lives to bring ?
Who will leave the world's side ?
　Who will face the foe ?
Who is on the Lord's side ?
　Who for Him will go ?

By Thy grand redemption,
　By Thy grace Divine,
We are on the Lord's side,
　Saviour, we are Thine.

The God of our fathers hath chosen thee, that thou shouldest know His will, and . . . thou shalt be His witness.—Acts 22 : 14, 15.

Jesus . . . findeth Philip, and saith unto him, Follow Me.—John 1 : 43.

Jesus Christ! Race and clime and caste and kindred, were nothing to Him. Neither beauty nor virtue, nor power, on the one hand ; nor misery nor weakness nor want on the other, counted anything with Him. In His great quest for the souls of men He passed by all those things. His appeal almost disregards the temporal, the passing and perishing in us, and calls to the eternal part—to conscience, to memory, to faith, to will, to love—to all that belongs to the *soul*. Christ could not be satisfied with less than rescuing men from sin. *He was a lover of their souls*.

Let us follow Him, then, in our quest. To go in this fashion after the souls of all whom *we* can influence, *that* would indeed be *following Christ*. Not merely believing on Him ; finding our own Salvation in Him ; resting all our hopes upon Him for the world to come. It would be more than all that : it would be really *following* Him ; going after the deliverance of men's souls ; not merely cheering them or instructing them or making things as agreeable as possible for them, but mounting up to the highest in them, *seeing* and *loving* and *seeking the soul*.

Jesus calls me, I am going
Where He opens up the way.

Knowing that Christ being raised from the dead dieth no more ; . . . likewise reckon ye also yourselves to be dead indeed unto sin, but alive unto God through Jesus Christ our Lord.—Romans 6 : 9, 11.

This is still the dividing principle. Those who are with Jesus Christ have been made alive from the dead by believing in Him. Those who are against Him care nothing for His resurrection ; to them He is but ' a root out of a dry ground.'

It will be the power of His resurrection which will work out your deliverance. Hold on in the dark, and the Land of the impossible life and light and love and power will come to you. Do not give up ! Do not complain ! He seems to be dead, but He is alive for evermore. He hides His face for a little while, but He loves you with an everlasting love. It seems as though He has forgotten you, but He cannot forget.

' Before the Throne my Surety stands
    And pours the all-prevailing prayer,
Points to His side, uplifts His hands,
    And shows that I am graven there.'

Jesus, when He came out, saw much people, and was moved with compassion toward them, because they were as sheep not having a shepherd : and He began to teach them many things.—Mark 6 : 34.

Behold, I say unto you, Lift up your eyes, and look on the fields ; for they are white already to harvest.—John 4 : 35.

Dwell on those matters likely to move your own spirit and draw out your affections toward God—His holiness, His struggle with sin, His sympathy with and longings after sinners and His sacrifice for them. Go to the graveyard, the prison, the hospital, the lunatic asylum ; go down into the slums and the dens of Hell on earth, where the Devil is transforming men and women into fiends and training little children to grow up to be damned ; go and look and think until you feel, until your whole soul rises up and cries out to God : ' Who is sufficient for these things ? ' Mingle your tears with the tears of those who weep ; groan and travail and struggle with those who are in darkness ; wring your hands for those who sink ; say with Paul : ' I could (even) wish that myself were accursed from Christ for . . . my kinsmen according to the flesh.'

> Arise, my tenderest thoughts, arise ;
> In sorrow flow, my streaming eyes.
> And thou, my heart, with anguish feel
> Those evils which thou canst not heal.
>
> See human nature sunk in shame ;
> See scandals poured on Jesus' name :
> The Father wounded through the Son,
> The world abused, the soul undone.

**Those things which are revealed belong unto us
and to our children for ever.**—Deuteronomy 29 : 29.

One of the most important and most promising
branches of Salvation Army work is that directed to
the Salvation of the children and their training in
goodness and virtue. The old notion that religion
does not touch children, except with a long pole of
propriety and silence and so forth, has gone—
shattered, I hope, for ever ! We have had something
to do with bringing in the new ideas. We have led
the way in associating in the children's minds the
service of God with a life of happiness. We have
shown how it is possible, even amongst the poorest
and roughest of the populations, to join together
true worship and true obedience and true service with
the jolliest music and singing and the brightest
Meetings. And we have done more than this.

We have established a great Movement in the world
for bringing children into recognized fellowship with
the Church of Christ and have, in some measure at
any rate, revived the idea of child Salvation.

Blessèd Jesus, save our children !
  Be their Guardian through life's way ;
From all evil e'er protect them,
  Walk Thou with them, come what may.
In white raiment let us meet them
  When earth's shadows flee away.

255

Beloved, let us love . . . : for love is of God. . . .
He that loveth not knoweth not God ; for God is
love.—1 John 4 : 7, 8.

He . . . made His own people to go forth . . .
and He led them on safely, so that they feared not.
—Psalm 78 : 50, 52, 53.

We all know something of love. Even if we have
never loved—we have been loved. Even if we have
never been loved, still we have loved. Even if we
have ' loved and lost '—all is not lost, love is not
dead. So when I say love—love souls—every one
knows what I mean.

I want all the lonely and solitary ones who seem
to have none to love or care for—to love souls. I want
all the lovers who are hoping to win the heart of the
one they love—to love souls. I want all the husbands
and wives who live in the sweet and faithful love of
each other—to love souls. I want all the mothers—
and they really know how to love—who love their
precious children, to love souls. I want all the
children and young people, whose love for father or
mother is a kind of heaven on earth for them—oh, I
want them to love souls ! I want all who love their
dear dead—ah, how deeply some of us love our dead,
our dear living dead !—well, I want all who love their
dead, to love souls.

Ready for all Thy perfect will,
  My acts of faith and love repeat,
Till death Thy endless mercies seal
  And make the sacrifice complete.

Who is like unto the Lord our God . . . ! He raiseth up the poor . . . He maketh . . . a joyful mother of children.—Psalm 113 : 1, 5, 6, 7, 9.

Jesus . . . said, . . . whoso shall receive one such little child in My name, receiveth Me. —Matthew 18 : 2, 3, 5.

Lay up . . . My words in your heart and in your soul, . . . and ye shall teach them your children, speaking of them when thou sittest in thine house. —Deuteronomy 11 : 18, 19.

Being asked to account, apart from religion, for the happiness of Army marriages, and in view of the fact that divorce is practically unknown amongst us, I replied that if religion *could* be left out, I should say that there were three auxiliary conditions which conduce to this happiness. (1) The position of the woman being properly recognized before her marriage makes her position straightforward and natural. (2) Large families. My observation in every part of the world has been that nothing helps to keep the home sweet and united like children. (3) The way in which the interests of The Army are intertwined with the life of the children gives a new objective to, and outlook upon, human affairs generally, and tends to that variety and gladness which come from the recognition and service of God.

> Happy the home when God is there
> And love fills every breast,
> Where one their wish and one their prayer,
> And one their heavenly rest.
>
> Happy the home where Jesus' name
> Is sweet to every ear,
> Where children early lisp His fame,
> And parents hold Him dear.

God hath . . . chosen you to salvation through
sanctification of the Spirit and belief of the truth :
. . . Therefore, . . . stand fast, and hold the
traditions which ye have been taught.—2 Thessalonians 2 : 13, 15.

Wherever men meet, east or west, north or south,
and Salvationists are the subject of their thought or
debate, whether the result be to applaud or condemn
us, to praise or to blame us, it is our religion which
takes the first place in attention. It may attract, or
it may repel ; it may be a reason for approval, or a
ground for hatred ; but there it is.

And so, when we appear among our fellows, there
is a kind of universal instinct which, without knowing
it, brushes aside the nonsense which is sometimes
talked about us, and by an involuntary act of both
intelligence and conscience acknowledges that, first
and foremost, *we stand for God.*

> Lord, we come, and from Thee never
> Self nor earth our hearts shall sever ;
> Thine entirely, Thine for ever,
>   We will fight and die.
> To a world of rebels dying,
> Heaven and Hell and God defying,
> Everywhere we'll still be crying,
>   ' Will ye perish—why ? '

258

Christ . . . formed in you.—Galatians 4 : 19.
**That He might be the firstborn among many
brethren.**—Romans 8 : 29.

The life of Jesus in Palestine was a foreshadowing
of His life in all who accept Him. God appointed
Him a Saviour, not only because He should bring
redemption nigh by a sacrifice which He alone could
offer, but because He was also appointed to be the
first-born of many brethren, to be the head of a new
family, the beginning—the new Adam—the first of a
new line, in which character should cease to be merely
human, even though perfect with all human per-
fections, and should become a union of the human
and the Divine ; in which, in fact, the body and mind
and spirit of man should continue to exhibit the
wonder of Christ's Incarnation and show forth God
clothed with man.

> Thou hast my flesh, Thy hallowed shrine,
>   Devoted solely to Thy will :
> Here let Thy light for ever shine,
>   This house still let Thy presence fill ;
> O Source of life, live, dwell and move
> In me, till all my life be love.

Then Jonah prayed unto the Lord his God out of the fish's belly, and said, I cried by reason of mine affliction unto the Lord, and He heard me ; out of the belly of hell cried I, and Thou heardest my voice.—Jonah 2 : 1, 2.

Whenever we think about God, or give our hearts a chance to turn to Him, we know how *instinctively —how easily—we feel that we can speak to Him*, no matter where we are. Even bad men in some measure feel this. I have often thought so when I have heard men using blasphemous language, especially if they happened to be aroused by some wrong done to themselves and were really in earnest. The very fact that such implications were possible seemed to me to imply that the speaker believed God was there —to be appealed to, whether for evil or for good. How much more is this so with those of us who know Him and love Him ! In times of trial and sorrow, of great joy or satisfaction, we think of Him—we speak as though He were actually present. We feel that He is. In all those experiences in which the soul is greatly stirred, whether by failure or grief, by temptation or sin, the thought of His eye being on us is in harmony with our own instincts and nature. We live, as John Milton said, ' *as ever in our great Task-master's eye.*'

God . . . giveth grace unto the humble.—James 4 : 6.
He hath put down the mighty from their seats, and exalted them of low degree.—Luke 1 : 52.

The occupation chosen for the early life of Jesus was a humble one. He learned the trade of a joiner, and worked with Joseph at the carpenter's bench. His associates and friends were of the village community and He ' whose name is above every name ' passed to and fro and in and out among the cottage homes of the poor as one of themselves.

Is there not something here for us ? Does not the lowly origin of our comrades make them hesitate on the threshold of great efforts, when they ought to leap forward in the strength of their God ? Let them remember their Master, and take courage. Let them call to mind the unfashionable, uneducated, uncultivated surroundings of Nazareth. Let them bear in mind the humble service of the family life. Let them, above all, remember the gentle Mother and the meek and lowly One Himself, and in this remembrance let them go forward.

> If so poor a soul as I
>   May to Thy great glory live,
> All my actions sanctify,
>   All my words and thoughts receive ;
> Claim me for Thy service, claim
> All I have and all I am.

He that hath My commandments, and keepeth them, he it is that loveth Me : and he that loveth Me shall be loved of My Father, and I will love him, and will manifest Myself to him.—John 14 : 21.

Nothing was more emphatic and distinctive in the teaching of Jesus Christ while He was on earth than His assertion of His Presence with those who lived for Him. In these amazing statements He stands absolutely alone among men. No other moral or religious teacher, true or false—Moses, Buddha, Mohammed, Zoroaster, Confucius, Socrates or Plato —ever made such a claim. We are so familiar with His words that we are apt to lose the sense of wonder in them. With one breath He speaks to the disciples of the agonizing and shameful death which awaits Him a few hours ahead, and with the next He declares He will abide with them for ever ! And again, after His resurrection, in the very last moments of His presence with them before He is taken up into the clouds, He utters the glorious declaration : ' Lo, I am with you alway.' Again and again during His last days on earth He assures not only His disciples, but all who He knew would come to believe on Him through their word, of this blessed fact. We no longer have to go to Jerusalem and the holy hill. Jerusalem and the holy things go with us !

Unto every one of us is given grace according to the measure of the gift of Christ. . . . Till we all come in the unity of the faith, and of the knowledge of the Son of God, unto a perfect man, unto the measure of the stature of the fulness of Christ.
—Ephesians 4 : 7, 13.

Whereas the best that the other great teachers and prophets of the world's past could do for us was to set up and explain the truths they had to proclaim, Christ did much more. He did all that ; but, oh, so much in addition ! He proclaimed the truth. He also left us an example that we should follow in His steps. He came to change our whole being so as to make us able not only to receive His message, but to become like Himself. Yes, like Him in this wonderful two-fold likeness. Like Him as a faithful fighter with evil—a lover of the strife against evil, with a dread-nought heart for God and righteousness. And like Him in this gentleness and meekness of the Lamb ; silent in provocation ; patient in suffering and trial ; meek in the hour of wrongful accusation ; able to be still when the storms go raging round us ; kept in peace with the peace of God in the midst of strife.

Within my heart, O Lord, fulfil
The purpose of Thy death and pain,
That all may know Thou livest still
In Blood-washed hearts to rule and reign.

**Who shall separate us from the love of Christ ?
. . . neither death, nor life, . . . nor things present, nor things to come . . . shall be able to
separate us from the love of God, which is in
Christ Jesus our Lord.**—Romans 8 : 35, 38, 39.

**He that loveth father or mother more than Me
is not worthy of Me : and he that loveth son or
daughter more than Me is not worthy of Me.**
—Matthew 10 : 37.

Just because love is of such high origin, and is the
greatest power in human life, it is often captured and
held by the Devil as his last stronghold against God.
The heart is at once the strongest and the most
sensitive part of our nature ; and it is here, therefore,
that we often find the most blessed and profitable
opportunities for self-denial.

That pleasant companionship, so grateful, so full
of joy, and yet so likely to tempt me from the path of
faithful service, ' Lord, I deny myself of it.' That
love of home and friends and circle which is so powerful a factor in life and enters so constantly into all the
arrangements and details of our conduct, influencing
so largely all real plans for doing God's work—' Lord,
I will deny it, when it is in danger of lessening my
labours for Thee and Thy Kingdom.' The pleasant
hour, the quiet evening, the restful book, ' I will lay
them at Thy feet, for Thy sake, when they hinder me
from doing Thy will. It is between me and Thee
alone ; it is the sacrifice of love.' How precious it
must be to God to see such self-denial !

The word of God is quick, and powerful, and sharper than any twoedged sword, piercing even to the dividing asunder of soul and spirit, . . . and is a discerner of the thoughts and intents of the heart . . . all things are naked and opened unto the eyes of Him with whom we have to do. —Hebrews 4 : 12, 13.

Go, stand and speak . . . to the people all the words of this life.—Acts 5 : 20.

Is there not manifested in all the activities of this life, determination, daring, cost ; to an almost unbelievable extent ? And the same principle applies in our unspeakably important business of saving men. All around us are the sinners—in their dug-outs of pleasure or greed or lust or crime. Nothing will arouse them to their danger but an invasion from the outside, attack, the forcing of the barriers of pre-occupied minds. Cannot we start a *Compelling Club* and make the people face the truth ? Every Soldier could join.

Tell the sinners, tell them again and yet again the whole truth about sin. Advertise its deceitfulness ; its deadening paralysing inroads upon all that is best and noblest and most Godlike in them ; its abominable cruelty. Advertise how sin ruins the sinners themselves, their families, their neighbours and all whom they influence, dragging all down, down, to the depths of eternal misery. And testify ! Personal experiences of Salvation cannot but capture attention ; they reveal men to themselves and accentuate the difference between the slave of the Devil and God's happy free man.

Jesus answered them, Verily, verily, I say unto you, Whosoever committeth sin is the servant of sin. . . . If the Son therefore shall make you free, ye shall be free indeed.—John 8 : 34, 36.

What men want is *Personal, Individual Liberty from sin.* Given that, and a slave may be free. Given that, and the child in the nursery of iniquity may be free. Given that, and the young man or maiden held in the charnel-house of lust may be free. Given that, and the victim of all that is most cruel and brutal in life may still be free. Oh! blessed be God, he whom the Son makes free is free indeed!

This, and this alone, is the liberty for the new century—the Gospel liberty for the individual soul and spirit, without respect of time or circumstance; and here alone is He who can bestow it—Jesus, the Lion of the Tribe of Judah.

> I am saved! I am saved!
> Jesus bids me go free!
> He has bought with a price
> Even me, even me!
>
> Hallelujah! Hallelujah!
> Hallelujah to my Saviour!
> Hallelujah! Hallelujah!
> Hallelujah! Amen!

All the people rejoiced for all the glorious things that were done by Him.—Luke 13 : 17.

The power of God is always the same power but when that power is shown forth in the spiritua and the moral nature of man, the wonders achieved are far grander and more enduring than when He works among the passing forms of nature, even though they be suns and seas and skies, or when the issue be life or death itself.

Stand in awe, then, when God works—especially when His work is seen in the deathless fabric of a soul. Take your shoes from off your feet in His presence. Believe and rejoice, and worship Him when you hear the sinner cry for mercy or see the slave of evil made free, for that is God making Himself visible in your very midst.

> For my blindness I thought
> That no power could have wrought
> Such a marvel of wonder and might ;
> But 'twas done, for I felt,
> At the Cross as I knelt,
> That my darkness was turned into light.

Whatsoever the Lord pleased, that did He in heaven, and in earth.—Psalm 135 : 6.

The works of the Lord are great, sought out of all them that have pleasure therein. . . . He hath made His wonderful works to be remembered. —Psalm 111 : 2, 4.

Country to-day very beautiful. I have lived such a crowded life, and have from my earliest years been occupied with affairs which have seemed so momentous if only because they have had to do with eternal things, that I have had little time for the beauties and charms of nature. All the same, when I do, in passing along the ways of life, give myself for a moment to her, she returns double to me in inspiration and—yes, even in revelation of her Maker and Lord. The vivid images and tender impressions of these hills and vales remain with me, associated with the deeper thoughts of God and of the goodness and liberality and beauty of the works of His hands.

> All things bright and beautiful,
>   All creatures great and small,
> All things wise and wonderful,
>   The Lord God made them all.
>
> He gave us eyes to see them,
>   And lips that we might tell ;
> He gave us hearts to love Him
>   Who doeth all things well.

The Lord searcheth all hearts, and understandeth all . . . : if thou seek Him, He will be found of thee.—1 Chronicles 28 : 9.

God finds pleasure in being sought after by men. Just as the happiness of earthly parenthood is increased by the desire of our children to tell us of their deeds and needs and devotion, so the great Father delights to have us seek Him in communion and prayer. The fact that He knows all, or more than all, we have to tell Him, does not greatly alter this. We are quite as pleased when our children confide in us concerning matters about which we are already fully informed, as when we hear from them about those of which we know little or nothing.

The great thing is that they seek us—that of their own heart's desire and trust they lay their treasure of joy or their burden of sorrow at our feet. And so God finds Divine satisfaction in His children's confidence. It is this—the will to seek Him—the heart-hunger for His help and presence—which really makes true prayer, and which renders of so little importance the form of words we may use or the manner we may adopt, or even the particular request which we desire to urge.

> Beloved . . . ye should earnestly contend for the faith which was once delivered unto the saints . . . the Lord cometh . . . to execute judgment upon all, and to convince all that are ungodly . . . of all their ungodly deeds.—Jude 3, 14, 15.

It seems to me that the New Testament teaches that the people of Christ—the company of all those who really love and follow Him, who are sometimes called in our language ' The Church of Christ '—I say that His people, whatever they are called, must be the *Rebukers* of the world—the *Intruders* upon its selfishness and pleasure life—the *Demanders* from it of its dues and duty to God, its Maker and Judge. No greater mistake could be made than to suppose that our sole business with the world is to serve it or reveal to it the sympathies and benevolences of God. We are to condemn its sin and command its repentance and foretell its doom. And it seems to me that, this being so, we shall never get help or sympathy on a large scale either from the world itself or from those— no matter what they may be called—*who don't do it* !

> Yes, our warfare is great and our enemy strong,
>   Our aim he will ever oppose ;
> But the battle's the Lord's and to Him we belong,
>   And with Him we shall conquer our foes.

God said, Let us make man in our image.
—Genesis 1 : 26.
**The Lord God formed man of the dust of the
ground, and breathed into his nostrils the breath
of life ; and man became a living soul.**—Genesis
2 : 7.
**Let love be without dissimulation . . . con-
descend to men of low estate.**—Romans 12 : 9, 16.

Dust ! If one had searched the whole sphere of
existence, could there have been found anything more
unlikely, more unpromising, out of which to produce
so noble a result ? But that He might be glorified,
that He might show forth His power, that none
might share the honour with Him, He took dust,
and made man !

Ah ! What a lesson is written here for me, and for
you, my comrades. It is still from the degraded dust
—from the ashes of wasted lives, from the drunkards
and the Magdalenes, from the liars, the idolaters and
the unclean—yes, indeed, from the dust—that we
are called to gather in the material that He will
change into a ' *new creation.*'

From the dust ! Well, then, are you doing this ?
Are you, like your Lord, ' condescending to men of
low estate ' ? Are you seeking amongst the worst
for the material out of which is to come the new man
in Christ Jesus ? Are you seeking for the dust to
which God will again speak those wonderful words :
' Let Us make man in Our image ' ?

**The Lord shall reign for ever, even thy God, . . .
unto all generations.**—Psalm 146 : 10.

Many good people are, I know, shaken and nervous.
But that is nothing new. Indeed, that is usually so
in big storms. Especially when God's anger is poured
out, there are always some ready to give up hope in
God altogether. They act as if He had changed,
because they cannot understand His ways ! We must
cheer them and hold them up. Time is on His side.
Right is immortal. Love can never die. The interests
with which the sons of God are concerned are eternal
interests. Kingdoms and thrones, armies and navies,
victories and defeats, earthly pomp and power, pass
away like the leaves on the trees, like the grass of
the field, which to-day is, and to-morrow is cast into
the oven.

Come, then, and let us hope in God. Out of this
fiery furnace the gold will come forth, and in the
midst of the fire we shall find One like unto the Son
of God, . . . and of the increase of His government
and peace there shall be no end. Hallelujah !

> Though we pass through tribulation,
>   All will be well !
> Ours is such a Full Salvation ;
>   All, all is well !
> Happy, still in God confiding,
> Fruitful, if in Christ abiding,
> Holy, through the Spirit's guiding ;
>   All must be well !

The God of Israel is He that giveth strength and power unto His people.—Psalm 68 : 35.

Jesus said unto them, . . . My Father giveth you the true bread from heaven. For the bread of God is He which cometh down from heaven, and giveth life unto the world.—John 6 : 32, 33.

God is the great Giver. It is not merely that giving is one of the great principles of action with Him, or one of the leading laws which He has laid down for His government ; it is more than that—it is His nature. He gives, not by rule and rote merely—He gives as the eternal outflow of a loving heart. Giving, with Him, is like the rolling forth of a mighty river which cannot be restrained. He gives because He loves to give—because He cannot help it. Now, how can men be like God unless there is something of the same kind in them ?

He walks with God, who, as he onward moves,
Follows the footsteps of the Lord he loves,
And, keeping Him for ever in his view
His Saviour sees and His example too.

When the Pharisee which had bidden Him saw it, he spake within himself, saying, This man, if He were a prophet, would have known who and what manner of woman this is that toucheth Him : for she is a sinner. And Jesus answering said unto him, . . . Her sins, which are many, are forgiven ; for she loved much : but to whom little is forgiven, the same loveth little. And He said unto her, Thy sins are forgiven.—Luke 7 : 39, 40, 47, 48.

That heart-nearness to the thief had nothing to do with the nearness of the crosses. Every one knows what a gulf may be between people who are very near together—father and son—husband and wife ! No, it was the nearness of a heart deliberately trained to seek it ; a heart delighting in mercy and deliberately surrendering all other delights for it ; hungering and thirsting for the love of the lost and ruined.

> ' The hart panteth after the waters,
>   The dying for life that departs,
>   The Lord in His glory for sinners
>   For the love of rebellious hearts.'

And so He is quite ready, at once, to share His Heaven with this poor defiled creature, the first trophy of the Cross. Again—what a lesson of love ! How different, all this, from the common inclination to shrink away from contact and intercourse with the vile ! Oh, shame, that there can ever have been such a shrinking in our poor guilty hearts ! The servant is not above his Lord. He came to sinners. Let us go to them with Him !

Thy throne, O God, is for ever and ever : a sceptre of righteousness is the sceptre of Thy kingdom. . . . Thou, Lord, in the beginning hast laid the foundation of the earth ; and the heavens are the works of Thine hands : they shall perish ; but Thou remainest ; and they all shall wax old as doth a garment ; and as a vesture shalt Thou fold them up, and they shall be changed : but Thou art the same, and Thy years shall not fail.—Hebrews 1 : 8, 10–12.

All things that touch the life of man are marked for change. As knowledge advances, and men come nearer to the secrets of the world in which they live, they find how true indeed it is that man is but ' a shadow dwelling in a world of shadows.'

Everything is changing—everything but God. The sun, the astronomers tell us, is burning itself away. The everlasting hills are only everlasting in a figure ; for they, too, are crumbling day by day. Time is writing wrinkles on the whole world and all that is therein. But, above it all, I see One standing—my unchanging God.

> Oh ! may this bounteous God
>   Through all our life be near us,
> With ever-joyful hearts
>   And blessèd peace to cheer us ;
> And keep us in His grace
>   And guide us when perplexed,
> And free us from all ills
>   In this world and the next.

God . . . will render to every man according to his deeds : . . . for there is no respect of persons with God.—Romans 2 : 5, 6, 11.

The wronged wife suffering in silence ; the children destroyed in their innocence ; the servant defrauded of wages rightly earned ; the sick and the solitary cheated in their weakness ; the widow and the fatherless robbed of their due—do not these all seem to say in their misery, and do not we who know of their wrongs feel instinctively with them, ' This ought to be set right ; there ought to be a day of reckoning— a day of account ' ?

The Judgment described in the word of God meets this universal cry of the human spirit. According to that word, it will be a day when the fire will try every man's work of what sort it is, and will bring to light the hidden things of darkness, and will make manifest the counsels of the heart. The Judge cometh !

> Thou Judge of quick and dead,
>   Before whose bar severe
> With holy joy or guilty dread
>   We all shall soon appear,
> Our wakened souls prepare
>   For that tremendous day,
> And fill us now with watchful care
>   And stir us up to pray.

As many as received Him, to them gave He the right to become children of God, even to them that believe on His name.—John 1 : 12 ; R.V.

Holiness has three aspects. First, it is *purity* ; the cleansing of the soul from all impurity by the sacrifice of Jesus.

The second aspect is *the utter change in the preferences of the soul*, and that correction of the will which brings submission to God in every detail of life. Not only the choice of, but the preference for, what He wants, because He wants it.

The third aspect of the truth is that together with this change of preference comes the *impartation of Divine Power*—the power to walk in purity and live in harmony with the new preferences of the soul. To have the most blessed desires for the will of God, but to have no power to fulfil it, would not only belie His majesty and belittle His might, but would be a positive torture for us. But God's response to the soul's preference for the right is power to fulfil that preference. He gives that power by the gift of His own mighty nature He comes into His temple He ascends the throne of our hearts. That is the kingship of God, the Divine rule, the Divine government. Hallelujah ! It is the victory promised by Jesus Christ to every soul of man.

Deborah arose, . . . a mother in Israel.—Judges 5 : 7.
The Lord giveth the word ; the women that publish the tidings are a great host.—Psalm 68 : 11 ; R.V.

I am more and more convinced that The Salvation Army is greatly indebted for its very self to the Mother of The Army.* I am far from saying—as some of our unhappy critics like to say when they want to belittle our dear Father—that it was really she who made The Army. I do not think that. But I do think that she led us forward on this momentous subject. She had the sense to see the absurdity of leaving out half the human family when trying to save the whole world, and the wit to say so, and the fine courage to act so. Yes, she took up the cross and sustained it in the fiery trial, and made a way for woman to represent her Master, at least as freely as hitherto woman had been allowed to represent on the stage the frivolous or murderous characters of this world's history.

Strife and sorrow over,
The Lord's true faithful Soldier
  Has been called to go
  From the ranks below
To the conquering hosts above.

*Promoted to Glory on October 4, 1890.

**For there is no difference : . . . all have sinned,
. . . redemption . . . is in Christ Jesus : whom
God hath set forth to be a propitiation through
faith in His blood, . . . for the remission of sins
that are past.**—Romans 3 : 22–25.

The only really satisfactory test of any faith, or
system of faiths, lies in its treatment of sin. Human
consciousness in all ages, and in all conditions of
development, bears witness to the fact of sin with
universal and overwhelming conviction. Men cannot
prevent the discomfort of self-accusation which ever
follows wrongdoing. They cannot escape from the
bitter which always lies hidden in the sweet. They
cannot forget the things they wish to forget. Even
when they are a law unto themselves, they are compelled to judge themselves by that law. It is as
though some unerring necessity is laid upon every
individual of the race to sit in judgment upon his own
conduct, and to pass sentence upon himself. He is
compelled to speak to his own soul of things about
which he would rather be silent, and to listen to that
which he does not wish to hear.

The proof that this is so is open, manifest, and in-
disputable. No system of philosophy, no school of
scientific thought, no revelation from the heavens
above or the earth beneath can really weaken it. It is
not found in books, or received by human contact,
or influenced by human example. It is revealed in
every man. It is felt by all men. They do not learn
it or deduce it or believe it merely. They know it.
All men do. You do. I do.

One Mediator between God and men, the man Christ Jesus ; who gave Himself a ransom for all. —1 Timothy 2 : 5, 6.

' He saved others—He saved others—Himself He cannot save ! ' Amidst the din of discordant voices, this taunt sounded out clear and loud and fell upon the ears of a dying thief. Perhaps the strange words made the poor criminal think. ' " Others "— " others "—He saves others—then why not me ? ' Presently he answered the railing unbelief of his fellow-prisoner and then, in the simple language of faith, said to the Saviour : ' Lord, remember me when Thou comest into Thy Kingdom.'

Jesus Christ's reply is one of the great landmarks of the Bible. It denotes the boundary line of the long ages of dimness and indefiniteness about two things— assurance of Salvation in this life and certainty of immediate blessedness in the life to come. ' To-day thou shalt be with Me in Paradise ! ' It is as though great gates, long closed, were suddenly thrown wide open. The whole freedom and glory of the Gospel is illustrated at one stroke. Here is the Salvation of The Salvation Army ! To-day—without any cere- monies, baptisms, communions, confirmations, with- out the mediation of any priest or the intervention of any sacraments : such things would indeed have been only an impertinence *there*—to-day. ' *To-day* shalt thou be with Me.' Indeed, the gates are open wide at last !

God hath chosen the weak things of the world to confound the things which are mighty ; . . . and things which are not, to bring to nought things that are.—1 Corinthians 1 : 27, 28.

He that cometh to God must believe that He is, and that He is a rewarder of them that diligently seek Him.—Hebrews 11 : 6.

How many people I have known—I do not need to go farther afield than my own observation in this matter—whose mental powers have been of the very simplest type ; people who have had practically no education, no reading, no mental training ; and yet who out of weakness have been made strong in His cause and have been mighty with ' the mind that was in Christ ' !

Now, I am well aware that such a transformation as this can only be accomplished by dint of industry, patience, self-restraint, self-control, self-denial. Nothing which is worth having in this world can be had without these things. But, at the same time, I am convinced that these means alone would not have sufficed to bring about such a change. Indeed, these means would probably never have been employed even, much less have been effectual, had it not been for the presence of that other force—faith.

> Fully trusting in the battle's fray,
> Fully trusting Jesus all the way,
> Fully trusting—this the surest stay,
>   Trusting alone in Jesus.

The Lord spake unto Moses . . . as a man speaketh unto his friend.—Exodus 33 : 11.

Ye are My friends, if ye do whatsoever I command you.—John 15 : 14.

Peace with God depends upon coming over on to God's side. Giving up the struggle and pulling down the rebel flag and surrendering the citadel is not enough. There must be a covenant of everlasting friendship. The rebel must not only cease his rebellion, but he must, if he wants peace, be ready to be an obedient and faithful subject. Some well-meaning people never enter into this covenant. Even some of those who want peace, and talk a great deal about it, and are willing to make some sacrifices to get it, are never willing to be counted as God's friends, and so they never get His peace.

One of the strangest things I have met with in my journey through life is that men can be *ashamed* of their *Maker*, and shrink from wearing His colours and sharing their Saviour's Cross.

> Ashamed of Jesus—that dear Friend,
> On whom my hopes of Heaven depend ?
> Whene'er I blush, be this my shame,
> That I no more revere His name.
>
> . . . .
>
> And oh, may this my glory be,
> That Christ is not ashamed of me.

**Why call ye me, Lord, Lord, and do not the
things which I say ?**—Luke 6 : 46.
**Having a form of godliness, but denying the
power thereof : from such turn away.**—2 Timothy
3 : 5.

Religion is an essentially practical thing—not
merely a matter of theory or theology, but a thing
of life and conduct. I am sure that many of us ought
to be far more thankful to God than we are that,
under the teaching and practice of The Army, it has
been made almost impossible to fall into the error, so
common even in these days, of confusing listening to
the things of God and being convinced of their truth
with the personal enjoyment and practice of them and
the pressing them upon others. Theory there is, of
course, and must be. Man is a reasoning being. But
the theory of religion, no matter how correct, how
beautiful, how convincing, is a totally different thing
from religion itself.

How easy for the forms of religious service, the
listening to eloquent sermons, the music and cere-
monies and sacraments associated with religious
worship—inspiring, beautiful, and full of meaning in
themselves as they may be—to become a deadly
danger by being mistaken for vital godliness of
heart and life and conduct.

> Whate'er I say or do,
>   Thy glory be my aim ;
> My offerings all be offered through
>   That ever-blessèd Name.

Who is among you that feareth the Lord, that obeyeth the voice of His servant, that walketh in darkness, and hath no light ? let him trust in the name of the Lord, and stay upon his God.—Isaiah 50 : 10.

Are there not strange events, unlooked-for catastrophes, heart-breaking bereavements, mysterious contradictions, unfathomed problems strewed along our path in which it seems as though by some sudden combination the very heavens are blotted out ? Do we not sometimes feel like the pelican in the wilderness, or the sheep among wolves, or the stranger left by the caravan in the desert to die alone in a dry and thirsty land where no water is ?

In times of great trial the test is in many cases most severe, in regard to a man's material possessions of prospects. ' You can't live,' the temptation goes, 'without this or that, and this trial or upheaval will deprive you of it unless you act quickly.' It is the great trial of faith.

> When we cannot see our way,
> Let us trust and still obey !
> He who bids us forward go,
> Cannot fail the way to show.

We are troubled . . . perplexed . . . persecuted, but not forsaken ; . . . that the life also of Jesus might be made manifest in our body.
—2 Corinthians 4 : 8–10.

Jesus said : Lo, I am with you alway.—Matthew 28 : 20.

The finest pine-trees grow in the stormiest lands. The tempests make them strong. Surgeons tell us that their greatest triumphs are often those in which the patients have suffered most at their hands—for every stroke of the knife is to heal. The child you most truly love is the one you most anxiously correct. And ' whom the Lord loveth He chasteneth.' Oh, do believe that by every blow of disappointment and sorrow He permits to fall upon you He is striving to bring you to the measure of the stature of a man in Christ Jesus. Do work with Him in the full knowledge that He will not forsake you. He, the Man who has penetrated to the heart of every form of sorrow, and left a blessing there ; He who has watched in silence by every kind of earthly grief, and found its antidote ; the Man who trod the wine-press alone—He will be with you. And, since He is with you, see to it you acquit yourself well in His presence.

Wherefore to Thee I all resign :
    Being Thou art of Love and Power ;
Thy only will be done, not mine ;
    Thee, Lord, let Heaven and earth adore.
Flow back the rivers to the sea,
And let my all be lost in Thee.

Praying always with all prayer and supplication in the Spirit, and watching thereunto with all perseverance and supplication for all saints.—Ephesians 6 : 18.

Love is strong as death.—Canticles 8 : 6.

The teaching of the New Testament clearly is that we should ' pray without ceasing.' The truly godly man will talk to God about everything, just as the true lover talks about everything to the one he loves, or the true wife makes her husband a partner with her in every concern of her life. The real lover—whether before or after marriage—no more thinks of dividing his life up into compartments and saying, ' This I will speak to her about, but that I won't,' than he thinks of putting an end to his affection. The man who is in right relations with God, with his work and with himself, will pray about everything, and thus will, in fact, pray without ceasing !

> My dwelling-place art Thou alone ;
> No other can I claim or own ;
> The point where all my wishes meet,
> My law, my love, life's only sweet.
>
> Then let me to Thy Throne repair
> And never be a stranger there ;
> There Love Divine shall be my guard,
> And peace and safety my reward.

In all things approving ourselves as the ministers of God, . . . by kindness, by the Holy Ghost, by love unfeigned.—2 Corinthians 6 : 4, 6.

Among the evidences that we are really the ministers of God, is kindness. It is a humble qualification, which often influences people more than gifts which are, perhaps, more sought after ; and is just as necessary in the minister of Christ as is patience or pureness or knowledge or love. There are few human hearts that are not moved by it. Where preaching and learning and miracle-working have failed, kindness, by a charm and force which are all its own, has often succeeded. Some one has said that ' kindness is a language which the dumb can speak and the deaf can understand.' Many a heart, cold and still, has been warmed into flowing life again by one kind act. Many a sweet and tender memory, buried long ago and forgotten, has come forth from its grave alive with blessing and happiness under the gracious influence of one kind word.

> Help me the slow of heart to move
> By some clear, winning word of love ;
> Teach me the wayward feet to stay,
> And guide them in the homeward way.

The Lord God planted a garden eastward in Eden ; and there He put . . . man whom He had formed.—Genesis 2 : 8.

Our Father . . . Thy will be done in earth, as it is in heaven.—Matthew 6 : 9, 10.

His will must be done in you, as it was done in the earth in those first days of that new spring time. Your life must be in Him, and His in you. Your law must be His wish ; your body with all its powers must be His, and in His hands, as really as was that sweet garden earth in Eden ; your love must be kept pure and undefiled by the presence of His ; your will must be linked to His for better or for worse, for joy or for sorrow, just as Adam's was on that the earth's first Sunday morning. There must be no opposition to Him, no holding back from Him. The will of God must be gladly and fully done. And then the inward rest of God, the Sabbath of the soul, will begin for you.

> Lord, I make a full surrender,
>   All I have I yield to Thee ;
> For Thy love, so great and tender,
>   Asks the gift of me.
> Lord, I bring my whole affection,
>   Claim it, take it for Thine own ;
> Safely kept by Thy protection,
>   Fixed on Thee alone.

Jesus rejoiced in spirit, and said, I thank Thee, O Father, Lord of heaven and earth, that Thou hast hid these things from the wise and prudent, and hast revealed them unto babes ; even so, Father ; for so it seemed good in Thy sight. —Luke 10 : 21.

It pleased God, who . . . called me by His grace, to reveal His Son in me.—Galatians 1 : 15, 16.

Christ's birth and infancy, His childhood ; His youth, His manhood, His perfected or completed life following Calvary and the Resurrection : every one of these phases or sections of His wonderful experience of earth has its continuing lessons for us. All speak aloud to us of His purposes and plans, and reveal to us the power and force of His inner life in the outward or public appearances and acts which belong to each. God has hidden many things from us—mysteries of nature, of grace, of eternity ; but this mystery of God's relations to man He has exhausted His resources in order to make plain. Before all else the life of Jesus is a revelation of the mind and methods, the principles and practices of God, as they ought to appear and as they ought to work out, amid the surroundings and limitations of Humanity.

> Centre of our hopes Thou art,
>   End of our enlarged desire ;
> Stamp Thine image on our heart,
>   Fill us now with heavenly fire ;
> Overflowed by love Divine,
> Seal our souls for ever Thine.

The Spirit also helpeth our infirmities : for we know not what we should pray for as we ought : but the Spirit itself maketh intercession for us with groanings which cannot be uttered. And He that searcheth the hearts knoweth what is the mind of the Spirit, because He maketh intercession for the saints according to the will of God.—Romans 8 : 26, 27.

Some people have great difficulty as to what they should pray for. They want some particular gift or blessing or deliverance, but they are in doubt whether or not they ought to ask for it ; because, while they are anxious that God's will should be done, they do not know what His will in the matter may be. Well, now, it seems to me that Jesus Christ Himself gave us the solution of the difficulty when He said : ' If ye abide in Me, and My words abide in you, ye shall ask what ye will, and it shall be done unto you.' He means that if there is such unity of spirit with Him that His life is our life, and His rule is our rule, we shall know what to ask for, and if there be likeness of character to Him, as there is likeness of nature between the branch and the tree, then, as He said in another place, we cannot ask amiss. His Spirit teaches us—leads us—actually intercedes for us and joins His intercession with ours.

**Blessed is he whose transgression is forgiven.
. . . I acknowledged my sin unto Thee, and mine
iniquity have I not hid. I said, I will confess . . .
unto the Lord ; and Thou forgavest the iniquity of
my sin.**—Psalm 32 : 1, 5.

The soul with unconfessed guilt upon it is like the
troubled sea, it can never rest. The conscience with
unconfessed sin upon it has a burden which nothing
can take away. This is true of all men. It is not
confined to murderers and seducers, or the inmates of
prisons, or to the great crowd of those who spend their
lives in fleeing from the discovery of crime. It con-
cerns all who have sinned—all classes, all ages. Even
the little child that stands before its parents knowing
the wrong it has done feels it. The parents feel it also.
Without confession there will be no rest. David said
that while he kept silence about his sin his bones
waxed old within him. 'For day and night Thy
hand was heavy upon me.' But when he said, ' I
will confess my transgressions,' then he was forgiven
and at peace.

Now there is no denying these things. They are
facts of which human consciousness itself attests the
truth. No amount of theorizing or weeping or
suffering can get away from them. Confession is an
essential part of repentance.

He took the blind man by the hand, and led him out of the town ; . . . He put His hands again upon his eyes, and made him look up : and he was restored, and saw every man clearly.—Mark 8 : 23, 25.

Jesus Himself drew near, and went with them.—Luke 24 : 15.

There is something very wonderful in the principle of contact as illustrated by the life of Jesus. Just as to save the human race He felt it necessary to come into it, and clothe Himself with its nature and conform Himself to its natural laws, so all the way through His earthly journey He was constantly seeking to come into touch with the people He desired to bless. He touched the sick, He fed the hungry, He placed His fingers on the blind eyes and put them upon the ears of the deaf and touched with them the tongue of the dumb. He took the ruler's dead daughter ' by the hand, and the maid arose.' He lifted the little children up into His arms and blessed them ; He stretched forth His hand to sinking Peter ; He stood close by the foul-smelling body of the dead Lazarus ; He took the bread, and with His own hands brake it and gave it to His disciples at that last farewell meeting. He even took poor Thomas's trembling hand, and guided it to the prints in His hands and the wounds in His side. Yes, indeed, it is written large, in every part of His life, that He really came, and that He came very near to lost and suffering men.

See that ye refuse not Him that speaketh.
—Hebrews 12 : 25.

Every impulse to goodness of which Christ's
followers are aware in themselves is the work of God
and a sign of His Presence in them. The unexpected
call to speak to a soul ; the inward desire for the
Salvation of some one they see or think about ; the
flashing sight of some one's danger in sin ; the sudden,
urging desire for prayer—these are signs of the nearness of God. Altogether apart from the question of
the soul's obedience or disobedience to these promptings, the promptings themselves are proofs of the fact
of His Presence. Those who respond will become more
and more alive to the movements of the Spirit of God
within them.

> Let me hear Thy voice now speaking ;
>   Let me hear, and I'll obey ;
> While before Thy Cross I'm seeking,
>   Oh, chase my fears away.
> Oh, let the light now falling
>   Reveal my every need ;
> Now hear me while I'm calling,
>   Oh, speak, and I will heed.
>
> Speak, Saviour, speak !
>   Obey Thee I will ever ;
> Down at Thy Cross I seek
>   From all that's wrong to sever.

Serving the Lord with all humility . . . testifying both to the Jews, and also to the Greeks, repentance toward God, and faith toward our Lord Jesus Christ.—Acts 20 : 19, 21.

Not only does the existence of The Army, its uniform and its work, speak to men of the claims of God, but it goes further—it challenges men to account for their own conduct. It has, by God's blessing upon us, become almost impossible for a Salvationist to appear in any company in any part of the world without instantly arresting the attention of men and, merely by the silent testimony, of the uniform or some other outward sign of unity with us, compelling their thoughts to turn away for a moment from the trifles of time to the unanswered questions which relate to eternity, and to answer the great inquiry : ' Am I right, or am I wrong ? '

> Are you ready for the battle,
>   Ready armed with holy might ?
> Ready now to help The Army,
>   Ready now to come and fight ?

Go and proclaim these words . . , and say, Return, thou backsliding Israel, saith the Lord ; and I will not cause Mine anger to fall upon you : for I am merciful, saith the Lord, and I will not keep anger for ever. Only acknowledge thine iniquity.—Jeremiah 3 : 12, 13.

Think of the prodigals who never come home. My comrades, what a thought is that ! And yet it was their intention to return. I believe that all backsliders promise themselves again and again to return to the Father, confess their sin and seek forgiveness. Many, yes, very many, promise us ; some promise me ! But they are waiting for something to be altered or for something else to happen, and the years slip past, and while they wait for others the Devil is lying in wait for them—watching for his chance.

Poor broken things they often are—with broken vows, broken prayers, broken joys—broken love, broken strength and manhood ; sometimes with broken hearts. And in their broken condition they grow weak and ever weaker. And often just as they seem to be on the edge of better things—the Devil sends up against them some calamity, and catches them unawares. The blow falls and it is too late to save them—and they sink !

Make me, Holy Spirit, strong to fight
   For the Lord who died for me ;
Help me point the lost to Calvary's height,
   Where for sinners there is mercy.

Stand fast in one spirit, with one mind striving together for the faith of the gospel ; and in nothing terrified by your adversaries : . . . having the same conflict which ye saw in me.—Philippians 1 : 27, 28, 30.

It has ever been a common experience of God's leaders to have to meet the Devil in bitter personal conflicts before they put forth great efforts to rescue the souls of men. Is it to be wondered at, then, that so many Salvationists and other servants of God suffer such temptation and darkness ? It is the Devil ! Do not be distressed. Do not fear. Do not think that you are alone in these trying experiences. Hold fast to duty, and follow your Lord. He passed in triumph that way before you, and you shall go forward and triumph too.

His love in time past forbids me to think
He'll leave me at last in trouble to sink ;
Each sweet Ebenezer I have in review
Confirms His good pleasure to help me quite through.

How bitter that cup no heart can conceive,
Which He drank quite up that sinners might live.
His way was much rougher and darker than mine :
Did Christ, my Lord, suffer, and shall I repine ?

**After these things He went forth, and saw a
publican, named Levi, sitting at the receipt of
custom : and He said unto him, Follow Me. And
he left all, rose up, and followed Him.**—Luke 5 :
27, 28.

**All things whatsoever ye would that men should
do to you, do ye even so to them : for this is the
law and the prophets.**—Matthew 7 : 12.

Men are still demanding standards of life and
conduct. The open materialist, the timid agnostic,
no less than the avowedly selfish, the vicious and the
vile, are asking with a hundred tongues and in a
thousand ways, ' Who will show us any good ? '
The universal conscience, unbribed, unstifled as on the
fateful day in Eden—conscience, the only thing in
man left standing erect when all else fell—still cries
out, ' *You ought !* ' still rebels at evil, still compels
the human heart to cry for rules of right and wrong,
and still urges man to the one and withholds him from
the other.

And it is—for one reason—because Jesus can
provide these high standards for men that I say He
is the Man for the century. The laws He has laid
down in the Gospels and the example He furnished
of obedience to those laws in the actual stress and
turmoil of a human life afford a standard capable of
universal application.

> Only Thee, my soul's Redeemer !
> Whom have I in Heaven beside ?
> Who on earth, with love so tender,
> All my wandering steps will guide ?

My sheep wandered through all the mountains, and upon every high hill : yea, my flock was scattered upon all the face of the earth, and none did search or seek after them. Therefore, ye shepherds, hear the word of the Lord.—Ezekiel 34 : 6, 7.

The Son of man is come to save that which was lost. How think ye ? if a man have an hundred sheep, and one of them be gone astray, doth he not leave the ninety and nine, and goeth into the mountains, and seeketh that which is gone astray ? —Matthew 18 : 11, 12.

If you want the lost sheep you must go into the wilderness. One thing is certain. You will never find them in the fold. Ah, my comrade, where is your heart ? Where are your thoughts and plans mostly found ? Is it in the fold with the little flock —many of them gathered by the labour and tears of others rather than by your own—or is it out in the wilderness amidst the storms and where the wild beasts of Hell carry on their cruel business, where day by day those who might have been brought home give up and perish for ever ?

The safety and continued life of The Army depend not merely upon our shepherding and guarding those whom we have won, but upon our continuing to reach forth in ever-widening effort to those who are outside.

I would the precious time redeem,
And longer live for this alone :
To spend, and to be spent, for them
Who have not yet my Saviour known,
And turn them to a pardoning God,
And quench the brands in Jesus' Blood.

Paul was pressed in the spirit, and testified to the Jews that Jesus was Christ. . . . Then spake the Lord to Paul in the night . . , Be not afraid, but speak, and hold not thy peace : for I am with thee.—Acts 18 : 5, 9, 10.

How many thousands, nay, how many tens of thousands, who cannot get up courage to invite it— in offices and shops and marts and mills and amid the cares of life—long to hear the word of truth spoken from hearts touched with the light and fire of Love Divine !

My comrades, will you not begin again this very day to take full advantage of your opportunity in this matter ? Personal testimony for Christ has exercised a far greater influence on the world than the pulpit and the platform put together. It was so in the early days of our holy faith. It has been so in every great religious awakening since religious awakenings began. It has been so in the history of The Salvation Army. The Holy Ghost will work with those who take up their cross in this matter. He will guide and help with wisdom and love.

I have glorious tidings of Jesus to tell,
How He unto me hath done all things well ;
And I love Him for stooping, in sin when I fell,
Where His strong arm of mercy did reach me.

Giving thanks unto the Father, . . . who hath delivered us from the power of darkness, and hath translated us into the kingdom of His dear Son : in whom we have redemption through His blood, even the forgiveness of sins.—Colossians 1 : 12–14.

And if God so regards men, how shall we set a true value upon them ? Ah ! is it not possible to be satisfied—are not some of us in danger of being satisfied—with our world, its goings and comings, its workings and plannings, its news and its meetings, its joys and sorrows, its ambitions and desires and struggles, forgetting that without men restored to the image of God it is all a failure ? An Army, a Corps, a Division, an Officer, a Campaign which does not make men, which does not restore them to the likeness, and add them to the Kingdom of Christ, may do many other wonderful things, but it is not working the great work of God.

Give us all more holy living,
　Fill us with abundant power ;
Give The Army more thanksgiving,
　Greater victories every hour.
　　Bless our Army !
Be our Rock, our Shield, our Tower.

God is love : and he that dwelleth in love dwelleth in God, and God in him.—1 John 4 : 16.

Now is the very time to let men see that love can make us brave and true to stand alone for the right. That to snatch men from the condemnation of sin and the banishment of Hell *is our war*, and that love is the spirit and soul of it. Love—the longer I live, the more I see that the Gospel of Jesus Christ is not much spread by anything else. Bibles can only go so far, and that not very far, without this. Money and music—no matter how beautiful—and Meetings and uniform and the multiplied agencies of a great and useful Organization do not amount to very much without this. Talk, even when it reaches the heights of eloquence, where men pour out the purest emotions in streams of beautiful thoughts and burning words, is just as powerless, without love, to spread our Gospel as is the sound of tinkling cymbals. Love is the true spreading power. Love that serves—love that goes to the bottom—love for which none are too weak or too repulsive or too near the dark night of despair.

> Give me more love, dear Lord, that I may
> Rush forth, Thy blessèd news to proclaim
> To all lost sinners, that there's one way
> By which they eternal life may obtain.

> Lord, with my all I part,
> Closer to Thee I'll cling ;
> All earthly things that bind my heart
> Dear Lord, to Thy feet I bring.

Give ear ; . . . for the Lord hath spoken. . . . But if ye will not hear it, my soul shall weep . . . ; and mine eye shall weep sore, and run down with tears, because the Lord's flock is carried away captive.—Jeremiah 13 : 15, 17.

The treasure of Heaven itself is to be found in the very poorest. But we shall only see all this, and love it, just as we seek after it and come to know men in their misery and sin and to understand how gloriously Christ's Salvation fits the soul which accepts Him.

And so I would say again, seek after the highest— the soul. Tell men the thoughts of God about them. Speak to them of hope and Heaven as well as of sin and Hell. Believe that they need pardon, and that they know it. Pray with them. Pray for them. Cultivate a patient and tender heart toward all men, but especially toward those you know. A tear shed over a barren and fruitless soul will sometimes turn into a fountain of living waters. Remember that Jesus Christ ' pleaded with strong crying and tears ' and that the prophet put those solemn words into His lips, ' I am poured out like water ; all My bones are broken ; My heart is like wax.' It was to win our souls !

> The love of Christ doth me constrain
> To seek the wandering souls of men,
> With cries, entreaties, tears to save—
> To snatch them from the gaping grave.

Ye sorrow not, even as others which have no hope. For if we believe that Jesus died and rose again, even so them also which sleep in Jesus will God bring with Him.—1 Thessalonians 4 : 13, 14.

Yes! this was the meaning of that strange funeral of His—this was at least one reason why they buried Him. It was that He might hold a flaming torch of comfort at every burial of His people to the end of time. Sorrow not, then, as those that have no hope. He is hope. Your lost ones, perhaps, were strongly rooted in your affection, and your heart was torn when they were plucked up. You cried aloud with the prophet : ' Woe is me, for my hurt ! my wound is grievous. But I said, Truly this is a grief, and I must bear it : my tabernacle is spoiled, and all my cords are broken.' Ah, but remember He was buried also. He knows about the way. He was there. He has them in His keeping. They are His, and yours still. You have no more need to grieve over their burial than over Him. They live, they love, they grow, they rejoice. They are blessed for evermore.

If we find a loving Saviour now,
    And follow Him faithfully,
When He gathers His children in that bright Home,
    Then you'll be there, and I.

When the Comforter is come, whom I will send unto you from the Father, . . . He shall testify of Me . . . of sin, because they believe not on Me ; . . . of judgment, because the prince of this world is judged.—John 15 : 26 ; 16 : 9, 11.

The aggressive spirit is nothing if not courageous. You know how the Holy Spirit attacks sin in individuals, how He troubles their consciences, often follows them up day and night and never gives them up so long as there is the least chance of inducing them to abandon their sins. Very well, then, if our hearts are possessed by the Holy Spirit, ought we not to be making the like determined effort ?

> Give courage for the battle,
>   Give strength Thy foes to slay ;
> Give light to cheer the darkness,
>   Give grace from day to day ;
> Give rest amidst life's conflict,
>   Give peace when lions roar ;
> Give faith to fight with patience
>   Till fighting days are o'er.

The Son of man is come to seek and to save that which was lost.—Luke 19 : 10.

Your destiny is to seek and find and bring home the lost. You are to remember the forgotten ; to guide those who have wandered ; to snatch from final ruin those who have been scattered by the wolves of Hell and to find those who have not yet heard that the Shepherd gave His life for the sheep.

I want to say to every one : My comrade, what do you think and dream of ? What lies nearest to your heart ? Where is your ambition ? In what direction do your hopes lie ? Are you with the sheep which have been found, or is your heart outside with those which are lost ? They are all around you. There are whole flocks of them in every land, the Eastern nations especially teem with them. But you have no need to go to China, or the Sudan, or the Philippines. They are in your own town or city. They surround you in your own village. Nay, the wilderness in which they wander reaches right up to your door ! *Is your heart with them ?*

We're The Army that shall conquer
  As we go to seek the lost, and to bring them back to
    God ;
And His Salvation to every nation
  We will carry with the Fire and the Blood.

305

But He knoweth the way that I take : when He hath tried me, I shall come forth as gold.—Job 23 : 10.

Down with self and self-confidence, and up with God ! Surely that sums up the whole message of Job's experiences ! The strange dealings of God with him seem directed to bring him to an end of himself and his trust in merely temporal things, to subdue and purify and conquer his soul.

His friends treated it as though his afflictions were because of his *sin*, but we cannot forget that the very opening of the history shows Job to have been a ' perfect '—that is, a sincere—' man, and one that feared God and eschewed evil.' So that here we have the Almighty dealing with a man who was already *good*, and doing so in order that he may be refined and wholly sanctified.

I never think of this without reflecting upon the goodness of God in taking the trouble with us which He does to reach and cast out the roots of selfishness and false pride, and to lift us up to His holy hill.

> There is a holy hill of God,
>   Its heights by faith I see ;
> Now to ascend my soul aspires,
>   To leave earth's vanity.

> Lord, cleanse my hands and cleanse my heart,
>   All selfish aims I flee ;
> My faith reward, Thy love impart,
>   And let me dwell with Thee.

The churches . . . walking in the fear of the Lord, and in the comfort of the Holy Ghost, were multiplied. . . . The disciples were filled with . . . the Holy Ghost.—Acts 9 : 31 ; 13 : 52.

The great gift of the Holy Spirit is the gift of Love. By the Spirit-given Love comes the refined nature, comes the burning zeal, comes the fiery tongue. So that it is the Baptism of Love that is the greatest baptism of all.

The great Apostle wrote a splendid description of this ' love unfeigned ' in one of his letters. It comes home to us just now with a special force, if only because it was written at a time when he was suffering a living martydom for his Lord, and when the world was rocked, even as it is to-day, on the stormy waters of uncertainty and unrest. Here it is :

> ' Love suffereth long, and is kind ; Love envieth not ; Love vaunteth not itself, is not puffed up, doth not behave itself unseemly, seeketh not her own, is not easily provoked, thinketh no evil ; rejoiceth not in iniquity, but rejoiceth in the truth.'

> Jesus, Thine all-victorious love
> Shed in my heart abroad ;
> Then shall my feet no longer rove,
> Rooted and fixed in God.

> Refining Fire, go through my heart,
> Illuminate my soul ;
> Scatter Thy life through every part,
> And sanctify the whole.

307

They remembered that God was their rock, and . . . their redeemer. Nevertheless . . . their heart was not right with Him, neither were they stedfast in His covenant. But He, being full of compassion, forgave their iniquity.—Psalm 78 : 35–38.

No amount of enthusiasm or sacrifice will take the place of rightness, any more than glorious stonework on a building will compensate for a faulty plan or a shifty foundation.

Many are willing to make great sacrifices for God and The Army, and yet they fail in some perfectly simple matter of *rightness* in their own lives and experience. You know that when I speak thus of rightness I am not thinking of outward manifestations, but of inward things—of *being* right.

To begin with, there is the question which always arises, of clearing up old darkness, failure, mistake, sin. These things belong to the past, but they seriously affect the present if they have never been fully brought into the light.

> While in Thy light I stand,
>   My heart, I seem to see,
> Has failed to take from Thy own hand
>   The gifts it offers me.
> O Lord, Thy plenteous grace,
>   Thy wisdom and Thy power,
> I here proclaim before Thy face,
>   Can keep me every hour.

Christ also suffered for us, leaving us an example, that ye should follow His steps : . . . who, when He was reviled, reviled not again ; when He suffered, He threatened not.—1 Peter 2 : 21, 23.

Let us not complain because, like our Master, we are sometimes forsaken by those we would so gladly have kept with us in the struggle ; or because, like Him, we are sometimes betrayed, denied and denounced by those who promise so loudly to be true to the Cause ; or because, taking advantage of our rule of silence, they sometimes say of us what is not kind or even true. Let us submit, and take care to be true ourselves. Let us carry our own heavy cross as He carried His, and go steadily on with our great work of dying daily for those around us, as He went on with His. It will, no doubt, sometimes seem in the eyes of men a weak and foolish thing to do. But the foolishness of God is wiser than men, and the weakness of God is stronger than men. To Him be the glory !

How much will you suffer for Jesus ?
For the hate of His cause is the same,
Would you seek to gain by His sufferings,
Whilst shirking to share in His shame ?

Seeing then that all these things shall be dissolved, what manner of persons ought ye to be in all holy conversation and godliness, looking for and hasting unto the coming of the day of God, wherein the heavens being on fire shall be dissolved, and the elements shall melt with fervent heat ?—2 Peter 3 : 11–13.

What a contrast there is between the Worker and His work, between the Creator and the creature ! We see it in a thousand things ; but in none is it so manifest for the wayfaring man, or written so large upon the fading draperies of time, as in this : ' *They shall perish, but Thou remainest.*' And greater changes yet lie ahead. A universal instinct points to the time of the restitution of all things. The day of the Lord will come. ' As the lightning cometh out of the east, and shineth even unto the west ; so shall the coming of the Son of man be.'

What a combination of astounding catastrophes is here ! Earth and stars are to meet in awful shock ! Sun and moon to fail ! Cloud and sky to disappear ; the elements to melt with fervent heat—a world on fire ! But, above it all, the Lamb that was slain will take His place upon the Throne—unmoved, unchanged, amidst the tumult of dissolving worlds. *My* God, *my* Saviour, in *Thy* unchanging love *I put my trust.*

> Jesus, Thy Blood and righteousness
> My beauty are, my glorious dress ;
> 'Midst flaming worlds, in these arrayed,
> With joy shall I lift up my head.

God shall bring every work into judgment, with every secret thing, whether it be good, or whether it be evil.—Ecclesiastes 12 : 14.

It is impossible to overestimate the power of this truth as a motive for all that is holy and sincere in those who receive it. We see how it affected the Apostles. Opposed by all the forces of heathendom and standing, a tiny handful of simple souls, against a world infuriated against them by their witness, they ceaselessly appealed to it. On almost every record of their speakings and writings, especially of St. Paul's, we see that they actually live in the presence of the Great Day. The majesty of it is ever before them. It quickens their consciences. So it is with us of The Salvation Army. The great fact of our responsibility for our own actions and of our final accountability to Almighty God lifts the whole life we live up from the level of the cattle and the flies, on to the highway of men made in the image of God, coming forth from Him, charged with the accomplishment of His purposes and returning to Him to give our own account of the deeds we have done.

> To pray, and wait the hour,
>   The awful hour unknown,
> When robed in majesty and power
>   Thou shalt from Heaven come down,
> The immortal Son of Man,
>   To judge the human race,
> With all Thy Father's dazzling train,
>   With all Thy glorious grace.

Jesus . . . saith unto them, Have faith in God.
—Mark 11 : 22.

Jesus . . . said, Father, into Thy hands I commend My spirit.—Luke 23 : 46.

I trust in the mercy of God for ever.—Psalm 52 : 8.

The great lesson of this last word from the Cross of Jesus is the lesson of Abraham : that faith in the Father is the inner strength and secret of all true service.

Oh, dear comrade and friend, here is the crowning lesson of His life and death alike. Will you learn of Him ? In your extremity of grief or sorrow—if you are called to sorrow—will you not trust Him, and say, ' Father, into Thy hands I commend my bereaved and bleeding heart ' ? In your extremity of poverty —if you are called to poverty—oh, cry out to Him, ' Father, into Thy hands I commend my home, my dear ones.' In your extremity of shame and humiliation—arising, maybe, from the injustice and neglect of others—let your heart say in humble faith, ' Father, into Thy hands I commend my reputation, my honour, my all.' In your extremity of weakness and pain— if you are called to suffer weakness or pain—cry out in faith, ' Father, into Thy hands I commend this, my poor worn and weary frame.' In your extremity of loneliness and heart-separation from all you love for Christ's sake, if that be the path you tread, will you not say to your Lord, ' Father, into Thy hands I commend my future, my life ; lead Thou me on ? '

He was oppressed, and He was afflicted, yet He opened not His mouth : He is brought as a lamb to the slaughter, and as a sheep before her shearers is dumb, so He openeth not His mouth.—Isaiah 53 : 7.

Is it not that there was a passive side to our wonderful Saviour's nature ? That, together with the abundant life, the ceaseless conflict, and the untiring labour for others, there was this also in Him —this silent, submitting, patient grace of endurance. Do we not see that in Him (and therefore it may be so in us) the two things do and did go together ; the spirit of conflict with sin—the spirit of most desperate antagonism to and love of encounter with wickedness, dashing itself against evil ; and also the other—the patient humiliation of an utmost meekness, the gentleness and silence of a mind and heart really united with the Father's will and at rest in Him ?

> Oh, that I as a little child
>   May follow Thee, and never rest
> Till sweetly Thou hast breathed Thy mild
>   And lowly mind into my breast !
> Nor ever may we parted be
> Till I am one, my Lord, with Thee.

Take, my brethren, the prophets, who have spoken in the name of the Lord, for an example of suffering affliction. . . . Behold, we count them happy which endure.—James 5 : 10, 11.

Rejoice with them that do rejoice, and weep with them that weep.—Romans 12 : 15.

Here is a message of suffering, especially to us whose business is the winning of souls. Sorrow is permitted to us not only to call us to God ; not only to refine our spirits ; not only to strengthen our faith in the Friend who can never fail, but to make us perfect for the work of saving others, of reaching other hearts, of carrying the heavy burdens of others, of healing the wounds and woes around us.

Oh, you who are stricken and wounded, who may read these lines, let God's way be your way ! Let your griefs help you to the equipment, the tenderness, the completeness, which will enable you to take men and women by the hand and bring them by Christ's love unto Christ's glory.

> The light of His love shines the brighter
>   As it falls on paths of woe ;
> The toil of my work will grow lighter
>   As I stoop to raise the low.

Blessed is the man that endureth temptation : for when he is tried, he shall receive the crown of life, which the Lord hath promised to them that love Him.—James I : 12.

The forbidden tree in the Garden of Eden stood in the midst of the Garden—stood, that is, where all the paths would meet, and where Adam and Eve must pass that tree continually in the discharge of their daily duty. We are not now in the Garden, but temptation still appears in our very midst. It assails us where the roads meet in our lives, at the points we must so often pass, along the line of the duties that we cannot avoid.

And we may not complain. Without temptation we cannot know the triumph of the soul. It is the oft-recurring night which makes the returning day so sweet and so welcome. It is the hour of dangerous conflict which in due time gives the glory to the victor's honours. It is out of the hottest fire there comes the purest metal. This is that of which the Apostle speaks with the instinct of the highest wisdom, when he bids us ' count it all joy when ye fall into divers temptations.'

> Sometimes I'm tried with toil and care,
>   Sometimes I'm weak and worn,
> Sometimes it looks so dark everywhere,
>   Instead of the rose the thorn ;
> These are the times, when tempted sore,
>   A voice in my ear doth speak :
> Unsheathe thy sword, there's victory before !
>   Thy Saviour is mighty to keep.

John seeth Jesus . . , and saith, Behold the Lamb of God, which taketh away the sin of the world.—John 1 : 29.

The horrors and villainies of the war are only a kind of quick world-view, a view that is on a large scale, of what is going on all the time in the individual lives of those around us in every land. I do not, of course, say that sin is always manifested in all men after the manner in which we are able to view it just now. But in some way in every man it works toward the same end, comes at length to exactly the same spot—death and the disapproval and condemnation of God.

There are, there can be, no exceptions to this law. Sin is like some diseases of the body—once the poison has entered the system, no matter to what class the sufferer belongs, high or low, young or old, unless the horrid thing can be got out again, it goes steadily forward in its deadly work of disorganization and destruction to corruption and physical death.

My dying Saviour and my God,
   Fountain for guilt and sin,
Sprinkle me ever with Thy Blood,
   And cleanse, and keep me clean.

Greater love hath no man than this, that a man lay down his life for his friends. . . . These things I command you, that ye love one another. . . . Remember the word that I said unto you, The servant is not greater than his lord. If they have persecuted Me, they will also persecute you. —John 15 : 13, 17, 20.

' And the grace of God was upon Him.' Here was the promise of that entire sacrifice for men which culminated when a man cried out to Him on the cross : ' He saved others ; Himself He cannot save.' It is ever thus that God repeats Himself. When we are ready to be offered up for the blessing and saving of others, then grace will come upon us for the struggle as it came upon Him. When Christ formed in us finds free course for all His mind and all His passion ; when our eyes are opened to the great purposes of His life in the Salvation of the whole world ; and when we hear, through Him, the cry of those for whom He was born, and for whom He died, God will pour out on us grace to send us forth—grace sufficient, grace abundant, grace triumphant. Have you come to this ? Can you say He is thus dwelling in you and working in you, to will and to do of His good pleasure ?

Offences will come : but woe unto him, through whom they come ! It were better for him that a millstone were hanged about his neck, and he cast into the sea, than that he should offend one of these little ones. Take heed to yourselves : if thy brother trespass against thee, rebuke him ; and if he repent, forgive him.—Luke 17 : 1–3.

Every one of us is a God-appointed keeper of some other or others. We cannot escape from the obligation if we would. It is one of the great facts of human life. I *am* my brother's keeper.

Cain's conscience betrayed him when God spoke to him. In spite of the ready lie that was upon his lips when he said, ' I know nothing about it,' his conscience asserted itself and made him bring forward that other question about being his brother's keeper ; for, of course, if he were, that made the crime a hundred times worse, and increased his guilt and agony so much the more.

So now, the shame and sorrow and withering remorse which come from leading away from God, by word or act or example, even one of those who were entrusted to our care and love, cannot be measured or described.

> Help us to build each other up,
>   Our little stock improve :
> Increase our faith, confirm our hope,
>   And perfect us in love.

Daniel blessed the God of heaven . . . and said,
. . . He knoweth what is in the darkness, and the
light dwelleth with Him.—Daniel 2 : 19, 20, 22.
What time I am afraid, I will trust in Thee.
—Psalm 56 : 3.

Life's heaviest blows often come most unexpectedly.
Death appears, and our astonishment is even greater
than our grief.   Losses arise, and we are petrified
with surprise as our treasure disappears in the most
unlikely direction.   Friends or comrades fail us and
amazement almost chokes us.   Indeed it is true that
we know not the depth of any heart, we know not
what a day may bring forth.

Ah, do you expect to understand all God's ways
with you ?   Do you want a reason for every dis-
pensation, and explanation of every mystery before
you can trust Him ?   It is the darkness which makes
Faith a reality.   It is the ignorance which proves the
committal of the soul.

> ' The steps of faith
> Fall on the seeming void,
> And find the Rock beneath.'

Have mercy upon me, O Lord, for I am in trouble : . . . for I have heard the slander of many : . . . But I trusted in Thee, O Lord : I said . . . My times are in Thy hand.—Psalm 31 : 9, 13–15.

Slander is, in fact, a kind of pestilence that walketh in darkness, spreading its foul contagion by whispers and innuendoes, shady tales, doubtful hearsays, and the under chatter of spite and hatred. While it can run its course amid such favourable surroundings, it is often dangerous ; the moment it is compelled to face the day, and the slanderers can be tracked and tackled with the truth, it loses much of its attraction and most of its power.

. . . Be no party to any evil-speaking about any-one ; resolutely refuse to listen to a word that is un-kind until you have made it clear that you will report everything to the person condemned, and bring his slanderers to repeat their story before his face. Make no exception to this rule ; have done with the whole pestilential business except on these terms. Do unto others as you would that they should do unto you. Nothing that we can do in our own defence will be half so effective as what He will do, if we trust God and go on with His work, assured that He knows.

Put on therefore, as the elect of God, holy and beloved, . . . kindness, humbleness of mind, meekness, . . . forbearing one another, . . . forgiving one another . . . : even as Christ forgave you, so also do ye.—Colossians 3 : 12, 13.

Kindness is generally associated with small things. Do not think less of it on that account, for life is chiefly made up of little things. Many people, I think, would like to show kindness to others in great matters, or on a vast scale ; but then great matters only befall any of us now and then, while in many people's lives there is nothing that we can rightly term great. Kindness, therefore, must come into the little things, if at all. Do not, then, delay an hour the kind words and deeds that you can scatter around you. Small as they may seem, believe me, they are more important than your teaching—they will carry with them an influence for good in this world which cannot be exaggerated, and they will help to make the happiness of heaven for you.

> Oh, there's joy in every heart
>   When there's love at home ;
> There's a smile on every face
>   When there's love at home ;
> Voices have a kindly sound,
> Happiness beams all around,
> Peace and gentleness abound
>   When there's love at home.

I, even I, am the Lord ; and beside Me there is no saviour.—Isaiah 43 : 11, 12.

The Son of man hath power upon earth to forgive sins.—Luke 5 : 24.

It is God who saves. Nothing is so fatal to love, especially to love for the worst ; nothing is so ruinous to faith, especially faith for ourselves—as the introduction of any question or quibble as to this great truth.

Without God ye can do nothing. And this is the true word for to-day. Disorder, rebellion, corruption, uncleanliness, hatred—these are the chaotic elements into which man has been reduced by sin. These, therefore, are the materials out of which or in spite of which he must be made over again. And without God we can do nothing. Let there be no uncertainty here. Whatever other people may think about education and civilization and like human efforts, let there be no shadow of doubt in any Salvationist's mind as to the uttermost uselessness and hopelessness of any and every other remedy or palliative for fallen men, but *God*.

> There is a green hill far away,
>   Without a city wall,
> Where the dear Lord was crucified,
>   Who died to save us all.
>
> He died that we might be forgiven,
>   He died to make us good,
> That we might go at last to Heaven,
>   Saved by His precious Blood.

**I know the thoughts that I think toward you,
saith the Lord, thoughts of peace, and not of evil
. . . Call upon Me, and . . . pray unto Me, and I
will hearken unto you.**—Jeremiah 29 : 11, 12.

One thing is certain : *God wants peace.* He has no
love of contention with the souls of men ; in fact, if
anything can disturb the harmony and felicity of
God's own nature it must be the realization that His
own children are at war with Him. But, earnestly as
He desires it, there can only be peace with God on
certain conditions.

Those who want peace must ask for it ; and they
must ask for it with sincerity. God will not force His
favours on any one, nor will He listen to proposals
that are not honest and true. He hates make-beliefs.
If any man really seeks to be at peace with Him, then
He is ready to receive and reason with that man.
But He will not listen, He will not even look to a
man, let alone give Him peace, unless he will turn
away from every sham and come ' humble and
contrite ' to His feet.

> Joy, freedom, peace and ceaseless blessing,
>   All, all for thee,
> If, while your weakness still confessing,
>   To your Redeemer you flee.

323

O Lord, rebuke me not in Thy wrath : neither chasten me in Thy hot displeasure. For Thine arrows stick fast in me, and Thy hand presseth me sore ; . . . neither is there any rest in my bones because of my sin.—Psalm 38 : 1–3.

We also joy in God through our Lord Jesus Christ, by whom we have now received the atonement.—Romans 5 : 11.

The inward consciousness of approval in doing right, and the sense of condemnation in doing wrong, are sure signs of the presence of God. The simplest know something of these experiences. They are common to every class. The discomfort, the regret, the fear, the pain, sometimes the loathing which follows disobedience—what is it ? It is a manifestation of God and of His loving dealing with the soul. It reveals Him stirring with repulsion or anger or sorrow within us. And the opposite also—joy and peace in doing right—the assurance of approval and reward—what are these ? They are really the Spirit of God within us, lighting up our nature and shedding abroad His own joy in us.

> Oh, may the least omission pain
> My well-instructed soul,
> And drive me to the Blood again,
> Which makes the wounded whole.

**He that covereth his sins shall not prosper : but
whoso confesseth and forsaketh them shall have
mercy.**—Proverbs 28 : 13.
**If we confess our sins, He is faithful and just to
forgive us our sins.**—1 John 1 : 9.

Men and women who want peace with God must
render up what they have wrongfully taken from
Him. They have robbed Him, and there is no hope
of peace until they return to Him what they un-
lawfully took from Him—so far as it is in their power
to do so.

And more than this, God will only make peace with
those who act upon this principle of restitution
toward their fellows. If a man has filched his master's
money or cheated his servant—if he has deceived one
who trusted him—if he has wronged his wife or
defrauded his children, or oppressed the poor—he
cannot expect to have peace with God until, so far
as it is in his power to do it, he has made reparation
for the wrong. Let him give up his ill-gotten gain.
Let him set to work to earn what is needed to restore
that which he has taken away. Let him, at least,
acknowledge his sin and seek forgiveness at the hands
of those he has injured.

There can be no peace with God without restitution
and reparation for the abominable things of the past,
if restitution and reparation are within our power.

Praise the Lord, O my soul ; and forget not all His benefits, who forgiveth, . . . healeth, . . . saveth, . . . and crowneth thee with mercy and lovingkindness. — Psalm 103 : 2–4 ; Prayer Book Version.

Nicodemus . . . came to Jesus by night, and said unto Him, . . . no man can do these miracles that Thou doest, except God be with him. — John 3 : 1, 2.

A miracle is the testimony of God ; it is His own special witness to His own power. For example, we put a tiny seed into the ground, and in a few weeks it becomes a strong plant bearing a hundred or a thousand seeds ; but how this change has come about we do not know. We know that the mighty thing we call electricity is collected, so that it may be used for our benefit, but what it *is* is hidden from us. Because, however, these wonders are going on around us all the time, according to a system of things with which we have become familiar, they make but little impression upon us.

Now a miracle, being something out of the usual course and procedure, although it may not in itself be any more wonderful than some of the marvels we see every day, does, by its very strangeness and suddenness, compel us, in a special way, to acknowledge that it *is* the work of God.

> God moves in a mysterious way
> His wonders to perform ;
> He plants His footsteps on the sea
> And rides upon the storm.

As ye have therefore received Christ Jesus the Lord, so walk ye in Him : rooted and built up in Him, and stablished in the faith, . . . for in Him dwelleth all the fulness of the Godhead bodily, And ye are complete in Him.—Colossians 2 : 6, 7, 9, 10.

It is this manifestation of Jesus in His people for which the Apostle prays, ' My little children, of whom I travail in birth again until Christ be formed in you.' Nothing less will satisfy him, because he knew that nothing less will prevail against the power of the world, the flesh and the Devil, in any human heart. ' Christ formed in you,' Christ born again in them— that is his agonized prayer, his one hope for them.

In the workshops of human effort, no instruments, no skill, no motive power exists for the formation and development of character apart from the energizing vitality of God's Spirit dwelling in us. He is the indispensable foundation of any goodness or wisdom or beauty that can last. Purity begins and ends in Him. Faith finds her author and finisher in Him. Truth, which is the beauty of the soul, is but a reflection of His image, and love has no being but in Him. Let Him in !

> I give my heart to Thee,
> Thy dwelling-place to be ;
>   I want Thee ever in my heart ;
> Oh ! live Thy life in me !

Ye are My witnesses, saith the Lord, that I am God. Yea, before the day was I am He.—Isaiah 43 : 12, 13.
Be not thou . . . ashamed of the testimony of our Lord.—2 Timothy 1 : 8.

How great is the duty of witnessing for Christ, even among those who are quite unprepared to receive our testimony ! But how much greater that responsibility becomes when we know that all around us are those who actually expect that we shall make some effort to enforce the silent testimony of our uniform, or other mark of our association with The Army, by witnessing to the power of God in our lives !

' Why,' asked a fellow-passenger of a Salvationist on the railway the other day, as he put down his newspaper, ' why do you not speak to me about my soul ? ' From the moment he had seen the man in uniform enter the compartment he had been expecting the summons, and as it did not come he invited it.

> Wherever I may go,
>   Wherever I may stay,
> Whatever I may think,
>   And whatever I may say ;
> When I sing, when I speak,
>   When I preach or when I pray,
> I'll do it for the honour of King Jesus !

Do not err, my beloved . . . Every good gift and every perfect gift is from above, and cometh down from the Father.—James 1 : 16, 17.

The moment we really think of God at all we think of goodness, of the flowing fountain of all that belongs to goodness, of the over-flowing source of everything that is generous and benevolent. We think of One who is sending His rain alike upon the just and the unjust, upon the evil and the good, and making His mercy flow to all the generations of men.

Any other kind of God than this would really be repugnant to our whole notion of what is Divine. The God our hearts need for the bestowal of our love and trust and service, the God for whom we would be willing to suffer, the God for whom some would even be willing to die, must be the generous Being from whom there flows that loving stream of good toward all. Yes, this is the God we adore—the great Giver.

> This, this is the God we adore,
>   Our faithful unchangeable Friend,
> Whose love is as great as His power
>   And knows neither measure nor end.
>
> 'Tis Jesus, the First and the Last,
>   Whose Spirit shall guide us safe home ;
> We'll praise Him for all that is past
>   And trust Him for all that's to come.

Moses and Aaron among His priests, and Samuel among them that call upon His name ; they called upon the Lord, and He answered them.—Psalm 99 : 6.

Be careful for nothing ; but in every thing by prayer and supplication with thanksgiving let your requests be made known unto God.—Philippians 4 : 6.

Prayer is the act of petitioning God for those things which we cannot obtain without His co-operation or intervention. It is not merely thinking about God. It is not merely seeking His will. It is not merely hoping for God's help. Prayer is something more— it is asking Him for what we want.

Such asking is a perfectly usual and natural condition for us. Saved and unsaved alike, we know that day by day, from the cradle to the grave, men are accustomed to ask from their fellows what they need. And so with God ; prayer is asking Him for something which we feel we need and which He can give, and there is absolutely nothing unnatural or unreasonable in it. It seems to be the expression of a universal instinct, for, except where men have become utterly forgetful of God, all peoples pray to something —some to the living God, some to a representation of what they believe to be a God.

One thing stands out beyond dispute, that God's people of every age and of every name and creed have believed that they have received from Him answers to their prayers.

Jesus, moved with compassion, put forth His hand, and touched him, and saith unto him, I will ; be thou clean.—Mark 1 : 41.

Of some have compassion, . . . and others save with fear, pulling them out of the fire.—Jude 22, 23.

The enemy of souls is a very real enemy—a very cruel foe. He pays no attention to pity or weakness. Sin and Satan regard neither age nor sex, neither class nor condition. When they can, they sink all alike in that dark ocean of eternal night on which no ray of hope may ever fall and from whose dark waters no traveller returns.

My comrades, what shall we do about the wounded souls around us who are in this awful peril ? There can be only one answer—*Let us rush to the rescue !*

> Have you heard the voice of weeping ?
>   Have you heard the wail of woe ?
> Have you seen the fearful reaping
>   Of a soul that sinks below ?
> Rouse, then, who by Christ are freed,
> Heed, oh, heed the world's great need ;
> To save the lost, like Him who saved you,
>   Forward speed !

For ye yourselves are taught of God to love. —1 Thessalonians 4 : 9.

He first loved us.—1 John 4 : 19.

Love—the great driving force of our warfare—is from God. It is not only God-like, but it springs from Him,—begins in His nature and thence spreads to ours, and from us spreads abroad again to others. This is what makes it so infinitely valuable for us to know with the assurance of certainty that God loves us—that He loves us because it is His nature to love, just as it is the nature of the sun to give heat and light. Loving us is just being God.

Do we realize how lovingly and generously God feels toward us ? Do we rest on that love and hold fast to it ? Do we say, ' I am loved of God, unworthy though I be, poor though I am ; yea, though I am lean and weak in the great qualities of His nature. When I forget Him, He does not forget me. I am an unprofitable servant even at the best. And yet my God does not overlook me or my needs—He surrounds me with His mercy—He holds me in the hollow of His hand and will hold me there so long as love can do me good.'

> One there is above all others ;
> Oh, how He loves !
> His is love beyond a brother's ;
> Oh, how He loves !
> Earthly friends may fail and leave us,
> One day kind, the next deceive us ;
> But this Friend will never leave us ;
> Oh, how He loves !

Let your light so shine before men, that they may see your good works, and glorify your Father which is in heaven.—Matthew 5 : 16.

Kindness is to be shown to others whether they show kindness in return or not. Like the rain, it descends upon just and unjust, upon the thankful and the thankless. It is a great mistake to suppose that we are to wait until we discover whether our acts of kindness will be welcomed or rejected. Never mind though some of them are not welcomed at the moment ; even though they only call forth unkindness then, they will bring forth fruit hereafter. I know of one in our ranks who, when a giddy worldling, was touched by seeing a Salvationist stop in the muddy street one day and pick up a little child that had fallen down and hurt itself. The kindness, of which the Captain saw no fruit, won that soul.

Surely, we are Christ's, sent forth to represent Him and His law to the world. Surely, we shall make manifest the kindness of our Father, who maketh His sun to shine upon the evil and the good.

**Be it known unto you all, . . . that by the name
of Jesus Christ of Nazareth, . . . even by Him
doth this man stand here before you whole. . . .
Neither is there salvation in any other : for there
is none other name under heaven given among
men, whereby we must be saved.**—Acts 4 : 10, 12.

We do not aspire to govern the world or, except
as to the influences of sympathy, even to participate
in its government. Nor do we wish to capture its
honours or its wealth, except so far as they may be
given us to further our work on its behalf. Thank
God we are outside its politics and independent of its
parties, of its statesmen and of its rulers. Nothing
the world has to give could induce The Army to part
with one shred of its own hallowed past or one
particle of the truths for which it stands or one duty
which it holds to be so sacred. No, what we want
with the world is to save it—to make all men see that
the only Salvation from their miseries is the Salvation
which begins with the forgiveness of sin by the Cross
of Jesus and goes forward to the building and victory
of a holy character against the day when God shall
judge us all by that Man whom He hath ordained.

> Salvation ! Sing Salvation !
>   Was e'er so grand a theme ?
> Sing on till every nation
>   Shall hear of Calvary's stream.
> Sing out the tidings glorious,
>   That ' God so loved the world,'
> Till Christ shall be victorious
>   And Hell be backward hurled.

**He said unto them, O fools, and slow of heart to
believe.**—Luke 24 : 25.

**Then saith He to Thomas, . . . be not faithless,
but believing.**—John 20 : 27.

Apart from the great fact of the Resurrection itself,
nothing in the whole story is more appealing to our
hearts than Jesus Christ's state of mind toward those
who had forsaken and left Him on the eve of His
crucifixion and death. It is revealed with wonderful
directness in the simple and yet lucid messages He
sent to them as the very first result of His re-appearance in the haunts of men. And we can see it also in
the reception He gave to some of them. Whether,
like Simon Peter and John at the grave, or Cleopas
and the other on the way to Emmaus, or Thomas and
the rest in the room with the closed doors, He met
them with an infinite patience, and gave them a
confidence that must have seemed overwhelmingly
wonderful when they reflected on the want of faith
in Him which He had found in them.

> Jesus Christ is now amongst us ;
>   Lord, I believe !
> He is here to bless and save us ;
>   Lord, I believe !
> He is loving, kind and gracious,
> And His Blood is efficacious :
> Every soul may feel Him precious ;
>   Lord, I believe !

Hereby we know that He abideth in us, by the Spirit which He hath given us.—1 John 3 : 24.

Before all else you will know that the new life entrusted to you is Divine ; that God has entered into your heart to make all things new. It is just the absence of this assurance which stamps so much of the Christianity of the present day as, in effect, a religion without God. Its professors have no certainty!

Salvation is of the Lord, and so is the assurance of it. Where there is the life of God, there will be His witness even in the heart of the weakest and slowest servant of all His household. If you are not clear about this first evidence of your Lord's coming, let me counsel you that there is something wrong. If Christ be formed in you, you will assuredly know it *beyond the power of men or devils to make you doubt.*

> To the heart where strife was reigning
> Jesus spake—dissension ceased ;
> From the bonds, so long enchaining,
> He hath wondrously released.
> Pardon full for past transgression,
> Grace for every time of need :
> With such treasure in possession,
> Happy is my lot indeed.

What ? know ye not that your body is the temple of the Holy Ghost which is in you, which ye have of God, and ye are not your own ? . . . therefore glorify God in your body, and in your spirit, which are God's.—1 Corinthians 6 : 19, 20.

It is when the body is full of youthful vigour and strength that all the natural appetites are most powerful and, therefore, most in need of government and control. It is then, in the spring-time of life, when the heart is fresh and innocent, when the mind is free from the harassing memory of wasted years, that evil works its most awful ravages. To be old and wicked, to be old and impure, to be old and the slave of your own body—that is bad, pitiably bad and sad. But to be young, and yet be unable to say No to your passions ; to be young and bright and strong, and with life before you, and yet to be held in degrading bondage to secret sin or to secret thoughts that you hate when you remember them in the daylight—that is worse still and sadder still. If it is not more hateful to God, it is certainly more ruinous to the soul and more destructive to the body. Impurity is the high road to death and hell.

> Henceforth may no unclean delight
> Divide this consecrated soul ;
> Possess it, Thou who hast the right,
> As Lord and Master of the whole.

337

Remember the words of the Lord Jesus, how He said, It is more blessed to give than to receive. —Acts 20 : 35.

Peter said, Silver and gold have I none ; but such as I have give I.—Acts 3 : 6.

We say that we are the children of God, not only because we are the work of His hands, but because we are united with Him through faith in the sacrifice— that is, the gift—of His dear Son. Ought not the children to resemble the Parent ? How, then, can we fairly claim our relationship unless there be something also of this wonderful giving nature in us ? How can we consider ourselves to belong to His family or to be really in the enjoyment of His favour unless, up to the measure of our ability and so far as we have been entrusted with what can be bestowed, we are givers also ?

> From each meagre storehouse,
>   From each heart and home,
> From rich heaps of plenty
>   More and more shall come ;
> Love for help is seeking,
>   Knocking at each door,
> All the world with gladness
>   Giving more and more.

I said, Lord, be merciful unto me : heal my soul ; for I have sinned against Thee.—Psalm 41 : 4.
Jesus Christ, who gave Himself for our sins, that He might deliver us.—Galatians 1 : 3, 4.

The consciousness of sin is the most enduring fact of human experience. From generation to generation, from age to age, amidst the ceaseless changes which time brings to everything else, this one great fact persists, the condemning consciousness of sin. It appears with men in the cradle, and goes with them to the tomb ; without regard to race or language or creed it is ever with us.

All attempts to explain it away, to modify its miseries, to extract its sting—whether they have come from the party of unbelief or the party of education or the party of amusement, have failed. Whether we look amongst the most highly civilized peoples or amongst the lowest savages ; whether we look into the past history of mankind or into its present condition, there is the stupendous fact of sin and there is the incontrovertible fact that everywhere men are conscious of it.

> Jesus ! the name that charms our fears,
>   That bids our sorrows cease ;
> 'Tis music in the sinner's ears ;
>   'Tis life and health and peace.
>
> He breaks the power of cancelled sin,
>   He sets the prisoner free ;
> His Blood can make the foulest clean,
>   His Blood avails for me.

If any man among you seem to be religious, and bridleth not his tongue, . . . this man's religion is vain.—James 1 : 26.

Let the words of my mouth, and the meditation of my heart, be acceptable in Thy sight, O Lord, my strength, and my redeemer.—Psalm 19 : 14.

For the development of the life of God in their souls, people must learn so to school their tongues that their words shall glorify Him. Many know by experience how sensitive are those faculties of the soul by which we apprehend and realize the presence of the Holy Spirit within us, how easily the spiritual ear is dulled so that we do not hear, and the spiritual sight dimmed so that we cannot perceive Him. Nothing more readily tends to this than unfitting or thoughtless speech.

I cannot help feeling that many of those who have suffered painful failures in the life of Holiness would have been kept if they had been instructed so to train and discipline themselves that their speech should be always of grace seasoned with salt, and would have gone on in the way of faith and love.

> Direct, control, suggest, this day,
> All I may think or do or say :
> That all my powers, with all their might,
> In Thy sole glory may unite.

Jesus said : **I will not leave you comfortless : . . . because I live, ye shall live also.**—John 14 : 18, 19.
Fear not ; I am the first and the last : I am He that liveth, and was dead ; and, behold, I am alive for evermore . . . and have the keys of hell and of death.—Revelation 1 : 17, 18.

In truth the death of some *is* a mystery. It is better that we should say so than that we should profess to be able to account for what we do not understand. This mystery is often the great bitterness in the cup. To die when so young ! To die when so much needed ! To die so soon after beginning to live. To die in the presence of so great a task. Oh, why should it be ? How much of gloom and shadow has come down on hearts and households I have known from the persistency of that ' Why ? '—intensifying every repulsion for the hideous visitor, adding to every other the greatest of all its terrors—doubt.

In the presence of such doubts, has not the death of Jesus Christ something in it to charm away the fears of those who know Him ? Does it not say to us, ' I have passed on before ; I that speak in righteousness, mighty to save. At My girdle hang the keys of life and death. I, even I, was dead—but I am alive for evermore !

Yes ; this is the crowning fact. Whether we live, therefore, or die, we are the Lord's !

I meditate on all Thy works ; I muse on the work of Thy hands.—Psalm 143 : 5.

God . . , He that created the heavens, and stretched them out ; He that spread forth the earth, and that which cometh out of it—Isaiah 42 : 5.

This God is our God for ever and ever.—Psalm 48 : 14.

All I have said about enthusiasm and zeal in pursuit of the great objects for which we live, and their manifestation to the world, has also an application to our pursuit and knowledge of God Himself. Like all lovers, He loves those who seek Him with zeal and enthusiasm ! How it must give Him joy of heart to see us going about the world ever reminded of Him, ever recognizing and acknowledging Him. Seeing God in events, and saying : This is my God ! Seeing Him in the wonders of nature, and saying : This is my God ! Seeing Him in the outstretched heavens and the mighty seas, and saying : This is my God ! Seeing Him in the delivery of souls from the bondage of sin, and saying : This God is my God !

What joy to Him when He sees us holding all the treasures of life as His gifts, crying out daily in return for all He gives : ' O my Father, I thank Thee ! '

> Now thank we all our God,
>   With hearts and hands and voices,
> Who wondrous things hath done,
>   In whom His world rejoices ;
> Who from our mother's arms
>   Hath blessed us on our way
> With countless gifts of love,
>   And still is ours to-day.

I would ye should understand, brethren, that the things which happened unto me have fallen out rather unto the furtherance of the gospel ; so that my bonds in Christ are manifest in all the palace, and in all other places.—Philippians 1 : 12, 13.

I read lately of an old saint chained for weary years to a dungeon-wall, unable even to feed himself, whose testimony for Jesus was powerful to the deliverance of many of his persecutors. He was killed at last, lest, one by one, he should convert the jailers also who were employed to supply him with food.

Are you ' bound ' in some way ? Are you chained fast to some strange trial ? Are you appointed to serve in what seems like a den of beasts ? Are you under the compulsion of some injustice ? Are you made to feel helpless and useless without the support of those around you ? Ah, well, do not repine. Do not forget that God's call comes often—oh, so often to just such as you—to witness for Him in spite of ' these bonds,' to declare the truth, to dare to reprove sin. Above all, do not doubt your God. You may be very dependent to-day, but you may be more than victorious to-morrow.

343

I charge thee therefore before God, and the Lord Jesus Christ, who shall judge the quick and the dead at His appearing and His kingdom ; preach the word ; be instant in season, out of season ; reprove, rebuke, exhort.—2 Timothy 4 : 1, 2.

I am thinking of the mighty influence of personal contact with souls ; the great truth that those who walk with God bring a light with them which penetrates the darkened spirits of those to whom they witness, bringing to mind things that are hidden in the black past and discovering to men how they actually stand in the sight of the living God.

Use this method. Spread this light. Plunge into attack whenever you have the chance, whether in the palace or the prison, in the saloon or the slum, whether in dealing with those you are accustomed to meet or with the stranger. Whether in season or out of season, be faithful. Attack, and again attack, and you will find that around you are multitudes who, behind the mask of an ordinary life of work, or pleasure, of sickness or something else, are hungering for they know not what, conscious of sin, dissatisfied and wretched and condemned.

> I will spread the fame abroad
> Of the mercy of my Lord,
> That other souls to God may be restored
> Through the Blood of my Redeemer.

Jesus said . . , I came down from heaven, not to do Mine own will, but the will of Him that sent Me. . . . And this is the will of Him that sent Me, that every one which seeth the Son, and believeth on Him, may have everlasting life : and I will raise him up at the last day.—John 6 : 35, 38, 40.

Ours must be a practical and present care. We must come right down to the souls we want to save, as our Master did. Our own blessedness and peace must stand aside for the company of those on whom the curse and conflicts of sin have fallen. We may truly long to be with Christ in His Heavenly Kingdom, and, as Paul says, feel that it is far better ; but we must be ready to be with those who have no Christ, and know no Heaven. Our sweetest songs must be the songs we sing to those who cannot sing. Our deepest joy must be joy with the Father when the prodigals come home from the far country of backsliding and sin.

> Can we, whose souls are lighted
>   With wisdom from on high,
> Can we to men benighted,
>   The lamp of Life deny ?
> Salvation ! oh, Salvation !
>   The joyful sound proclaim,
> Till each remotest nation
>   Has learnt our Saviour's name.

345

We trust in the living God, who is the Saviour of all.—1 Timothy 4 : 10.

The fact is, that mere religiousness is nothing. Churchism and sacramentalism, chapelism and pulpitism, Salvation Armyism—or, if you like to use a hard word, ecclesiasticism—are all nothing. The world will not be blessed and saved by these things without another thing which is far more important than they are—nay, which is more important than all of them put together. It is this : that only Jesus Christ—the Son of Man, the Son of God—giving His Blood on the Cross, showing His power over the grave, making Himself known to men, can change them in their purpose and desire and life.

Yes, that is it ! Christ the Saviour ! Not merely Christ the Helper of the poor, or the Feeder of the hungry, or the Father of the prodigals, or the Brother of the Magdalene, or the Comfort of the sorrowful ; but Christ the Saviour from condemnation and guilt, from stains and filth, from the love and power and presence of sin.

Precious Lamb, by God appointed,
   All our sins on Thee were laid ;
By almighty love anointed,
   Thou hast full atonement made.
All Thy people are forgiven
   Through the virtue of Thy Blood ;
Opened is the gate of Heaven,
   Peace is made 'twixt man and God.

346

Jesus . . . said, . . . I pray not that Thou shouldest take them out of the world, but that Thou shouldest keep them from the evil. . . . Sanctify them through Thy truth.—John 17 : 1, 15, 17.

God . . . sanctify you wholly ; . . . your whole spirit and body be preserved blameless.—1 Thessalonians 5 : 23.

God's plan is not to tinker with symptoms or fruits, but to deal with the disease itself, purifying the heart by faith and sanctifying it wholly, so that the whole spirit and soul and body may be preserved blameless in the sight of God. That is Full Salvation.

When God sanctifies a man or woman He neither destroys the powers of the body nor prohibits their lawful exercise. What He does do is, He cleanses them and restricts their exercise to their proper purposes and occasions.

The nature of sanctified man remains wholly human—not mutilated or emasculated nature, but a nature sanctified and controlled by the indwelling presence and government of the Spirit of God. So possessed and controlled, every faculty of his body, soul and spirit can be exercised in purity and to the glory of God. Our God is on high. He will come down to men, but He will lift men up to Himself.

Can any hide himself in secret places that I shall not see him ? saith the Lord. . . . Is not My word like as a fire ?—Jeremiah 23 : 24, 29.

Blessed are they that hear the word of God, and keep it.—Luke 11 : 28.

Man is a thinking creature, and think he must ! Above all, think about himself, about his future, his past. A great French writer—and not a Christian writer—says, ' There is a spectacle grander than the ocean, and that is the conscience. After many conflicts man yields to that mysterious power which says to him, " Think." One can no more prevent the mind from returning to an idea than the sea from returning to a shore. With the sailor this is called " the tide." With the guilty it is called " remorse." God, by a universal law, upheaves the soul as well as the ocean.'

On these unerring and resistless tides He sends into the human soul His messages. He visits men. He arouses them. He compels their attention. In His providence, by acts of mercy and judgment, by sorrow and loss, by stricken days and bitter nights—to prick them to the heart—in order to lead them to recognize and to confess and to turn away from sin !

> All that I was, my sin, my guilt,
>   My death, was all mine own ;
> All that I am, I owe to Thee,
>   My gracious God, alone.
>
> The grace that made me feel my sin,
>   Bade me in Christ believe ;
> Then, in believing, peace I found,
>   And now in Christ I live.

For this thing I besought the Lord thrice, that it might depart from me. And He said unto me, My grace is sufficient for thee : for My strength is made perfect in weakness.—2 Corinthians 12 : 8, 9.

I do not know what that sore trial was which Paul called the ' thorn in the flesh.' It may have been some physical infirmity, it may have been some weakness or insufficiency intimately associated with his spiritual life and with his work as an Apostle. All we know is that he cried to God thrice that it might be removed. But it was not removed. On the contrary, instead of being taken away, it received a kind of confirmation from God as a part of the Apostle's life. He said, in other words, Paul was to be made strong while in his weakness ; he was to struggle on, conquering, not by reason of his strength, not by reason of miracle-workings, transforming his nature, but conquering by simple, child-like, common-place faith in the ever-present power of his Saviour's grace.

> Oh, for trust that brings the triumph
>   When defeat seems strangely near !
> Oh, for faith that changes fighting
>   Into victory's ringing cheer—
>   Faith triumphant,
>   Knowing not defeat or fear !

But I know you, that ye have not the love of God in you.—John 5 : 42.

Whatsoever ye do in word or deed, do all in the name of the Lord Jesus.—Colossians 3 : 17.

I see how possible it is to have a kind of charity toward one's fellow-men, expressing itself in humanity, in philanthropy, in sympathy and generosity, and yet to have no religion in the Bible meaning of the term ; that a man might lay down his life or give his body to be burned for his neighbour or his country, and yet be without one spark of God's life and God's grace. It has been a sheet-anchor to me during these forty years, amid the problems arising out of our dealings with the outside world, with governments and communities who would press The Army into philanthropic and social work, that I have seen clearly that the world's great need was not the so-called 'religion of humanity,' but the humanity of religion —the religion of Jesus Christ.

> For His love that fills my soul,
>   For His gift of grace Divine,
> He shall have my life, my all,
>   And His will henceforth is mine.
> Where He calls me, I will go,
>   Serving Him who for me died ;
> Only Jesus will I know—
>   Jesus crucified.

The fear of the Lord is to hate evil.—Proverbs 8 : 13.

What unnumbered woes, what dreadful forebodings, what appalling enmities against goodness and against God, the life of man under his delusions has to show ! What a face he has to put upon the world ! What means of self-indulgence, what instruments of hatred, cruelty and violence, what instigations and incitements to shameful appetite and abominable pleasures he has invented and contrived !

* * *

Oh, sin, arch-enemy of man ; we hate it ! Yes, and will ! Here afresh we dedicate ourselves to this great mission of holy hatred ! The hate of selfishness ! The detestation of pride and envy and hypocrisy ! The uttermost abhorrence of the destroying vices of the people ! The loathing of what is unclean ! Here is the true Gospel of Hate ! *The hate of sin.*

> Oh, may I love like Thee,
>   In all Thy footsteps tread ;
> Thou hatest all iniquity,
>   But nothing Thou hast made.
> Oh ! may I learn the art
>   With meekness to reprove,
> To hate the sin with all my heart,
>   But still the sinner love.

I have chosen thee in the furnace of affliction.
—Isaiah 48 : 10.
**Knowing this, that the trying of your faith
worketh patience. But let patience have her
perfect work, that ye may be perfect and entire.**
—James 1 : 3, 4.

Here I find a word of help and courage and cheer
for you and me, my precious comrade. I am not sure
that you could receive any more valuable Christmas
gift than the full realization of this truth—that your
advance from the infancy to the manhood of your
life in God will not be hindered and delayed, but
rather will be helped and quickened by the storms
and trials, the conflicts and sufferings, which will
overtake you. As our dear Lord was made perfect
through suffering, so are His saints. We are ' chosen
in the furnace of affliction,' and often cast into it,
too ! And yet He who chooses all our changes
might have spared us every trial and conflict, and
taken us to victory without a battle, and to rest without a toil. But He knows better what will make us
men, and it is men He wants to glorify Him—men,
not babes.

> I'll go in the strength of the Lord
>   To conflicts which faith will require ;
> His grace, as my shield and reward,
>   My courage and zeal shall inspire.
> Since He gives the word of command,
>   To meet and encounter the foe,
> With His sword of truth in my hand
>   To suffer and triumph I'll go.

Who through faith . . . wrought righteousness, . . . out of weakness were made strong.—Hebrews 11 : 33, 34.

Many of the greatest of God's warriors have been very weak and feeble creatures physically. The history of the world teems with examples of great works accomplished for God and man by those whose flickering lives became literally the vital force of the services they rendered. Nor does this apply only to the past, for unto this very day we have constantly before our eyes the achievements of those who are the weak, the delicate. We have seen the shy, nervous, hesitating girl rise up, completely forgetting her weakness, while her appeals laid hold of the crowd. We have seen the heart crushed by personal grief, or worn by ceaseless care, readily and lovingly taking more and more on itself of others' griefs and cares. Faith has been the secret of it all. Faith in God, in duty, in the opportunity, in the future : above all, faith in the Divine Call.

Do you find anything of this kind in your experience ? Is it not sometimes too easily accepted as a reason for not doing some unpleasant duty, or for not facing some serious difficulty, that you are not well enough, or strong enough—in fact, that you are weak ? Was that the true reason ? Was not the real difficulty a want of faith ?

**God dealeth with you as with sons : for what son
is he whom the father chasteneth not ? . . . Now
no chastening for the present seemeth to be joyous,
but grievous : nevertheless afterward it yieldeth
the peaceable fruit of righteousness unto them
which are exercised thereby.**—Hebrews 12 : 7, 11.

Again and again I have seen how incomprehensible
are many of the trials of the righteous. We are called
on to suffer, and do not know why. Sorrows and
deprivations overtake us as they overtook Job, and
we question within ourselves, ' Can God really have
anything to do with this ? Now one lesson of Job's
experiences is just that—*God has to do with it !* He
is watching it. He is in the very centre of it. His
eye is on the fruit !

Here was the great mistake of Job's friends in
dealing with him. They did not see that the bereave-
ment and sorrow and poverty and suffering were all
to open Job's eyes, to show him the vanity and un-
reality of earthly things in comparison with the
spiritual, the *Divine*. Do not let *us* fall into that same
blunder in dealing with ourselves ! No matter how
unpleasant the chastening, nor how strangely it may
seem to wound us, God and His purpose are in it,
and His eye is upon the peaceable fruit.

> Art Thou not touched with human woe ?
>   Hath pity left the Son of Man ?
> Dost Thou not all our sorrows know,
>   Who hadst a share in all our pain ?

By the hands of the apostles were many signs and wonders wrought among the people.—Acts 5 : 12.

Add to your faith virtue ; . . . and to godliness . . . kindness.—2 Peter 1 : 5, 7.

Do not, for your own sake as well as for your Master's, move about amid your own people, or among those to whom God and The Army have given you entrance, as one who has little in common with them. Go into their houses, put your hand sometimes to their burdens, take a share in their toils, nurse their sick, weep with them that weep and rejoice with them that rejoice. Make them feel that it is your own religion, rather than the Army system, that has made you come to them. Let them see by your sympathy and kindness that love is the over-mastering influence in your life, the influence that has brought you to them. Compel them to turn to you as a warm-hearted unselfish example of the truths you preach. Let them feel that you are indeed come from God to take them by the hand, as far as may be, and lead them through this Vale of Tears to the City of Light and Rest.

> 'Mid the homes of want and woe,
>   Strangers to the living word,
> Let the Saviour's herald go,
>   Let the voice of hope be heard.

355

They could not enter in because of unbelief. Let us therefore fear, lest, a promise being left us of entering into His rest, any of you should seem to come short of it. For unto us was the gospel preached, as well as unto them : but the word preached did not profit them, not being mixed with faith in them that heard it. For we which have believed do enter into rest.—Hebrews 3 : 19 ; 4 : 1–3.

Is your heart a temple, set apart and separated from unclean things and from the world and the love of the world, and really made fit for the occupation of your Saviour, so that He is able to fulfil His great promise, ' I will dwell in you, and walk in you ' ?

> ' To come with grace and love,
> And never hence remove.'

Blessed be His Holy Name, that is the Sabbath of a Full Salvation. But this rest was only entered after the work—that is, the will—of God was done. His whole purpose had been completed. Everything was then according to His will. The disorder and the darkness were both gone. *That* is the only way to obtain rest in *your* world.

There's peace in believing, sweet peace to the soul,
To know that He maketh me perfectly whole ;
There's joy everlasting to feel His Blood flow,
'Tis life from the dead my Redeemer to know.

**Beware that thou forget not the Lord thy God, in
not keeping His commandments, . . . lest when
thou hast eaten and art full, and hast built goodly
houses, and dwelt therein ; . . . and thy silver
and thy gold is multiplied . . . ; then thine heart
be lifted up, and thou forget the Lord thy God.**
—Deuteronomy 8 : 11–14.

Nothing is much more astounding to those who
know the reality of evil and its terrible consequences
to the human spirit than to see multitudes of intelligent men eat and drink and dress, rise up and lie
down, go out and come in, get their gains and spend
them, and do it all as though they had no sin—as
though indeed they had no souls. They leave God to
Himself.

Pride, no doubt, has something to do with this
silence about sins, at any rate in some men. They
say they are not like others. They do not drink, or
blaspheme, or commit adultery, or cheat in business,
or tell lies. They do the best they can. They pay
their way. They are straight and decent. They are
kind to their families. . . . . They are well-meaning,
hoping people, but they never get beyond that.
They never confess their sins or cry shame upon
themselves for that greatest sin—leaving God out
of their lives.

> I'll keep well in mind how He bought me,
> I'll keep well in mind how He sought me ;
>   When tempted to leave Him,
>   Or stray, and so grieve Him,
> I'll think of His dying for me.

They saw the young child with Mary His mother, and fell down, and worshipped Him.—Matthew 2 : 11.

Christ . . . was crucified through weakness, yet He liveth by the power of God. For we also are weak . . , but we shall live with Him by the power of God.—2 Corinthians 13 : 3, 4.

What a service of imperishable worth to all the world was rendered by His mother in her loving care of Him ! That little Child was to become the greatest Example, the greatest Teacher, the greatest, the only Saviour, the greatest Healer of the sorrows of men, the greatest Benefactor, the greatest Ruler and King. Upon Him and upon His word, who lies there in His virgin mother's arms, dependent upon her breast for life and warmth, unnumbered multitudes were to rest their all for this life and the next—in the face of inexpressible agonies were to trust to Him their every hope.

Let not, then, your heart be troubled because you also are so dependent on others—so hedged in by your circumstances, so limited by sickness and pain, so incompetent through inexperience and ignorance, or that you are so compelled to stand and wait when you would fain rush on and do or dare for your Lord. All this may be even so, and yet you may be called to share in the same high vocation as your Saviour.

To day the Lord will appear unto you.—Leviticus
9 : 4.
**Adorn the doctrine of God our Saviour in all
things, For the grace of God that bringeth salvation hath appeared to all men.**—Titus 2 : 10, 11.

What is the history of man ? What is the story the
Bible has to tell ? What is the testimony of all time ?
That God has ever been speaking to man, opening now
his eyes and now his understanding and now his
heart, and making an everlastingly new revelation to
the soul that God in him is his sole hope of glory.
And His Christmas message to-day is still the same.
To you, if you are willing, Christ will come as really,
as sensibly, as wonderfully—nay, a thousand times
more so—as He came to Mary and to Bethlehem.
In truth, a second coming ; but in many and wonderful ways like unto the first.

Come in, my Lord, come in,
    And make my heart Thy home ;
Come in and cleanse my soul from sin,
    And dwell with me alone !
Thyself to me be given,
    In fullness of Thy love ;
Thyself alone wilt make my Heaven,
    Though all Thy gifts remove.

My Lord, Thou dost come in ;
    I feel it in my soul ;
I hear Thy words, my Saviour-King :
    ' Be every whit made whole ! '
Glory to God on high !
    Let Heaven and earth agree
My risen Christ to magnify
    For lo ! He lives with me.   W. B. B.

The angel of the Lord . . . said unto them, Fear not . . . For unto you is born this day . . . a Saviour, which is Christ the Lord.—Luke 2 : 9–12.

Jesus Christ . . . in whom we have redemption through His blood.—Ephesians 1 : 5, 7.

> Oh, may we keep and ponder in our mind
> God's wondrous love in saving lost mankind ;
> Trace we the Babe, who hath retrieved our loss,
> From His poor manger to His bitter cross ;
> Tread in His steps, assisted by His grace,
> Till man's first heavenly state again takes place.

If the Babe had not been laid in the manger, then the Man would not have been nailed to the tree, and the Lamb that was slain would not have taken His place on the Everlasting Throne. If, on the human side, our Redeemer's origin and circumstances were of the humblest and we are thus enabled to see His humanity, as it were, face to face, there was united with it the Divine nature ; so that as our doctrines say, ' He is truly and properly God, and He is truly and properly man.' Many mysteries meet at the side of that manger, some of them to remain mysteries till God Himself reveals them to our stronger vision in the world to come. But, blessed be God, some things that we cannot compass with our mental powers are very grateful to our hearts !

> ' How Thou canst love me as I am,
> Yet be the God Thou art,
> Is darkness to my intellect,
> But sunshine to my heart.'

And she brought forth her firstborn Son, and wrapped Him in swaddling clothes, and laid Him in a manger ; because there was no room for them in the inn.—Luke 2 : 7.

God . . . hath in these last days spoken unto us by His Son, whom He hath appointed heir of all things, by whom also He made the worlds. —Hebrews 1 : 1, 2.

Great weakness may be quite consistent with true greatness and goodness. It is unnecessary to dwell even for a moment on the weakness of the Infant Jesus. The Scripture has left no possible doubt about it.

Unable to speak, to walk, indeed to do anything for Himself—weak with all the weakness of the human race ; the Holy Child was laid in the manger hard by the beasts that perish.

And yet we know that there was the Divine Son, the express Image of the Father, the everlasting King, the Enthroned One, the Creator, ' without whom was not anything made that was made ' ! It is indeed a contrast which first astounds us and then compels our adoration and love. Our God is a consuming Fire—our God is a little Child. Holy, holy, holy, is the Lord of Hosts ; the whole earth is full of His glory—and yet He is there in fashion as a Babe for whom, in all His sweet innocence, they cannot find a room in the crowded inn.

**The disciple is not above his master, nor the
servant above his lord. It is enough for the
disciple that he be as his master, and the servant
as his lord.**—Matthew 10 : 24, 25.

Side by side with evidences of His Divinity, the
infancy and childhood of Jesus revealed His dependence and weakness ; that is, *the reality of His human
nature*. The first recorded act of His mother shows
us one aspect of that weakness after a fashion which
appeals to the tenderest recollections of the whole
human family, '*She wrapped Him in swaddling clothes*';
and then, as though to make for ever the perfection
of dependence, the history goes on, ' and laid Him in
a manger.' It is the perfect union of Him ' who was,
and is, and is to come,' with him who flourisheth as
the flower of the field ; the wind passeth over him,
and he is gone !

Even so may Christ be formed in you. The purity
and dignity of His life will be all the more wonderfully
glorious in the eyes of men and angels because it is
linked with dependence and trial and weakness and
sorrow. As it was at Nazareth, so it is now. Hand in
hand with Divinity walked hunger and weariness,
disappointment and toil. Did we think it would be
otherwise ? Did we, do we, sometimes wonder why
the road is so rough, the burden so heavy and the
sky so dark ? Is there an echo of murmuring at these
bonds, infirmities and drudgeries of daily duty and
common sorrow ?

Christ Jesus . . . took upon Him the form of a servant, and was made in the likeness of men.
—Philippians 2 : 5, 7.

The Divine condescension never appears so new and so real to us as when we stand at the side of this lowly cradle. Here are no high-sounding doctrines, no hard words, no terrible commands, no far-off thunders of a new Sinai, no rumblings of a coming Judgment. Here we see Jesus, and Jesus only. Jesus showing Himself in our very own flesh and blood ; submitting Himself to the weakness of our infirmities ; voluntarily clothing Himself with our ignorance, and making God the present tangible possession of the whole human family, bringing Him ' very nigh to us.' And, more than this, God joined in that Babe His great strength to our great nothingness ; He bound us to Himself ; He robed us, as it were, with Himself. Henceforth the Tabernacle of God is with men. Henceforth every one of us may be conscious of an inward Presence, of which we may say in holy joy : ' Angels and men before Him fall, and devils fear and fly.'

> I'll let Thy glorious life in me
>   Be seen in all my ways,
> Then always I shall be
>   A credit to Thy saving grace.

Behold, the angel of the Lord appeareth unto Joseph in a dream, saying, Arise, and take the young child and His mother, and flee into Egypt, . . . for Herod will seek the young child to destroy Him.—Matthew 2 : 13.

The scribes and Pharisees watched Him, whether He would heal on the sabbath day ; that they might find an accusation against Him.
—Luke 6 : 7.

Are you, dear friend, tempted to complain of your narrow surroundings, of your small opportunity to shine before others, or of a want of appreciation of your service and gifts and powers by those who should know you ? Oh, remember the Babe, and the long years of His condescension to men of low estate, to the cramped surroundings of the carpenter's shed and the sleepy Jewish village. Are you tried sometimes because you have to suffer the hatred or jealousy, secret or open, of those for whom you feel nothing but goodwill, and who perhaps once thought themselves happy in your friendship ? Well, in such hours, remember your Master. Try to call to mind something of the secret, as well as the open, bitterness of men, religious and irreligious alike, which began to haunt Him while yet in swaddling clothes and which haunted Him still all through His days.

> Let the world despise and leave me,
>   They have left my Saviour too ;
> Human hearts and looks deceive me,
>   Thou art not like them, untrue.

Let us not be weary in well doing : for in due season we shall reap, if we faint not.—Galatians 6 : 9.

In our hours of deepest trial the Devil often argues, ' It is only reasonable and natural that you should do this or that. You cannot go on for ever on this high road of self-denial and nothingness. It must come to an end some time ; let it come to an end now ; do as others do.' Yes, it is the old attack. The very same Devil adopting, under varying disguises, the very same tactics that he employed with our great Lord and Master. His reply was : ' Man shall not live by bread alone, but by every word that proceedeth out of the mouth of God.' As if He had said, ' Ah ! it is not bread—it is not the gratification of any desire, no matter how powerful, or how lawful, or how reasonable in the eyes of men—it is not My own I seek ; it is not for this, or by this, that I live, but by the call and purposes and promises of My God ; My meat is to do the will of Him that sent Me and to finish His work.'

That was His defence. That must be ours.

> Jesus, I'll trust Thee more and more,
>   Trust where I cannot trace,
> Trust when I hear the ocean's roar,
>   Trust when the foe I face.
> Thou wilt be more than life to me,
>   So broad, so high, so deep ;
> Changing the thunder into glee,
>   Able to save and to keep.

Thus saith the Lord, the Holy One . . . I have made the earth, and created man upon it : I, even my hands, have stretched out the heavens, and all their host have I commanded. . . . I will direct all his ways.—Isaiah 45 : 11–13.

Do not be deceived by the modern talk about the laws of nature into forgetting that they are the laws ordained by your Father for the fulfilment of His will. Every day that dawns is as truly God's day as was the first one. Every night that draws its sable mantle over a silent world sets a seal to the knowledge of God who maketh the darkness. Behind the mighty forces and the ceaseless activities around us stands the Sovereign of them all. The earth is the Lord's and His chosen portion is His people.

It is with some such thoughts as these that I send out a brief New Year's greeting to my friends. I wish them a happy New Year, because I feel that God has sent it ; that in all the changes it may bring He will be planning with highest benevolence for their truest welfare. Whether, therefore, it holds for them sorrow or joy, it will be a year of mercy, a year of grace, a year of love.

> If in mercy Thou wilt spare
> Joys that yet are mine,
> If on life serene and fair
> Brighter rays may shine,
> Let my glad heart, while it sings,
> Rise by faith's exultant wings,
> And, whate'er the future brings,
> Glorify Thy name.